Peace Be
with
You

ALSO BY GREG STONE

Taming the Wolf: Peace Through Faith

The Secrets of Peacemaking

PEACE BE
with
YOU

*Peacemaking
and the
Theology of Pope Benedict XVI*

Greg Stone

Peace Be with You: Peacemaking and the Theology of Benedict XVI

All rights reserved. For permissions, contact tamingthewolf.com.

ISBN: 978-0-9848853-4-3

Taming the Wolf Institute is a 501(c)3 that delivers peacemaking instruction and services.

Cover art by Tracy Stone.

Printed in the United States of America.

Contents

Introduction

ONE
The Peacemaking Journey

TWO
Faith and Reason: A Marriage

THREE
Christian Idealism & Divine Relationship

FOUR
Reason & Culture

FIVE
God Is Love

SIX
Healing Relationships: Human & Divine

SEVEN
Fallen World: Realm of Disordered Will

EIGHT
Managing Disordered Will

NINE
The Will of God

TEN
The False Self

ELEVEN
I & Thou

TWELVE
The Problem of Evil

THIRTEEN
Spiritual Warfare

FOURTEEN
Mystical Union: Eucharistic Reconciliation

FIFTEEN
Spiritual Healing

SIXTEEN
Peace in the End Times

Peace Be with You

INTRODUCTION
The Great Hunger

Hunger for peace is universal.

Daily, in our prayers, we call on God to grant us peace that will soften our hearts. We pray that peace will descend upon our world *like the dewfall.*

The Advent of Peace

Amidst worldly struggle, we all long for tranquility. We long for peace in our families, workplaces, communities, and nations. However, all too often, serenity is confined to our dreams while turmoil and conflict become constant companions. Cries of human suffering clash with sweet promises of heavenly peace. In a fallen world, mankind shares and laments a great disappointment—the failure to secure lasting peace.

When our efforts to resolve conflict prove inadequate, disappointment turns into apathy. We retreat from relationships in the hope we can avoid suffering. We pray that unsettling events will leave us untouched. We avert our gaze from the clashes of discordant human wills.

Such avoidance may alleviate our present pain and discomfort, but it fails to satisfy our hunger for peace or quench our thirst for tranquility. Broken relationships continue to haunt us. A sense of loss nags at our soul. Troubled thoughts persist. Before long, we abandon any hope for peace of mind.

Hope reemerges during the Holy Mass. For a moment, fears are set aside. During the Eucharist,[1] we hear Jesus' words of comfort: "Peace I leave with you; my peace I give to you." His promise continues: "Not as the world gives do I give it to you. Do not let your hearts be troubled or afraid."[2]

In response, many are inspired to pray: "Lord, make me an instrument of your peace."[3] Together we pray: "Lord, grant us peace." They exchange signs of peace and, later, they are commissioned to go forth and bring peace to the world. In such moments—when sacred words promise heavenly peace—hope is restored and we dare wonder: *is it possible for men to hasten the arrival of peace?*

In the following pages, I hope to convince you, the aspiring peacemaker, that the answer is yes. To ensure our success, we turn to the writings of Pope Benedict XVI.

---

[1] The Eucharist is a sacramental rite instituted by Jesus Christ during the Last Supper. As he shared bread and wine with his disciples, referring to them as his body and blood, Jesus instituted the rite to be performed "in memory of me." In the sacrament, Christians recall Christ's sacrifice on the cross and come into his Real Presence.
[2] John 14:27, *New American Bible*.
[3] Leonardo Boff, *The Prayer of Saint Francis: A Message of Peace for the World Today*, trans. Philip Berryman (Maryknoll: NY, Orbis Books, 2001).

His words motivate us to "put on spiritual armor" and battle for peace in our time, while his insights into men's souls provide us with the wisdom needed to carry out a robust reconciliation ministry that will hasten the arrival of an era of peace.

The Journey

Fortunately, we do not journey alone on the path to peace. Saints throughout all history have shared our yearning. For example, Benedict recounts how Saint Bonaventure postulated the advent of an age of peace within history:[4]

> "It is a peace which God Himself will establish in this world which has seen so much blood and tears, as if at least at the end of time, God would show how things could have been and should have been in accordance with His plan."[5]

Yet mankind still raises swords high, signaling that the time of fulfillment is not the present.[6] Regardless, aspiring peacemakers have ample reason to be upbeat, as the "mystery of hope remains for Christianity," which leads to "a concrete hope for transformation of the world."[7]

Thus, while we must acknowledge the harshness of present reality, we must not cease working for peace. We

---

4 Joseph Ratzinger, *The Theology of History in St. Bonaventure*, trans. Zachary Hayes OFM (Chicago, Illinois: Franciscan Herald Press, 1971), 56.
5 Ibid., 162.
6 Ibid., 13.
7 Ibid., 16.

seek to soften hearts, one by one. We cannot retire to the sidelines and wait for our arrival in the next world. That is not an option. Instead, we actively pursue the peace Christ promised:

> "Augustine and Bonaventure know that the Church which hopes for peace in the future is, nonetheless, obliged to love in the present; and they both realize that the kingdom of eternal peace is growing in the hearts of those who fulfill Christ's law of love in their own particular age."[8]

This sentiment prompts each of us to assess how we "love in the present." Do we love unconditionally, with all our heart? Or do we tremble and retreat from relationships? Do we become the peacemakers Jesus commended in the Sermon on the Mount? Or do we avoid challenge and possible heartache? Are we passionate when it comes to satisfying our hunger for peace or do we succumb to apathy? Do we abandon our dreams and accept a flawed world?

These types of questions inspired my earlier work, *Taming the Wolf: Peace through Faith*,[9] a mediation manual that marries contemporary conflict resolution with the peacemaking legacy of Saint Francis. *Taming* launched a preliminary effort to develop a robust faith-based reconciliation discipline. That effort continues with *Peace Be*

---

8 Ibid., 163.
9 Greg Stone, *Taming the Wolf: Peace through Faith* (Westlake Village, California: Taming the Wolf Institute, 2011).

with You, which seeks to lay the theological foundation for a reconciliation ministry.

Initially, the study of theology may seem daunting. However, do not become troubled or intimidated. Our journey has been blessed with the extraordinary gifts of Benedict, the leading theologian of our time. Allow his words to speak, first and foremost, to your heart. Take time to engage in reflective reading. Do not be in a hurry. Remain open to the guidance of the Holy Spirit.

Establishing this solid theological foundation for a reconciliation ministry would be impossible without Benedict's guidance. Thus, it is with gratitude that I share his wisdom with you, tomorrow's peacemakers.

Preparations

Peace Be with You presents a comprehensive framework for a reconciliation ministry based on insights from Benedict's theology. When I mediated in the courts and for the Catholic Church, I found this theological foundation to be the missing link. Repairing this missing link is vital—never has there been a more pressing need for a theological framework to enhance peacemaking.

The enormous size of the task demands parsimony. This volume seeks only to lay out the basic principles of faith-based peace ministry. Case studies, anecdotes, training drills, and role-plays will be delivered later—in seminars, workshops, and training materials.

In addition, given that conflict manifests in a variety of ways, examples I might choose may not be germane to the specific situation of a reader. Therefore, I encourage readers to compile their own storehouses of personal examples by journaling thoughts and recollections. This collection of personal anecdotes, when tied to basic principles of theology, will later prove valuable in your practice.

The journey charted in *Peace Be with You* is one of contemplation. As you read, you will want to reflect on prior conflicts. Hopefully, the concepts presented in this book will shine a new light on old disputes and challenge long-held assumptions. As you progress in your studies, your personal theology and your view on conflict may evolve.

A word of caution is warranted: personal reflection that touches on prior conflict unearths upset. Therefore, you are *strongly advised* to schedule time for leisurely pursuits between reflections. Perhaps you will want to schedule walks or visits to pleasant retreat settings. As a rough guideline, spend as much time placing your attention on a pleasant external reality as you spend in reflection. Allow the space and the time needed for your reflections to fully mature.

Aspiring peacemakers will also soon discover the important role the faith community plays in reconciliation ministry. For that reason, it may be advantageous to study *Peace Be with You* in a parish setting. Parish-based study groups accrue considerable value when they integrate prayer or adoration with the study. The rationale for augmenting peace studies with the participation of the faith community becomes clear once peacemakers engage in the ministry.

Let us now start the journey. May your path to peace be blessed.

ONE

The Peacemaking Journey

Peacemakers inspired by the theology of Benedict must prepare for a life-changing journey. They must learn new skills, acquire fresh knowledge, and shape a personal theology. They must grasp conflict resolution fundamentals, master the basic premises of theology, and prepare to dispel any doubt and confusion that threatens to sabotage their ministry. Their study begins with an introduction to basic conflict resolution concepts and fundamental theology.

Conflict Resolution Basics

Peacemaking involves the prevention, management, and resolution of conflict. Before conflict can be resolved, it must first be understood. It is a mediator's job to study the dynamics that fuel the most common types of conflict.

We begin with a key principle: during a conflict, each party strives to satisfy personal desires, needs, or interests. A second principle follows: disputants often assume they must oppose and defeat another person's interests in order to satisfy their interests.

When they arrive at mediation, each party opposes the other party's desires. They are caught up in an apparent win-lose situation: *if one party is to win, the other party must lose.* This is a faulty assumption that sabotages peacemaking. In order to clarify and remove such faulty assumptions, the peacemaker assesses party needs and interests.

What does each person desire? What do they need to be, to do, or to have? What do they wish to avoid being, doing, or having? As you mediate a dispute, you may find that each party is pulling toward them things they want to be, to do, or to have and each party is pushing away things they refuse to be, do, or have. In this way, we discover push-pull dynamics.

Take a moment to reflect on your past conflict experiences. Recall times when you felt peace was possible *only if* your opposition would allow you to *be, do*, or *have* what you wanted. Recall times when you felt peace was possible *only if* the opposition would not force you to *be, do,* or *have* something you did not want. Recall how opposing intentions escalated conflict. You may find that a basic axiom applies: *when people seek to satisfy opposing desires or intentions, their exercise of free will fuels conflict.*

As you recall past conflicts, ask yourself: *What did I want, desire, or need? What did I want to be, do, or have that another opposed? What was the other party forcing me to be, do, or have? Why did they oppose my desires? Why did I oppose their desires?*

In this way, conflict forces us to confront the challenges of human free will. A principle soon emerges: *peacemakers facilitate difficult conversations between people who have exercised free will in a way that has resulted in a conflict entanglement.*

Parties who are embroiled in a conflict usually fail to identify the opposing intentions in play. They rarely understand why they're fighting. Mediators can help them by assessing the drivers of conflict. They ask the key question: what is fueling this fight? When we assess the drivers of conflict, we engage in the type of creative problem-solving designed to resolve party differences.

As you hone your peacemaking skills, this analysis will become second nature—you will automatically assess the interests and needs in play; you will naturally begin to analyze intentions. Eventually, you will gain the skill needed to help parties correctly identify opposing intentions.

Conflicts versus Problems

One common pitfall deserves special mention: *problems* may be incorrectly identified as *conflicts*. Problems tend to be mechanical or logistical in nature, while conflict typically involves two or more conscious agents exercising free will. A peacemaker focuses on repairing *free will* and *clashing intentions*, rather than on managing problems.

For example, moving a boulder up a hill against the force of gravity qualifies as a *problem*. The effort does not involve a conflict—unless someone *intentionally* pushes the boulder in the opposite direction, down the hill. Sometimes a problem morphs into a conflict—but *only* when a conscious agent intentionally opposes a solution to the problem. The hallmark of conflict is a conscious counter-intention.

Sometimes we inadvertently create conflict. When we wrestle with a problem, for example, we may misdiagnose the nature of our troubles and accuse someone else of wrongdoing. Blame provokes a hostile reaction. The wrongfully accused person becomes resentful; they may even attempt to sabotage the reconciliation process.

Though conflicts do not always emerge out of underlying problems, the dynamic is sufficiently common to warrant an assessment. Mediators should ask each disputant if they might have antagonized others after they became frustrated with a problem. Did they inadvertently generate resentment that fomented opposition? This line of questioning helps warring parties correctly discern the events that precipitated conflict.

In many instances, an assessment uncovers the flawed exercise of free will. A thorough investigation may even pinpoint the conflict drivers that are causing emotional, mental, and spiritual turmoil, such as opposing intentions responsible for lost friendships, broken families, and workplace clashes. A basic axiom guides the assessment: *when conscious agents exercise free will in a manner that generates opposing intentions, the result is conflict.*

A word of caution: when problems morph into conflicts, people may become defensive and deny any wrongdoing—they were simply struggling with a problem. No one should take offense at their behavior. They may deny they played a role in escalating the problem into a conflict when they blamed others. They may be unaware that their frustration and dark mood led to them insult others.

Mediators who discover this situation should gently probe the person's defenses, asking, "Is it possible that the other party felt you blamed them for the problem? Can you see how that might have happened? Did your frustration send the wrong message to those around you?"

Mediators can prepare for this assessment by recalling times when they struggled with a problem, became frustrated, and then antagonized another person, thereby inciting conflict. Upon reflection, they may understand the need to disentangle opposing intentions from the underlying mechanics of the problem.

When peacemakers learn these conflict resolution basics, they walk the path to peace with less trepidation. In a similar manner, they can prepare for the ministry by studying the basics of theology.

Introduction to Theology

Theology is the discipline that studies God's nature and the nature of God's relationship with individual souls. Most aspiring peacemakers already possess an informal sense of theology: a concept of God informs their worldview and guides their lives. An informal theology, however, is not sufficiently robust for this ministry. A peacemaker seeks a theology powerful enough to inspire and lift up those he serves. This requires study, reflection, and contemplative prayer.

Pope Benedict XIV's theology grounds our study of peacemaking. As you reflect on his words, compare his views with your own personal philosophy. Do you agree with his view of salvation history and the role of the Church, or will you approach the problem of faith from a different perspective?

Consider Benedict's most fundamental premise: his view of God. As you read, you will discover that he avoids descriptions that objectify God and turn Him into a two-dimensional icon worthy of idolatrous worship. Neither does he propose a deistic view of the Creator as a distant, impersonal force. Instead, he views God as a being capable and willing of forming relationships with humanity:

> [P]erfection attributed to God comes to be reinterpreted in fundamentally dynamic, relational terms. God comes to be known as the One who speaks and who, in speaking, shows himself not only to be creative, intelligent, and intelligible but also essentially communicative and loving.[1]

Benedict's theology aligns perfectly with reconciliation axioms. They both support the following logic: *if souls emerge into existence in a relationship with God, then*

---

[1] Christopher Collins, *The Word Made Love: The Dialogical Theology of Joseph Ratzinger / Pope Benedict XVI* (Collegeville, Minnesota: Liturgical Press, 2013), 65.

all their subsequent relationships build on the pattern of that first relationship. Thus, all human relationships echo divine relationship. It is for this reason that our work in mending human relationships requires the study of theology.

The reason is simple. Unlike psychologists, who focus on healing human relationships, and priests, who work to restore man's relationship with God, faith-based peacemakers mend relationships along both the human and the divine axes. Although mediators recognize the difference, they must nevertheless be careful when splitting relationships into two separate disciplines—human and divine. Instead, they must understand how they are linked:

> [B]y the inner structure of faith our relationship to God and our fellowship with man cannot be separated from each other; the relationship to God, to the "You," and to the "We" are intertwined; they do not stand alongside each other.[2]

Benedict's dialogical theology suggests that success in healing personal relationships rests on an understanding of *divine* relationship. A reconciler who does not understand divine relationship never fully grasps personal relationships. The link between these two facets of human relationships leads to the marriage of peacemaking with theology.

---

2 Cardinal Joseph Ratzinger, *Introduction to Christianity,* trans. J.R. Foster (San Francisco: Communio Books, 1969), 93.

When we delve deeper into Benedict's theology, we discover a God who enters into history and into our lives. This is not a completely new idea but one with a profound history:

> The experience of the God who conducts a dialogue, of the God who is not only *logos* but also *dia-logos*, not only idea and meaning but speech and word in the reciprocal exchanges of partners in conversation—this experience exploded the ancient division of reality.[3]

Jesus initiated the New Covenant and placed divine relationship at the center of Christianity. Benedict echoes the New Covenant with a theology centered on the "dialogical principle in which the Eternal Word is continually being spoken in history, in human words."[4]

You may already appreciate this theology as a result of reading scripture or listening to homilies. The Roman Catholic Church adopted this dialogical viewpoint in *Dei Verbum*,[5] the Vatican II document describing revelation as a dialogue between God and humanity unfolding in history.[6] This teaching guides the Church: "This posture of receptivity to the Word is at the heart of what has come to be known as '*communio* ecclesiology,' one of whose

---

3 Ibid., 183.
4 Collins, *The Word Made Love*, 18.
5 Austin Flannery, O.P, ed., *The Basic Sixteen Documents of Vatican II* (New York: Costello Publishing Company, 1996).
6 Collins, *The Word Made Love*, 54.

most prominent advocates has been Joseph Ratzinger."[7]

In this view, the Church is defined as "those who listen to God." It is a community of individuals in relationship with God:

> Christian faith is more than the option in favor of a spiritual ground to the world; its central formula is not "I believe in something", but "I believe in you." It is the encounter with the man Jesus, and in this encounter it experiences the meaning of the world as a person.[8]

As peacemakers contemplate the nature of sacred relationship, they may ask: how well are the principles of divine relationship articulated in my parish setting?

I-Thou Relationship

Benedict's dialogical theology was inspired in part by the writings of Martin Buber, especially *I and Thou*.[9] This seminal work calls for a transition from a faith based on logical propositions to a lived faith:

> Rejecting the objectification of God...Buber reintroduces his reader to God as divine subject with whom the human person is able to enter into

---

7 Ibid., 105.
8 Ratzinger, *Introduction to Christianity*, 79.
9 Martin Buber, *I and Thou*, trans. Walter Kaufman (New York: Touchstone, 1970). I discovered Buber's *I and Thou* while enrolled for a semester at Chicago Theological Seminary, University of Chicago.

real relationship and thereby actualize authentic human identity.[10]

Buber anticipated the emerging discipline of faith-based reconciliation when he argued that healing the "sickness of alienation" is contingent upon a return to dialogue with the "Eternal Thou."[11] It is here, in the sacred I–Thou dialogue that we discover the very heart of peacemaking. The ability to make peace, for self or others, is contingent upon an ability to reconcile divine relationships. In this regard, a quote from Benedict deserves reflection:

> The philosophical God is essentially self-centered, thought simply contemplating itself. Whereas...the God of faith is basically defined by the category of relationship.[12]

Peacemakers seek to infuse their ministry with dialogical divine presence. This presence is consistent with Benedict's vision of Communio ecclesiology:

> The church is, by definition, a collecttion of subjects who make up the "people of God"...who are given their corporate identity by being in dialogue with the living God.[13]

Mediators typically work in a secular atmosphere, but

---

10 Collins, *The Word Made Love*, 14.
11 Ibid., 13.
12 Ratzinger, *Introduction to Christianity*, 147.
13 Collins, *The Word Made Love*, 117.

they should never forget that they also serve the faith community, healing spiritual estrangement as they resolve conflict between people. When peacemakers reconcile souls with each other and with God, they forward the Church's core mission of saving souls, thereby advancing the goals of peace and salvation.

Reflection

Preparation for the journey begins with reflection on the nature of human relationships. Those who wish to take up the mantle of faith-based peacemaking might find inspiration in a "theology of relationship."

We also take into account the lessons of the conflict resolution profession and discern best practices. However, we discover that secular mediators, who lack a foundation in theology, enjoy only intermittent success. Ultimately, they fail to hasten lasting world peace.

Students of peacemaking are encouraged to reflect on a key axiom: sacred dialogue with a living God forms the cornerstone of all peacemaking. With that in mind, they may want to think of ways to facilitate dialogue in the presence of the Holy Spirit.

They might consider mediating in a retreat setting to allow for deeper reflection on divine relationship. They may want to incorporate prompts into their reconciliation sessions. Recognizing that faith-based ministry demands special skills, they may want to further their study of theology and spirituality.

How students approach the ministry remains a personal matter, based partly upon circumstances and partly upon their particular faith tradition. That being said, they should begin to formulate a plan for incorporating basic theological principles into their peacemaking protocols.

With that in mind, students should compile resources into peacemaking "toolkits." On their journey, they will gather more knowledge and enlarge their toolkit.

A word of caution: when problems morph into conflicts, people may become defensive and deny any wrongdoing. They may insist they were simply struggling with a problem and no one should take offense at their behavior. They may deny they played a role in escalating the problem into a conflict when they blamed others. In some cases, they may be unaware that their frustration and dark mood led to them insult others.

Mediators who discover this situation should gently probe the person's defenses. They should ask, "Is it possible that the other party felt they were being blamed for the problem? Can you see any way that might have happened? Do you believe your frustration might have sent the wrong message to those around you?" With such open-ended questions the mediator is likely to prompt an epiphany—the person may likely recall an unkind word or gesture that ignited the conflict.

At this early stage, regardless of the level of enthusiasm newcomers bring to the ministry, questions and doubts may arise. Is it really possible to achieve the dream of peace? Are the odds stacked against success? A mediator may even question whether they possess sufficient courage or skill to resolve intractable conflict.

Rather than push these concerns aside, peacemakers must learn how to integrate private reflections into their journey. As they wrestle with self-doubt and the emotional challenges presented by conflict, they create a textured personal story. This narrative may prove to be a valuable asset when it comes time to help others face fears and doubts.

TWO

Faith and Reason: A Marriage

When peacemakers first attempt to resolve a dispute, they may become confused. What really happened? Conflicting narratives may frustrate attempts to establish an objective account of events. Is one party lying? Are faulty memories to blame? Is there more than one explanation for events?

In extreme cases, mediators may become disoriented, like sailors lost at sea with no land in sight. If they hope to understand what happened, they must first reestablish their bearings. This task requires two vital "navigation" tools—faith and reason.

Only after dispelling their own confusion with the help of faith and reason will peacemakers be able to rescue drowning souls set adrift in the stormy seas of conflict. Only after reorienting themselves will they be able to help disputants chart their coordinates in mental, emotional, and spiritual spaces. Only when they have a firm grasp on reality will they be prepared to help parties discover what is real and what is unreal.

In the course of their study, aspiring mediators realize that success depends largely on their ability to lay a strong philosophical foundation for their practice. With that in mind, they may want to reflect on the following questions: *What is reality? What is truth? What is man's essential nature? What are the properties of an immortal soul? What is a soul's relationship with God?*

The study of theology and philosophy can help peacemakers shape a comprehensive worldview. In particular, the marriage of faith and reason, of the natural and supernatural, deserve their attention. Discussion of mediation and investigation techniques, in particular, can help them move beyond abstract theory into practical questions regarding the nature of personal inquiry. To put it simply, mediators are searching for the skills they need to conduct "reality checks."

The Reality Check

Peacemakers minister to real people. These people experience real crises. Mediators must be able to address these life-altering events. In extreme cases, they may have to prevent one party from harming another. In short, the ministry is practical.

Real-world conflict resolution begins with assessment. Mediators want to know how parties perceive reality in general and how they view the conflict events in particular. What happened? Which scenarios seem most real to them and which appear to be unreal? Listen closely to narratives and seek to grasp "what happened" from the party's viewpoint.

Assessment can be challenging, as parties embroiled in conflict experience an unsettling sense of unreality. Their certainty is shaken; they cannot understand why others would want to do them harm; they cannot imagine themselves as a valid target of an attack. For this reason, conflict events do not seem anchored in reality.

Mediators recognize this disconnect from reality. They must build a bridge back to stability and certainty. They begin bridge construction by assessing what seems most real to each party: *which account of the events makes the most sense?* They sort through clues, trying to decipher party viewpoints. In essence, they conduct "reality checks."

The assessment path is not smooth, paved, and tree-lined. Rather, it is muddy, twisted, steep, and lined with bramble bushes. Distorted perceptions obscure vision. Negative emotions explode like smoke bombs. As embattled parties suffer through the fog of war they fail to "track with reality."

Peacemakers thus face an overgrown jungle of dark emotions, mental confusion, and ingrained bias. Nonetheless, peacemakers serve as a stable presence in the storm as they help parties assess their recall (*are their memories reliable or fuzzy?*) and inspect their perceptions (*has their vision been impaired?*).

This narrative assessment, or "reality check" creates an opportunity for parties to discard misperceptions, jettison alterations, and clear obfuscations. Parties set aside misperceptions and rewrite their stories. During the rewriting process, parties share revised narratives of "what happened." Peacemakers facilitate these difficult conversations as reality is restructured. Eventually, such drafting shines a brighter light on the actual drivers of conflict.

Reality Check Phases

A Phase One "reality check" assesses basic facts and seeks to align narrative accounts. *Does each party to the dispute tell the same story? Does their recall align with known evidence or is it at odds with the facts?*

A party involved in a traffic accident dispute, for example, may insist the light was green while a witness may insist it was red. A mediator who encounters such contrary claims or facts recognizes the need for an assessment to detect altered, inhibited, or biased perceptions.

The mediator might ask: Did drugs or alcohol play a role? Is it possible that illness or incapacity altered perception? Have disturbed emotions muddied memories? If possible, he matches perceptions with tangible evidence and seeks to weave varied accounts into a consensus view of events.

The mediator does not seek to impeach party accounts, as might take place during a trial. Rather, he helps parties secure a more accurate picture of reality, a better understanding that improves their narrative of "what happened."

During a "reality check," parties revise, redraft, and fine-tune narratives. Inconsistencies are not discarded, but rather integrated into a revised mega-story that creatively melds different points of view into a single comprehensive narrative.

The *Phase Two* "reality check" transitions to increasingly subtle factors. A mediator surfaces attitudes, prejudices, and emotions; he inspects a rich tapestry of subjective views. Some of these views will emerge in the form of accusations: *"You were angry; you showed disrespect; you refused to trust me; you tried to deceive me; you lied and cheated; you were acting crazy."*

Such emotionally laden views rarely blend seamlessly and completely into one unified viewpoint. Instead, individual strands of shared reality are woven into a consensus tapestry. For example, one party might say, "Though I don't agree with you, I can see why you feel that way. I can understand how that is real for you." In this way, conflicting views are embraced and integrated into an overall story.

Reality checks may also bring unintended consequences to light. As each party reflects on how their decisions have affected others, as they come to appreciate the harm caused by their actions, they begin to assume responsibility for outcomes, past and future.

During this exchange, mediators may practice framing claims and demands in a way that avoids triggering negative emotions. They may also demonstrate how to express interests in ways that avoid insult. By practicing a collaborative style of negotiation, they increase the chances of a successful reconciliation.

Even as parties make progress, they will instinctively work to impose their views on one another. It is natural for people to want their view of reality to prevail; they want others to see the world as they do. These attempts to impose reality on others are usually covert or unconscious: impulses take shape "under the radar." For this reason, mediators work to surface hidden intentions and place them "on the table" for negotiation. Slowly, parties regain certainty; the sense of unreality dissipates; events make more sense, and the future looks a little brighter.

A *Phase Three* "reality check" is unique to faith-based reconciliation. Parties explore the supernatural aspects of reality and reflect on fundamental, or ontological, aspects of creation. They view events through spiritual lenses and assess their choices in the context of ultimate reality.

In Phase Three, parties begin to grapple with questions of truth and justice. They reassess relationships based on deeper insights into the true spiritual nature of a person. They seek a comprehensive view of reality, one that integrates natural and supernatural elements.

Suggested Phase Three reflections include: *Have supernatural influences been overlooked in this conflict? Did an absence of divine relationship contribute to this conflict? Would the situation be different if events were viewed through a spiritual lens?*

In this phase, mediators can introduce prompts that help parties contemplate the nature of prayer: *Do prayers of petition prompt divine intervention? Does the Holy Spirit function as an advocate? Does the Holy Spirit reveal truth or play a role in healing?* Short reflections on faith inspire confidence and encourage humility. They help parties rediscover their true essence as a soul, remind disputants that they are not alone, and encourage them to seek divine assistance. Sometimes, such prompts are enough to put parties in the appropriate mindset for reconciliation.

More complex disputes may call for deeper reflection on scripture and theology. When dealing with complicated issues, long-standing conflicts, or intractable disputes, mediators may want to search for references that provide specific insights on managing relationships. They might ask parties to compare their personal conflict narrative with stories or parables found in sacred texts. They may encourage parties to attend spiritual retreats to contemplate their immortal nature. They may even enlist the help of spiritual directors well-versed in the faith traditions of the disputants.

The Phase Three "reality check" resembles spiritual formation. Both processes mine the basic truths of existence. As a practical matter, it is rare for a mediator to undertake a "reality check" of such depth. In most instances, parties pay little heed to bedrock worldviews that lie so far beneath the surface. Instead, they buffer small disagreements with social habits. Manners lubricate the friction of everyday social interactions. When disputes arise out of day-to-day social friction, Phase One and Two reality checks may suffice.

This changes once a serious dispute erupts. In the midst of conflict, parties tighten their grip on entrenched worldviews. Habit and prejudice color their evaluation of right and wrong. Worldview bias justifies misdeeds. While parties rarely articulate their deepest underlying viewpoints, such worldviews nonetheless fuel their hostility.

When peacemakers embrace the goal of building a solid foundation for world peace, they no longer rely on repairing surface reality. Instead, they conduct deep-dive "reality checks." They consult theology and philosophy as they attempt to reconcile faith and reason. Using Phase Three "reality checks," they go to work repairing fundamental worldviews.

Navigating the chaos of conflict requires considerable skill. The next section explores how peacemakers can prepare to restore clarity, reason, and vision.

The Peacemaker's Worldview

People embroiled in major conflict find their sense of reality torn asunder. They lose their bearings and become disoriented, confused, and detached. Before conflict escalated, their personal assumptions, biases, and prejudices marked their path. Decisions regarding right and wrong were most likely made without reason, often dictated by social pressure. Previously, they probably failed to discern truth and failed to engage in contemplation; they followed vague feelings and untrained intuition instead of relying on verifiable facts and rational thinking.

When major conflict arises, however, the dynamics change. Uninspected worldviews crumble; doubt twists perspectives; fear motivates defensive postures. At this point, peacemakers are called upon to pick up the pieces and restore civility.

The conflict resolution ministry begins with "reality checks"—peacemakers assess party viewpoints. They address not only *what* parties viewed but also *how* they viewed. Peacemakers inventory mental, emotional, or spiritual filters that color or alter perceptions. They help parties root out bias and faulty assumptions.

However, before peacemakers can conduct sophisticated "reality checks" with others, they must have fully explored their own worldview. They must shape a personal philosophy, for if they do not stand on solid ground, they'll be unable to bring order out of chaos. If they lack a sound worldview, they will resemble an inebriated skipper in a wobbly rowboat who reaches out to a drowning man only to be pulled overboard and drowned.

Peacemakers must avoid drowning in the stormy seas churned by chaotic worldviews. They must turn to the timeless truths of philosophy and theology. They do not seek academic expertise but rather practical knowledge that can be applied. They seek robust tools used to construct accurate worldviews.

The first step in this rebuilding process is site excavation—old perspectives are tossed and emotional debris is discarded. Prejudices, biases, and assumptions are dumped. After old faulty structures are removed, new construction begins. Pillars of wisdom, strong enough to weather any storm, are erected to support a peacemaker's personal worldview.

Aspiring peacemakers acquire skills used to diminish confusion, doubt, and fear—they become proficient in the use of contemplative prayer. They shore up the weak structures in their worldview with supernatural or mystical insights. They marry faith and reason and thus arrive at a comprehensive worldview, built with natural and supernatural components.

After peacemakers reshape their worldviews, they often begin to recognize the extent of the cultural wreckage caused by philosophical materialism. In the past, most people were oblivious to this carnage. Although they knew unwanted conditions denigrated the human condition, they failed to pinpoint the source of the problem.

Once peacemakers recognize that a destructive worldview is the primary source of the damage, they understand that developing valid worldviews is time well spent. Once they are trained, they can more easily identify the sources of turmoil. They realize the only peace that will endure is peace rooted in a comprehensive worldview with both natural and supernatural aspects.

Peacemakers, once trained, come to realize they cannot allow those of limited reality to foreclose their mystical gifts. They learn that "knock on wood" materialist reality often distracts us from perceiving deeper reality. They discover that the mystical life is often the most real. Mystical and spiritual reality cannot be ignored. In order to illustrate this point, we consider the mystical wisdom of Saint Paul.

Knowing with the Heart

Peacemakers heal broken relationships, but such healing can be blocked by misunderstanding. If parties hope to achieve reconciliation, they must acquire a greater understanding of their opponent and of themselves. They must seek wisdom.

Saint Paul, in his letters, captured the type of understanding that mediators should nurture. Benedict summarizes:

> Knowing "from a human point of view," in the manner of the flesh, means knowing solely in an external way, by means of external criteria... Although one may know someone in this way, nevertheless one does not really know him, one does not know the essence of the person. Only with the heart does one truly know a person.[1]

Paul's insight flows from mystical wisdom gained through a dramatic conversion, as well as years of contemplative prayer.[2] He noted the difference between external knowledge—which has come about "in the manner of the flesh"—and mystical knowledge. Paul's axiom—*one truly knows another only with the heart*—motivates peace-

---

1 Pope Benedict XVI, *St. Paul* (San Francisco: Ignatius Press, 2009), 43.
2 Paul's conversion account can be found in Acts 9.

makers to move past external concerns to "matters of the heart."

The shift from mundane to spiritual views often begins when parties share their conflict narratives. As they listen to one another, they increase understanding of self and other, gaining a new kind of wisdom.

As parties trade stories and concerns, a common myth is shattered. There is no such thing as a reality separate from subjective views. Mediators do not address a stand-alone objective reality, complete with objective facts to be adjudicated. Rather, they work with subjective personal narratives, as Benedict notes:

> Pure objectivity is an absurd abstraction. It is not the disinterested person who comes to knowledge; rather, interest...is itself a requirement of the possibility to know.[3]

The truth underlying a dispute does not lie somewhere "out there" in an isolated objective realm, but rather lives in the hearts and minds of disputants. Truth is subjective and relational. Parties respond with subjective perspectives when asked, *"What happened?"* Likewise, they offer subjective views when asked: *What did you see or hear? What did you experience? How did that experience make you feel?* Their responses capture reality *as they experienced it.*

---

3 Emery de Gaál, *The Theology of Pope Benedict XVI: The Christocentric Shift* (New York: Palgrave Macmillan, 2010), 111.

Thus, in the discovery phase, *mediators choreograph subjective disclosures and facilitate a collaborative search for a shared narrative reality.* They facilitate the search for overlapping mental, emotional, and spiritual spaces. They help parties find a shared reality that they previously overlooked.

The process of redrafting conflict narratives is not limited to human relationships. A party to a dispute may also need to rewrite the account of his or her relationship with God. When tasked with rethinking the nature of divine-human interaction, the interested party would do well to consult sacred texts and engage in contemplative prayer. By seeking a deeper understanding of their relationship with sacred truth, by "knowing with the heart," people begin to reveal God in a personal manner:

> Revelation refers to an act in which God shows himself to a particular receiving subject. Without an actual receiver, no revelation occurs. There must be someone who becomes aware of it.[4]

Any recipient of divine revelation comes to "know with the heart." In a similar manner, a "brother-to-brother" mediation, executed properly, becomes spirit-driven. Softened hearts become infused with mystical presence. Parties look inward at the same time they gaze "beyond." Individual spiritual consciousness co-mingles with divine consciousness.

---

4   Ibid., 88.

Mediators and parties who adopt a contemplative approach find the Holy Spirit opens doors to renewed relationship with God.[5] Once divine relationship is healed, parties begin to perceive the "spark of the divine" within others, including their conflict opponent. Paradoxically, once they know others in a spiritual manner, self-knowledge increases. They discover that their identity arises out of relationship:

> For man is the more himself the more he is with "the other." He only comes to himself by moving away from himself. Only through "the other" and through "being" with "the other" does he come to himself.[6]

This novel idea—*self is a function of relationship*—leads to a simple axiom: healing relationships restores self-knowledge and self-worth. After reconciliation, one begins to see through subtle falsehoods. Identities that once seemed meaningful turn out to be illusions.

Mediation serves as a "reality check," exposing faulty assumptions built into culturally "accepted" worldviews. Man may see reality "through a glass darkly," but the lenses can be cleaned and polished. When a peacemaker marries theology and philosophy, he learns how to remove smudges from the lenses.

---

5 See the Gospel of John for further description.
6 Ratzinger, *Introduction to Christianity*, 214.

Philosophy and Faith

Peacemakers who seek to resolve minor disputes may require little more than common sense and good communication skills; however, hastening world peace requires deeper wisdom. Reconcilers must learn how people construct their reality; they need to know how destructive viewpoints lead to conflict and hostility. Aspiring peacemakers must turn to theology and philosophy for answers.

However, in their search for answers they often encounter roadblocks. The popular culture informs them that faith and reason have been granted a divorce on the grounds they're incompatible. In centers of higher learning faith is barred, not unlike a feuding spouse obtaining a restraining order. Faith inadvertently comes to resemble a "crazy ex" who has been declared delusional and dangerous. In popular opinion, the divorce between faith and reason is final.

But can the marriage be saved? Is it possible to find a philosophy (a system of reason) suitable as a partner for faith? Many assume the mismatch, the divorce, is the fault of faith. However, when we analyze the split, we might find the fault lies with the discipline of philosophy. Contemporary philosophy, we may discover, has become unmoored from any valid roots. Perhaps philosophy is the crazy "ex" causing strive.

To render the search for a suitable philosophy partner easier, we can reduce the possible candidates to two opposing schools of philosophy: Materialism and Idealism. In the following discussion, I will highlight their dramatically different conclusions regarding the nature of life. Benedict's work will aid our analysis. His core sentiment is best expressed in Saint John Paul II's *Fides et Ratio*—a papal encyclical to which Benedict contributed:

> Faith and reason are like two wings on which the human spirit rises to the contemplation of truth; and God has placed in the human heart a desire to know the truth—in a word, to know himself—so that, by knowing and loving God, men and women may also come to the truth about themselves.[7]

Benedict, in his theology lessons, has restored balance to these wings. He began with a critique of the modern de-Hellenization movement—which had become a trend that diminished appreciation for the Platonic and Neo-Platonic philosophy that influenced early theologians.

Those early theologians found Greek philosophy (reason) compatible with Christianity. For example, Origen, the earliest theologian, brought Greek ideas into a Christian context. Augustine followed, finding the ideas of Plotinus consistent with Christian belief. Saint Paul, who was conversant with Greek philosophy, debated and converted many Greeks.

In those formative days of the Church, philosophy and theology worked in tandem. Patristic theology embraced

---

[7] Pope John Paul II, *Fides et Ratio: Encyclical Letter of the Supreme Pontiff John Paul II to the Bishops of the Catholic Church on the Relationship between Faith and Reason*, September 14, 1998 (Rome: Libreria Editrice Vaticana, 1998).

Greek philosophy. Emery de Gaál comments on the historic marriage:

> [T]he encounter between the Christian narrative and the Hellenic culture must be described as kairotic, a unique moment of divine providence in history.[8]

In a qualified sense, Benedict even considered himself a Platonist.[9] He applauded "Augustine's conjoining Neo-Platonic ontology and biblical insight in God."[10] In his view, Augustine provided a counterweight to Aquinas, and delivered a more profound and closer approximation of human existence[11]:

> Similar to Romano Guardini, Ratzinger discovered in Augustine and Bonaventure two original theologians quite unlike the more cerebral, Aristotelian Thomas Aquinas and later formalistic, neoscholastic thinkers.[12]

In the work of the early Church Fathers, we stumble upon a potential philosophy partner for Christianity—Platonic Idealism. Benedict goes a step further and builds a system of reason (a philosophy) from the ground up, resulting in a system that transcends all existing philosophy.

---

8 de Gaál, *The Theology of Pope Benedict XVI*, 112.
9 Ibid., 65.
10 Ibid., 76.
11 Ibid.
12 Ibid., 67.

He argues that Platonic Idealism—though compatible with Christian faith—cannot stand on its own as a complete system of reason. He goes on to argue that any philosophy lacking a personal God is too abstract to capture actual reality. If we accept a relationship with a living God as the foundation of all reality, then any philosophy that omits that relationship must be inaccurate or incomplete. Such reason is crippled. Benedict even "refers to reason that is not mindful of God as 'amputated reason.'"[13]

Thus, in this view, Idealism must be rebuilt on a foundation of theological truth. After we lay a theological foundation, we can then build a system of reason (a philosophy) using the building blocks of Idealism. In short, theology first informs philosophy; subsequently, philosophy compliments theology. In this model, faith and reason arise from the same ground of being. They're inherently compatible as they rest on a common foundation.

Benedict's theology eclipses Neo-Scholasticism,[14] a theology hobbled by the flaws of Aristotelian Realism. Benedict instead places a theological emphasis on mystical relationship with a living God and then insists reason or philosophy conform to the reality of divine relationship.

---

[13] Ibid., 74.
[14] Neo-Scholasticism developed from the Scholasticism of the Middle Ages during the latter half of the nineteenth century. Sometimes called neo-Thomism partly because St. Thomas Aquinas in the thirteenth century gave Scholasticism its final form. [Excerpted from https://www.catholic.com/encyclopedia/neo-scholasticism.].

He echoes the wisdom of early theologians:

> Closer examination reveals that in the cases of both doctors of the Church—Augustine and Bonaventure—the gravitational center is not dogmatic systemization for the sake of university lectures, but the historicity of faith and its mystical interiorization by a concrete human being.[15]

Benedict surpasses the goals set out in *Fides et Ratio*. He moves beyond mere philosophy to a marriage of faith and reason that displays a deep grasp of the sacred roots of reason. In accord with Augustine, he sees a transformation in which:

> [T]he mute and indescribable God of the philosophers becomes the speaking and listening God in Jesus Christ.[16]

Benedict thus offers a new benchmark for evaluating a marriage of faith and reason: *does the marriage respect and enhance man's divine relationship with a living God?* Aristotelian philosophy championed by Aquinas falls short on this measure:

> While Aristotle recognized the true God, Christian revelation provides a more profound and purer comprehension of God's essence.[17]

---

15   de Gaál, *The Theology of Pope Benedict XVI*, 67.
16   Ibid., 76.
17   Ibid., 75.

Aristotle's Realism, with its faults, weakens faith—it veers away from a God of relationship. Realism fails to embrace the intimate supernatural or mystical relationship captured so well by Idealism, a philosophy that acknowledges that creation emerges from the Mind of God. Only in Idealism do we find reason that acknowledges our intimate mystical relationship with God and all existence.

Benedict has reset the marriage table at a propitious time for peacemakers. His theology of relationship, partnered with Idealistic philosophy, delivers knowing-with-the-heart wisdom. Benedict delivers peacemakers from the pitfalls of abstract reason by grounding philosophy in personal relationship with God. He reveals the mystical roots of reason:

> The *ratio naturalis* (natural reason) is always personal and is never *ratio pura* (pure reason) which does not in fact exist—but rather *ratio purificata* (purified reason). Only the individual believer can be the bearer of a *cor punum* (pure heart).[18]

Benedict's approach demolishes conceptual walls separating mundane life from mystical awareness. In his work, natural and supernatural aspects of reality are knit into a comprehensive whole. In this way, he honors a key theological principle: every soul is endowed with the image and likeness of God. To put it another way, every soul is infused with spiritual consciousness, the medium

---

18 Ibid., 65.

through which man knows God, and the medium through which humans "know with their heart."

The marriage of faith and reason as laid out by Benedict serves as a tool for aspiring peacemakers. It motivates them to seek a renewed worldview augmented by supernatural insights. With Benedict as their mentor they discover a subjective universe resting on a foundation of divine relationship; they discover that Creation emerges from the Mind of God.[19]

Peacemakers are thus gifted with a path to a revised worldview rooted in previously overlooked spiritual foundations of reason. They are introduced to a philosophy that does not rest on abstraction or scholastic argument. Rather their worldview embraces the mystical aspects of reality found in sacramental rites and contemplative prayer. Along the way, the supernatural nature of consciousness is revealed, paving the way to divine relationship becoming the center of their lives.

It turns out that faith and reason were never incompatible. Their marriage, believed by many to have been a failed union, lies at the heart of Benedict's theology and the practice of peacemaking.

Reflection

If peacemakers are poorly grounded in reality, they risk failure. Those who lack a sound personal philosophy

---

19 For a comprehensive presentation of Idealism see Anglican Bishop George Berkeley's *A Treatise Concerning the Principles of Human Knowledge* (1710).

will flounder. Those who fail to prepare will be unable to conduct "reality checks." If they remain confused regarding the nature of reality, they will fail to rescue those who have become lost. Peacemakers who hope to hoist drowning men from angry seas must first stand on solid ground.

Thus, peacemaking preparation begins with a personal reality check that charts mental, emotional, and spiritual coordinates. Peacemakers calibrate their inner "compass" in preparation for the journey. They engage in contemplation and reflect on what it means to assert that the universe emerged from divine relationship. Consulting Benedict's theology, they revise stale assumptions about the nature of existence.

In addition, peacemakers discuss worldviews with friends and mentors. They conduct informal surveys to ascertain what others consider real or fantasy. They practice the inquiry as preparation for future discussions with disputants.

Peacemakers reflect on relationships as the building blocks of an idealistic universe. They contemplate what this means for their ministry. They catalog skills needed for healing relationships. They assess skills they possess and inventory skills they must develop. They reflect on how they might marry faith and reason in their lives and their ministry.

During this reflection, reconcilers experience considerable change, but also considerable discomfort. Some might begin to question whether or not they've ever known actual reality. As they uncover false assumption on top of false assumption, they may feel they have lived life in a fog. They might even worry that they will remain unable to accurately discern the nature of reality. However, they are warned to remember that they have just begun the journey. Much will be revealed. Challenges will be plentiful, but rewards will soon accrue.

Most of all, they must keep in mind the biblical admonition: *be not afraid.*

THREE

Christian Idealism and Divine Relationship

Aspiring peacemakers prepare for their ministry by integrating theology into their personal worldview. Mediators who base their ministry on the tenets of Christian Idealism, for example, work hard to dismantle materialistic biases that taint the disputing parties' view of reality. As they guide men and women to a peaceful settlement, they create personal "reality maps" based on insights gathered from both philosophical inquiry and personal experience.

Christian Idealism and the Narrative Tapestry

Picture a heated verbal debate over the existence of God. One side uses science and reason to attack the faith, while the other side counters with logical propositions in support of supernatural truths. The latter engage in a particular kind of philosophical debate called apologetics.[1]

---

[1] Apologetics is the systematic defense of religion, typically through argu-

Peacemaking should never enter the realm of apologetics. Peacemakers do not seek a debate; they seek a philosophy that enhances their ability to manage conflict. When they ask, "what happened?" they do not solicit philosophical propositions; they merely ask for the individual's subjective viewpoint. When they prompt reflections on faith, they are not looking for a theological debate; they are attempting to inspire attitudes of love, charity, and humility.

All actions are shaped by subjective views. Individuals hold viewpoints that motivate their behavior. Their actions, in turn, shape the subjective views of others, who then act on their beliefs.

Consider an example: a boss arrives at the decision to fire an employee. He feels the individual's character does not fit his company's culture. The employee, feeling hurt and wronged, adopts the view of a victim. He acts on that view, filing a lawsuit for wrongful termination. They battle back and forth, each party acting on the basis of what they feel is real, right, and just. Both can provide a mediator with a narrative account of why they do what they do, yet their reasons are almost entirely subjective.

In response to mediators' questions, parties weave a complex narrative, a tapestry composed of many overlapping views of reality. During mediation, peacemakers move about in this mental, emotional, and spiritual matrix. Empathy facilitates their movement through the

---

mentation and debate.

mental spaces occupied by the parties. Discretion leads them to reframe the conflict in terms upon which both parties can agree. Mediators soften attitudes and render previously rigid views more malleable.

A theme emerges: the integration of divergent worldviews is made possible by the inter-subjective nature of reality. If we live in a deterministic universe based on mechanistic principles—a machine-like world where every outcome is predetermined—then subjective viewpoints become largely irrelevant. However, if reality responds to subjective input—including love, beauty, and ethics—then the convergence of opposing views becomes possible. In order to succeed in their ministry, peacemakers must adopt a philosophy that captures the nature of this malleable inter-subjective reality.

Christian Idealism and Discovery

As mediators proceed with the discovery phase of the reconciliation process, they may find that they rarely rely on objective facts to understand what drives a particular conflict. They do not evaluate evidence and deliver verdicts; rather, they explore subjective, or inter-subjective, reality. They actively listen to personal narratives. They survey the human landscape and chart reality as seen by each individual.

Therefore, peacemakers must seek a personal philosophy, a system of reason, that recognizes the primacy of subjectivity. This focus on subjectivity does not arise simply out of a desire to accommodate personal narratives; rather, it is an expression of philosophical truth. It recognizes the subjective nature of reality in which conflict takes shape.

The sole philosophy that meets this standard is Idealism, which puts forth a theory of the universe as a subjective construct. Idealism, when built on a foundation of Christian revelation, advances a profound idea: Creation issues from the Mind of God.

Christian Idealism presents a stark contrast to prevailing cultural narratives, many of which are built on a foundation of secular materialism. Faith-based mediators who incorporate Christian Idealism into their ministry will soon discover the vital role Christianity can and should play in modern discourse. As mediators come to understand the axioms of Idealism, they find themselves gaining a "big picture" view of Creation.

Christian Idealism—God as Subject

Philosophy guides us through the mediation process. It gives us a glimpse into the nature of inter-subjective reality and helps us understand how to reconcile conflicting narratives. Similarly, theological reflection is required before reconciliation with God can take place. A passage from Benedict helps us understand why must reestablish and reaffirm our relationship with God before reconciliation can occur:

> Worship, then, that activity in which the human person addresses the personal God and allows *the*

God who is not object but subject to speak, is essential for healing the modern sickness of humanity.[2]

If this is true, if we must first understand and worship God before we can heal the sickness of conflict and alienation, then theology becomes central to the ministry of peacemaking. Furthermore, if we are dealing with the "God who is not object but subject," then all efforts at reconciling man's relationship with God must first precede from God. Divine initiative precedes human action. In this way, reconciliation with God is reconciliation with Absolute Subject.

A student of peacemaking may already be conversant with the idea that God is not a thing, not an idol or icon. He or she may know that God is not one object among many objects. But the student must now reflect deeper on *God as Subject*.

In contemplative reflection the peacemaker must come to know that God is both immanent *and* transcendent. God's presence pervades the universe but is not of this universe. In reflection, a peacemaker learns that God is present, knowing and loving. Reflection leads to the discovery that *God the Ultimate Subject is also the Subjective Ground of All Being*.

These spiritual discoveries do not come easy. Aspiring mediators may struggle with the idea that Creation issues from the Mind of God. How could Mind project material existence into being?

---

2   Collins, *The Word Made Love*, 15. Emphasis added.

As part of their study, students of theology may want to reflect on the nature of matter. They may ask questions such as: *Does physical matter "stand alone," independent of the Mind of God? Or is it contingent upon the Mind of God? Would matter cease to exist without God? Does matter exist separate from and independent of the supernatural?*

Initially, this reflection may prove quite difficult. We are conditioned to consider that objects exist independent of all thought—independent of God. It may take time to unravel this cultural conditioning.

Peacemakers should also reflect on the nature of an immortal soul. For example, what does it mean to say a soul is endowed with the image and likeness of God? Is a soul a subjective being? Do souls exist in subjective relationship with God? How is that possible? What is the nature of spiritual consciousness? Is the soul the seat of consciousness?

Peacemakers also reflect on the relationship between an immortal soul and God. Benedict directs our reflection with the following:

> No being can be thought of apart from God. God is the ground and measure of the human soul. Reason is also a divine attribute. Thus, there can be no measure outside the God and man relationship...[3]

In Benedict's view, a soul emerges out of the ground

---

3   de Gaál, *The Theology of Pope Benedict XVI*, 35.

of all being—God. A soul exists in the most profound relationship possible. When we encounter a soul, we encounter divine relationship with God.

Christian Idealism recognizes that souls exist in relationship with God and that souls participate in the subjective awareness of God. When souls perceive Creation, they perceive the Mind of God. Apart from the Absolute Subject, they have no true reality.

The universe of Idealism is a closed system comprised of three components: 1) God, who creates by projecting thought forms; 2) the mind stuff or "being thought forms" projected, i.e. creation; 3) immortal souls who interact with the Mind of God. These are the components of comprehensive reality—this is the reality in which reconciliation takes place.

The preceding skeletal outline is meant to prompt further reflection. In following sections, we will put flesh on these philosophical bones in order to ensure a deeper understanding. First, however, we will consider the opposite philosophy—secular materialism.

Materialism

Philosophical materialism—also called naturalism—recognizes only material causes and effects. In this view, nothing real exists beyond material conditions, and the sole basis of all reality is matter-energy, the world of material objects. In this scheme, "the objective" is primary, the subjective secondary.

Materialists argue that all consciousness, all subjectivity, emerges from the material substratum of the brain. Awareness and thought are considered emergent properties of matter—they arise from material conditions, from neurochemicals, from neurons and other brain structures. Based on these assumptions, materialists argue that religious belief is nothing more than an evolutionary artifact of primitive brains. Faith, in their view, is equivalent to a lingering fairy tale.

Contemporary culture, indoctrinated with secular materialism, has become vulnerable to these false assumptions. In spite of obvious shortcomings, materialism thrives, especially among passionate advocates of so-called objective science who denigrate faith. Benedict critiqued this faulty objectivity:

> Wherever an answer is presented as unemotionally objective, as a statement that finally goes beyond the prejudices of the pious and provides purely factual, scientific information, then it has to be said that the speaker has here fallen victim to self-deception."[4]

Skeptics wedded to materialism will no doubt challenge Benedict's assertion. They push materialist claims without discernment, but, if they look deeper, they find "objective science" fails to provide evidence or proof for their claims. The assertions of materialism do not rest on evidence or proof but rather they are rooted in bias.

---

4 Ratzinger, *Introduction to Christianity*, 175.

Claims that science has disproven the existence of the supernatural are especially fraught with faulty reason. For example, the claim that the universe spontaneously popped into existence, with no prior cause, ironically finds materialists relying on blind faith. They offer no coherent explanation of the spontaneous origins claim but rather they turn to blind faith to justify their unreasoned claim.

Most people consider materialist views to be relatively harmless; unfortunately, they're anything but. They block a person's understanding of their loving relationship with a living God. Such views toss divine relationship into the dustbin of old myths. They slam shut the doors to faith.

Christians rarely know how to respond to the vicious attacks of secular materialists. They feel awkward or intimidated. Some grudgingly accept the cultural narrative, secretly fearing their beliefs lack veracity. Eventually, they cease sharing their faith. Others privately reject the tenets of materialism, yet nonetheless withdraw from public dialogue. They avoid debating those who consider faith to be a delusion generated by brain chemicals.

However, once Christians grasp a strong theology augmented with sound reason, the dilemma vanishes. Christians come to know the subjective to be *that which is most real*. They come to understand that God, as Absolute Subject, is the ground of *all* reality, the Cause behind *all* material conditions.

> Christian belief...means opting for the view that what cannot be seen is more real than what can

be seen. It is an avowal of the primacy of the invisible as the truly real, which upholds us and hence enables us to face the visible with calm composure—knowing that we are responsible before the invisible as the true ground of all things.[5]

Materialism wilts under intense inspection. Its premises fail, as observation does not reveal a stand-alone material world that is the source of its own creation. No evidence, no proof, exists. In contrast, there is support for the alternative—Christian Idealism.

The Great Clash—Materialism Versus Idealism

The clash between Materialism and Idealism fuels the noisy conflict between secularists and Christians. On one hand, *men of faith argue that a universe comprised solely of material conditions cannot exist*. On the other side, materialists argue that the supernatural, or God, cannot exist. As long as these opposing worldviews generate conflict, we must place the dream of world peace on hold.

Materialism's denial of supernatural existence negates all paths to peace based on divine relationship. If God does not exist, there's no divine relationship: all paths to peace based on God's love are foreclosed.

Christian Idealism shines a light on spiritual truths. Unfortunately, the contemporary culture does not embrace Idealism. Instead, we encounter a vacuum of faith

---

5   Ibid., 74.

and reason, a denial of supernatural existence that blocks all paths to peace grounded on faith. If God does not exist, then there is no divine relationship. For too long materialistic atheism has stunted cultural growth and blocked the development of intellectual tools that could contribute to a more nuanced view of mankind and a more harmonious vision of society. Benedict recognized the danger:

> Atheism is deeper than the Nazi or Communist ideologies. It negates the eternity of the individual human soul and corrupts his conscience, rendering him unable to discern right from wrong. Because man is created in the image and likeness of God, man will free himself from materialist totalitarianism only by relating to the God-man Jesus Christ and by living sacramentally in this relationship.[6]

When we critique materialist philosophy, we're not engaging in polemics or performing an exercise in apologetics. Rather, we're alerting peacemakers to a worldview that has destroyed communities of faith and undermined efforts to establish peace throughout the world.

We are drilling down to practical concerns, trying to understand how people view self and others. If we assess the value that disputants place on human life, for example, we can anticipate how they will treat other people. When we know how they view reality, we can forecast future claims and complaints.

---

6 de Gaál, 19.

Christian Idealism and Theology

Peacemakers who build their ministry on Christian tenets should mine the theology of Benedict XVI for insights into divine relationship. His system of reason rests upon the idea of God as Absolute Subject, God as the source of the inter-subjective reality we call Creation.

Theistic Idealism is a philosophy that envisions creation issuing from the Mind of God. It is consistent with Platonic philosophy, which influenced both Origen and Saint Augustine, two leading theologians of the early church.

> Although Christian engagement with Idealism waned for centuries, some philosophers and theologians kept the tradition alive: For the ancient world and the Middle Ages, being itself is true, in other words, apprehensible, because God, pure intellect, made it, and he made it by thinking it. To the creative original spirit, the *Creator Spiritus*, thinking and making are one and the same thing.[7]

In spite of the emerging resurgence of Christian Idealism, many find the concepts challenging. A steady drumbeat of cultural materialism has skewed basic perceptions. Bias and blindness have occluded truth. Peacemakers must prune the dead branches of theology and invite the faithful to begin anew by contemplating the Gospel of John:

---

[7] Ratzinger, *Introduction to Christianity*, 59.

Ever since the Prologue to the Gospel of John, the concept of logos has been at the very center of our Christian faith in God. Logos signifies reason, meaning, or even "word"—a meaning, therefore, that is Word, that is relationship, that is creative.[8]

When John wrote his gospel, he fully understood that material conditions emerge from divine thought—the Word brings forth creation as being-thought. The Catholic Creed, even today, continues to speak of "all things visible and invisible." Men of faith realize that:

> [W]hat cannot be seen, what can in no wise move into the field of vision, is not unreal; ... on the contrary, what cannot be seen in fact represents true reality, the element that supports and makes possible all the rest of reality.[9]

Though scripture shines a bright light on these truths, it is not unusual to encounter Christians ensnared by materialism. They have been taught to distrust subjective awareness, including their own. They have been convinced that consciousness lacks inherent reality, that consciousness is a fleeting illusion, an emergent property of a material brain. They've been led to believe that biological determinism shapes and constrains our lives, reducing humans to the status of sophisticated bio-machines or herd animals. They've been induced to toss aside free will

---

8 Ratzinger, *Introduction to Christianity*, 26.
9 Ibid., 50.

and discard divine relationship. They have been tricked into following lazy thinking that negates their existence as an immortal soul.

In contrast, Benedict reminds us that free will is not an idle concept, and neither is the idea that our existence originates from divine thought:

> Christian belief in God means that things are the being-thought of a creative consciousness, of a creative freedom, and that the creative consciousness that bears up all things has released what has been thought into the freedom of its own, independent existence.[10]

Benedict celebrates free will and dismisses determinism. He recognizes that all creation is endowed with the divine gift of freedom. His thoughts, expressed in the following passage, warrant contemplation:

> [O]ne could very well describe Christianity as a philosophy of freedom. For Christianity, the explanation of reality as a whole is not an all-embracing consciousness or one single materiality; on the contrary, at the summit stands a freedom that thinks and, by thinking, creates freedoms, thus making freedom the structural form of all being.[11]

Mediators will find Benedict's powerful vision of

---

10 Ibid., 157.
11 Ibid.

faith—a view rarely expressed so beautifully—entirely accurate. The disputants sitting before the mediator are not programmed bio-robots; they're immortal souls endowed with free will. For this reason, peacemakers honor self-determinism and choice, applying a basic axiom: *mediators seek to restore party self-determinism and renew the conscious exercise of free will.*

When people antagonistic to faith attack the idea of free will with the faulty premises of materialism, men of faith can find a powerful defense in the robust tools of Christian Idealism. But before the faithful wield the power tools of reason, they will want to clear up any lingering confusions regarding Idealism. The subject has been so greatly misunderstood that only a handful of people remain who truly grasp its immense explanatory power.

Christian Idealism: Weak and Strong

Christian Idealism can be divided into weak and strong aspects. Though this division is arbitrary—as weak and strong aspects exist along a single continuum—the division into weak and strong aspects helps us discern important differences between the ends of the continuum. The weak aspect includes an individual's thoughts, perceptions, or mental images. The strong aspect is the *being-thought-forms* projected by God's consciousness. At the weak end, we find the mind of an individual soul; at the strong end, the Mind of God.

The strong aspect might be defined as *being-thought-forms* from the Mind of God. We shift away from talking about the "objective" to acknowledge the subjective nature of all causes and effects, which is consistent with Benedict's reflection on the nature of Idealism:

> Whoever looks thoroughly at matter will discover that it is being-thought, objectivized thought. So it cannot be the ultimate. On the contrary, before it comes thinking, the idea, all being is ultimately being-thought and can be traced back to mind as the original reality; this is the "idealistic" solution.[12]

The Mind of God, from the perspective of Christian Idealism, accounts for all natural and supernatural causes. This strong aspect plays a central role in creation, contrary to the weak aspect of the individual mind. Benedict distinguishes between the creative activity of the Mind of God and weak or *mere* idealism:

> [T]he Christian belief in God will say: Being is being-thought—yet not in such a way that it remains only thought and that the appearance of independence proves to be mere appearance to anyone who looks more closely."[13]

The preceding quote deserves to be parsed. "Be-

---

12 Ibid.,156.
13 Ibid., 157.

ing-thought" refers to substantial reality. Benedict warns against confusing this strong Idealism with weak idealism—with personal thought that "remains only thought." He contrasts being-thought emerging from Logos, from the Word, with ephemeral personal thoughts. Strong idealism represents the substantial being-thought that we recognize as creation. Weak idealism represents ephemeral personal thoughts that may "prove to be mere appearance."

A simple illustration may dispel confusion. Imagine—picture in your mind's eye—a common kitchen table. That mental image, derived from imagination or memory, is individual or personal thought that we categorize as a product of weak idealism. Personal mental images are a manifestation of weak idealism.

In contrast, the "actual" kitchen table is being-thought as a product of strong idealism. All people can independently view this being-thought-form—they can perceive the table. Both categories of thought are subjective, but one is individual and "weak," while the other is sufficiently strong for all to perceive.

Here we encounter the most troubling confusion regarding Idealism. When multiple subjective observers share a common perception—perhaps a kitchen table—we mislabel their *subjective agreement* as "objective reality." However, the perceptions of the multiple individual viewers always remain subjective. Each one retains a subjective viewpoint. And, in addition, the table continues to consist of subjective being-thought from the Mind of

God. The observers did not change, and the table's inherent nature did not change. The only thing that changes is that we simply have *subjective agreement* among multiple subjective viewers.

Thus, the table cannot be said to be truly objective—it does not possess *stand-alone existence independent of all subjective observers*. If we remove all conscious observers—*including the Mind of God*—the table no longer exists, as its true nature is being-thought.[14] If no conscious minds exist, there is no being-thought—and no table!

This realization may be quite startling. Skeptics will voice ironic objections. They may ask, how can you argue that the removal of all conscious minds leaves no objective world? The answer draws on simple logic: if you remove all conscious minds, all conscious observers, you are left with no way to observe or know what remains. If you remove all consciousness, you remove the only way anyone can know anything!

This last point warrants careful reflection. If we remove the only way men can possibly know anything—if we remove all consciousness—we hit a dead end, as beyond that point we cannot know anything. This conundrum exposes materialism's fatal flaw. Materialism assumes a stand-alone objective world independent of all consciousness—but no one can know if that claim is true. It is impossible to know whether or not an objective ma-

---

14 Note: If we remove all consciousness, no one remains to observe whether or not the table exists. Its "objective" existence must remain a matter of blind faith.

terial world exists separate from all conscious observers. When we remove all conscious agents, no one is left to observe whether or not anything "objective" continues to exist. This is simple logic.

In spite of this fatal flaw, materialists argue that a material or objective world exists *independent of all consciousness*. They hypothesize that first came a material universe, and then, later, consciousness emerged from matter-energy when brains developed. Materialists posit an independent, stand-alone objective world that is its own source of existence. However, such a world can never be observed—not even theoretically. Thus, philosophical materialism depends entirely on blind faith. Ironically, people who attack Christian belief as blind faith base their views on blind faith.

In contrast, Christian Idealism argues that all creation is being-thought-forms that issue from the Mind of God. These being-thought-forms are strong enough to be perceived by souls that share a *common subjective reality*. Let's examine that claim: Soul A perceives a being-thought-form that issues from the Mind of God—a table. Soul A perceives the table. Soul B also perceives the table. Soul A and Soul B agree. Their subjective perceptions match; they share inter-subjective reality.[15] A crude analogy would be a virtual-reality theater where souls gather to screen a 3-D movie projected by the Mind of God.

---

15 This is a simplified example. In an actual analysis, one might consider the constituent parts of the table to be the projection of the Mind of God. Such analysis is too complex and lengthy to be included in its entirety.

This conclusion is worth stressing. Multiple conscious observers perceiving in concert does not create a stand-alone objective reality. That which is perceived—being-thought-forms—remains subjective. Observers remain subjective. Multiple observers—conscious beings—perceive a *shared subjective creation. No phenomena exist independent of the Mind of God.*

Thus, at all times, man perceives subjective being-thought-forms, regardless of the number of observers. *All observations, including all scientific observations, involve subjective, conscious observers.* Even if we gather a million observers, we still have subjective observations of being-thought-forms.

Failure to reflect deeply on these principles leads to the faulty assumption that matter-energy exists independently. Those who assume the existence of a stand-alone material world—separate from all conscious observers, including God—do so as a matter of blind faith. Their assumption proves unverifiable.

This line of thought upsets a great number of people—it contradicts our common cultural conditioning. Atheists assume the physical world is primary and independent—God is unnecessary.

Secularists aren't alone. Many Christians unwittingly accept the premise of an independent material reality divorced from the Mind of God. They begin with the faulty premise of an independent material universe and then "add on" a God that fits the gaps.

The widespread rejection of Christian Idealism begs a

question: if the philosophy is valid, why is it not more broadly recognized? One reason is that critics fail to discern between the weak aspect—individual minds—and the strong aspect—the Mind of God. Centuries ago, Anglican Bishop George Berkeley addressed this issue, but his treatise has been largely overlooked.[16] To remedy this oversight, we will briefly consider the weak aspect and ask how a personal mental image could possibly have anything to do with the structure of reality.

In limited spheres of causation, an individual's thoughts play a creative role. For example, every conscious action we take is preceded by a thought. We make a decision and then act. All conscious actions are preceded by thought. As a trivial example, attempt to move your arm without first having the thought of moving your arm. It is not possible.[17]

Another example concerns mental images—imagination or memory. These images are strong enough to arouse emotions, sensations, and feelings that trigger bodily responses. For example, a person can recall a time of overwhelming emotion, either a time of great joy or a time of great distress. As they scan the memory or mental image, emotions, sensations, and feelings arise in their body. Simply scanning the mental image produces physical effects.

---

16   Bishop George Berkeley, *A Treatise Concerning the Principles of Human Knowledge.*
17   Ibid. Stimulus-response action, which bypasses consciousness, is mechanical action separate from consciousness.

In addition, ideas shape creative endeavors such as applied technology that alters the face of the earth. In these instances, creative thought applied to the physical world creates actual conditions. Stroll through a major city and take in the skyscrapers—those buildings were once an idea, and they now exist as imposing physical structures.

However, a divide exists between weak and strong idealism. Individual thought does not create "something from nothing." Weak "creating" is contingent on existing conditions; it is not original or ontological. Weak-aspect creation does not start with nothing; rather, it works with existing building blocks. In the example of the table, a carpenter executed a design with existing materials. He added to God's creation, rather than bringing something into existence from nothing. Only strong idealism, with being-thought issuing from the Mind of God, brings about fundamental creation.

Individual thought, however, does not differ *entirely* from the strong aspect of being-thought: Idealism's weak and strong aspects exist along a continuum. They share a common nature. Yet, because an immense distance separates the weak and strong poles, they may seem entirely different. A full clarification of the differences and the similarities would require an entire book.[18] For our purposes, therefore, we simply divide Idealism into weak and strong aspects and honor the differences.

---

18   Ibid.

Peacemaking Concerns

When mediators seek peace, they first assess the reality matrix: they want to know how a party's individual reality meshes with the inter-subjective reality of all parties. They seek to find or create a shared inter-subjective reality in which reconciliation can take place. Mediators who do not understand how subjective reality is shaped will struggle.

In a similar manner, mediators work to bring the individual soul's worldview into agreement with the comprehensive reality known as Creation. They explore the interface between weak and strong aspects of idealism—the intersection of a soul's consciousness with the Mind of God. This intersection or mystical union is the sweet spot of reconciliation. Parties who experience this mystical union begin to understand how prayer works, why miracles are possible, and why the dream of enduring world peace is legitimate and attainable.

Discernment and Reality

Materialism, based on blind faith in an "objective" world, turns out to be a cruel fantasy. Those who put their trust in the existence of such an objectively verifiable universe end up disappointed.

That's because the material world lacks stand-alone existence—it does not exist independently of thought, perception, and action, but rather depends upon an external cause for its existence. Christian Idealism adequately explains this cause—the Logos or Mind of God creates and projects thought-forms that individual souls perceive and experience as matter-energy.[19]

As reconcilers manage subjective phenomena unfolding in an idealistic universe, they must become familiar with the playing field of Creation and the minds of the players on the field. Just as we would not consult a bicycle repair manual to work on an expensive Maserati, so we would not consult inaccurate systems of reason to reconcile broken relationships.

Christian Idealism posits a malleable reality. It allows for a change in conditions leading to spiritual transformation. This is important: disputants require certainty that change is possible. They are not about to risk failure. If they believe man cannot be transformed into a better state, they will not attempt the arduous process of reconciliation. Peacemaking never truly convenes without real hope for meaningful change. Parties will convene only when they're confident they will find release from the bondage of conflict.

Worldviews that tout a machine-like world of deterministic outcomes do not impart confidence. As a result, such philosophies have no place in peacemaking. Instead, faith-based mediators should turn to Christian Idealism, which places the relationship between man and God at the center of reality.

In other words, faith-based peacemakers work within

---

19 Ibid.

a metaphysical reality in which spirit-to-spirit connection is recognized and honored. They invite and nurture divine love as the elixir that softens hearts. They utilize mystical affinity, wisdom, and various other perceptions that are non-existent in other worldviews. They lead souls out of bondage and guide parties beyond mundane realms to states of consciousness not even considered in other philosophies.

Materialism, in stark contrast, conceives human nature to be mechanistic and restricted by biology. Meaningful change is rarely considered possible. If change is considered, that change will be minor and not subject to self-determinism, but will rather be the result of coercive outside intervention. This viewpoint permits the use of manipulation, coercion, drugs, or psychological programming.

In a materialistic worldview, wisdom is reduced to computation; knowledge is reduced to data. Affinity is considered to be solely a product of evolutionary animal instincts related to procreation. Consciousness, devoid of spiritual qualities, is considered to be an emergent by-product of neurochemical processes, a mere epiphenomenon arising out of underlying material conditions. Materialists believe that our individual lives emerge from complex material systems. They believe society is an insentient system that they can predict using probability models.

As a result, materialists lack the means to bring about world peace. Their philosophy contains no system or method for facilitating cultural dialogue. The desired result—in this case, "enduring world peace"—would simply be one low-probability outcome among many. Peace would depend on a roll of the dice.

A mechanistic philosophy leads to mechanistic solutions. Control takes priority over collaboration. Mediators who rely on such flawed views of reality no longer seek to facilitate dialogue; instead, they try to re-program others in the hope of ensuring compliance.

To put it simply, philosophy matters. A peacemakers' worldview not only informs his personal approach, but may affect the outcome of the reconciliation process, determining the ultimate success or failure of the endeavor. For this reason, peacemakers should take the study of theology and philosophy seriously as they seek to become experts in assessing, discerning, and managing views of reality.

Reflection

Benedict XVI, expanding upon the legacy of his predecessor, Pope John Paul II, grasped the deeper message contained in the latter's encyclical:

> This is the deeper motivation behind the 1998 encyclical *Fides et Ratio*. Human reason must be capable of recognizing truth, lest it is unable to love.[20]

---

20   de Gaál, 169.

Benedict's discussion of faith and reason prompts reflection: why might the inability to recognize truth render us unable to love? One answer lies in the nature of deception. An intellect that is deceived, and thus not firmly grounded in reason, cannot discern truth from fantasy or fact from fiction. Rumors, innuendo, and slander destroy the foundation upon which healthy, loving relationships are built.

Deception may also to philosophical errors, such as materialism, which reduces man to a stimulus-response herd animal. Mediators must be prepared to help parties sort through such errors and biases.

Preparing for the peacemaking ministry requires diligent study and hard work, but the result is worth the effort. The goal is to help conflicting parties recover free will, discern truth, and regain respect for their opponents. With a solid grounding in Christian theology, faith-based mediators can begin to renew the foundation of love upon which sincere and lasting reconciliation can be built. Those who dedicate themselves to the cause of peace must rise to meet the challenge.

FOUR

Reason and Culture

Peacemakers often crash into cultural barriers, bringing reconciliation efforts to a halt. Mediation hits an impasse, dashing hopes for peace. Typically, cultural barriers that cause impasse operate subtly in the background of human consciousness. These worldviews, informed more by indoctrination than education, demand loyalty in subtle ways. They operate as invisible walls that constrain free will and creative thought. The barriers are so subtle that they're viewed as part of the reality landscape, exerting a subtle but pernicious influence.

As soon as we conduct a "reality check," cultural edicts that demand conformity rise to the surface and become visible. Enforced cultural viewpoints present a dilemma: on the one hand, parties have a strong desire to be liked, which causes them to conform, yet they also want to exercise free will. Conflicts exacerbate the dichotomy and fuel internal struggle.

Cultural indoctrination usually defeats free will. Party self-determinism suffers a loss. Internal voices echo cultural indoctrination, which dictates behavior. On one hand, the desire to be admired and accepted forces conformity while, on the other hand, free will reasserts itself and demands independence of thought and action. Those who find themselves at the mercy of such internal dynamics end up living roller-coaster lives, experiencing periods of tranquility interspersed by periods of hostility and conflict.

Effective peacemakers learn to unearth the subtle cultural influences that erect barriers to peace. Always wary of cultural views that sabotage reconciliation, they must train themselves to recognize the adverse influence of cultural beliefs and minimize their negative effects.

Reconciliation and Culture

Peacemakers prepare for reconciliation ministry by reflecting on their personal philosophy and renewing their commitment to their faith tradition. Only then can they can build a system of reason that guides their practical ministry.

Mediators who adopt a faith-based view may find themselves in opposition to their materialist counterparts in the dispute resolution field. They also might encounter parties who are strenuously opposed to faith-based views. A mediator will need to assess any such undercurrent of resistance or hostility.

Mediators may decide to recuse themselves or they may proceed with caution. In the early stages, before they guide the party through a reality check, they must maintain a delicate balance; they must unearth biases that threaten to sabotage reconciliation efforts while at the same time moving the process moving toward a worldview reality check.

Materialism Impedes Mediation

Materialists view humans solely as biological entities, physical products of evolution. Instead of addressing emotional or cultural concerns, they focus on underlying mechanical and biological factors and turn to techniques that others might find coercive—psychological programming tools, for example. Since they consider love, empathy, and compassion to be emergent properties of brain interactions, they endorse the use of psychiatric drugs to alter states of mind.

Materialists consider self-determinism to be an illusion. In their view, free will does not exist; rather, all behavior is biologically determined. They believe there is a low probability of significant personal change. In fact, they often believe that meaningful personality change is impossible since a person's psychology is dictated by immutable physical conditions. They find social engineering acceptable and even desirable. In their view, man resembles a herd animal; the species takes priority over the individual. Their core belief—that an organism's biological self-interest alone drives motivation—renders spiritual or transcendent concerns irrelevant. Some go so far as to claim that religious beliefs are evolutionary artifacts of primitive brains.

Materialists view party interests as temporal and fleeting. Morality—if it is considered at all—is utilitarian and relativistic. Absolute values are rejected. All meaning is ephemeral, considered to be an emergent by-product of brain activity. Knowledge is reduced to data and computations; wisdom plays no meaningful role. Searching for a deeper self (endowed with divine qualities) is considered a waste of time, as the sum total of a person can be found in mechanical, biological factors. A mediator who adheres to materialistic premises, consciously or unconsciously, limits potential reconciliation outcomes by placing limits on personal transformation.

Secularists may take offense at the the bleak and one-sided portrayal of materialistic philosophy. They may think the analysis is unfair. After all, even though they reject faith-based claims, they may still have a desire to reduce human suffering. They may be blessed with welcoming personalities, warm hearts, and sincere compassion. Perhaps they even deny their personal beliefs color their mediation. They claim impartiality. They see their views as "objective" scientific truth. This conviction is flawed and masks their bias.

In order to appreciate the stakes, we should evaluate the overall discipline of conflict resolution. In spite of the well-intentioned efforts of dedicated professionals, those under the influence of materialist philosophy have not advanced the cause of world peace. As a result, the world is no closer to its dream of attaining true and lasting peace.

Faith communities, in particular, have found their deep

beliefs and ancient traditions invalidated by those under the influence of secular views. When secular mediators impose a foreign view of reality, the faith community is left confused, angry, and disillusioned.

Why have peace efforts failed in the presence of so many well-intentioned practitioners? Something has gone wrong. Perhaps honed social skills and amenable personalities are not adequate? Mediators need to bring their faith traditions and expanded view of reality to bear on the discipline of dispute resolution. The most important factor in achieving long-term reconciliation success may be their worldview. The mediator's worldview, we discover, does make a difference.

Perhaps men and women of faith need to take responsibility for their own communities and bring their long-held traditions to bear on the discipline of dispute resolution. If they manage to prevail over their critics by staying true to their own beliefs, they may find that, for those of faith, *the most important factor determining long-term reconciliation success may well be the peacemaker's worldview.*

Faith Inspires Mediation

Peacemakers who adhere to the tenets of Christian Idealism honor free will and nurture party self-determinism. They believe personal views are malleable, which makes positive transformation possible and even likely. They believe parties can chip away vestiges of false self, layer by layer, until divine self is revealed. In their view, man's nature is not constrained by mechanical factors—man is not "hardwired." His life is not pre-determined and unchangeable.

Faith-based mediators believe spirit and mind transcend material conditions with divine qualities—compassion, love, and empathy. They believe human lives are sweetened with divine love, grace, mercy, and forgiveness. They anticipate times when love for others eclipses self-interest, times when people sacrifice self-interest for a higher value. Altruism, they believe, is not an evolutionary anomaly but rather a divine quality.

A faith-based mediator considers that all Creation arises from a conscious origin, not from spontaneous combustion of matter-energy. In a world that emerges from the Mind of God, mediation becomes imbued with a sacred quality. Faith-based mediators, keenly aware of each man's spiritual essence, know that each soul is endowed with the image and likeness of God. They come to realize that mystical union with God is the ultimate goal of reconciliation.

In the eyes of a faith-based mediator, the material world is fleeting and transient. Souls who cling to worldly phenomena later suffer disappointment when the objects of their attachment turn to dust. Mediators thus encourage parties to seek value beyond material conditions. The terms of settlements are expanded beyond mundane interests.

A significant difference between faith-based and secular mediators has to do with the time frame or scope of conflict resolution. Faith-based mediators believe souls experience an afterlife, a post-mortem continuity of consciousness. Mediators realize that the expanded time frame motivates an immortal soul to consider consequences that extend beyond this life. They know that someone who believes in the existence of a soul will be more likely to align their personal intentions with divine intentions, with the Will of God.

Reconcilers advocate sacred worship as a way to facilitate healing divine relationship. They encourage prayer as a tool that lifts a party beyond the mundane world into union with the supernatural. This mystical union fosters decisions consistent with a soul's spiritual nature. In these ways and others, faith-based mediators, viewing from a spiritual perspective, differ from secular mediators.

Each faith-based mediator holds a unique worldview; yet these individual views emerge from a shared faith, from a body of knowledge that presents fundamental truths regarding a comprehensive reality comprised of material and spiritual elements.

In contrast, though secular peacemakers may be caring individuals, they fail to base their work on fundamental truths regarding comprehensive reality. Their framework omits the spiritual; they suffer viewpoint contamination. Inaccurate and faddish concepts of human nature inhibit their success.

Faith-based peacemakers, on the other hand, seek truths regarding the essence of an immortal soul, truths grounded in divine relationship.

A discussion of the differences between faith-based

and secular mediators may remind readers of "culture war" debates. Peacemakers, however, do not care about debates. Rather, they seek to align mediation with "facts on the ground." If they fail to honor truths consistent with the deepest reality possible, they stumble. This basic sentiment will become increasingly clear in following chapters.

Peacemaking Assessment

Effective peacemakers bring their personality, spirituality, and wisdom to reconciliation. Therefore, periodically, they should inventory their personal assets and skills. They should evaluate their ability to know, to intuit, and to perceive. They should reflect on the following questions: *How do I know what I know? How do I determine what is real and what is unreal? How do I discern truth from fantasy or delusion?*

They will want to reflect on how they monitor their consciousness.[1] They will want to study their subjective interface with the world and ask how they might heighten their perception. As they reflect, they might recall times when they correctly identified factors driving conflict and times when they failed. They will need to hone their intuition, recalling times when *they knew that they knew.* They will want to recall moments when they were able

---

[1] The Jesuit Examination of Consciousness is one tool that peacemakers may want to use for this reflection.

to know with the heart—times when their perceptions transcended the mundane world. They will want to recall moments when the Lord's light made visible that which had been hidden. Benedict explains this heightened, infused knowledge:

> The human being Jesus is not only the Son of God, he—as John reminds one with haunting clarity in the prologue to his gospel—is the Logos, that is, the key to understanding the whole of reality and life. Human reason is unable on its own to reach such heights. However, provided with the Logos' wisdom and grace, it is capable of knowing the very condition and ultimate goal of its existence.[2]

This heightened awareness, delivered by the Logos' wisdom and grace, is vital for success in reconciliation ministry. Reconcilers must remain alert for moments when their awareness or perceptions dim. They must note times when they misperceive a situation or fail to observe the obvious. When they're distracted by the noise of the world, they note the lapse and refocus. They'll want to be aware of the degree to which they embrace the spirit of play and the spirit of discovery. When their passion for life dwindles, they'll want to make corrections that renew their vitality.

From time to time, they'll want to evaluate the soundness of their reasoning and ensure their intellect is infused with heart. They must engage in constant self-ap-

---

2 de Gaál, *The Theology of Pope Benedict XVI*, 184.

praisal and guard against slipping into stimulus-response behavior that leads them away from intentional and prayerful action.

Over the course of their studies, peacemakers should take self-assessment "snapshots" that reveal which areas are in need of improvement. The exercise prevents debilitating slides into doubt and ensures that mediators are not swept up unwittingly by faulty views. In some cases, these self-evaluations motivate students to seek pastoral counseling in an effort to "heal the healer."

Culture, Idealism, World Peace

After peacemakers complete a round of self-assessment, they're better prepared to address the conflicts that are troubling others. They learn, from their personal experience, how to construct an assessment that helps others.

The paradigm they construct should include assessing cultural influences that taint the parties' views. They seek to discern how cultural influences might inhibit or sabotage their reconciliation efforts. For example, a party who views his fellow man as a herd animal to be corralled, controlled, and manipulated, will also deny his own spiritual nature. He will adopt and cling to false-self ego identities. Mediators who detect this dynamic know they will need to help the party disentangle such false views and gain an accurate sense of their needs and interests.

Faith-based mediators realize that a culture that reduces people to the status of programmed bio-robots negates mankind's divine gift of free will. Individuals who lack free will cannot function in a self-determined manner: when they're called upon to make choices and decisions, they're easily swayed by opinion, prejudice, and bias. When a culture denies a person's status as an immortal soul, that culture condemns the person to live with a false identity. Assessments should be designed to pick up this adverse influence.

Cultural misdirection plays a harmful role in the arts and in public policy. Falsehoods create an adversarial social climate. While peacemakers do not seek to generate cultural debate, they must address worldviews that generate conflict. They function as teachers, life coaches, spiritual directors, and negotiation consultants. They teach disputants that faith and reason best inform life-altering decisions.

This assessment departs from the norm. Most people are hesitant to share their personal philosophy. Life moves too fast for such introspective endeavors. Out of expediency, people go along with the culture, letting popular assumptions shape their viewpoints and decisions. When conflict forces them to the mediation table, things change. They are forced to provide a rationale for their choices. Faced with the need to explain their worldview, they become confused. A well-designed assessment leads them into deeper reflection and helps them reconstruct their worldview.

Faith-Based Reconciliation and Culture

Faith-based reconciliation violates contemporary norms

that declare, with a whisper or a scream, that God is a delusion. This worldview tramples sacred joy, as Benedict notes in the following:

> Such joy faces two hurdles today: 1) philosophy nowadays rejects a metaphysics assuming a creator God, and 2) the reduction of reality to physical causes and effects can no longer consider the possibility of divine intervention.[3]

In an effort to restore this stolen joy, peacemakers encourage disputants to receive pastoral counseling or spiritual direction, processes that help them realize their essence as a soul endowed with the image and likeness of God. In guided contemplative prayer, parties explore the interface between spiritual consciousness and sacred reality. During spiritual exercises, they learn that the idea of brain-mind equivalency is false. Spiritual consciousness is not an epiphenomenon of the material brain as some assume but rather a phenomenon based in lived experience.

Benedict, in his description of mystical union, describes the loftier origin of spiritual consciousness:

> Man can rethink the logos, the meaning of being, because his own logos, his own reason, is logos of the one logos, thought of the original thought, of the creative spirit that permeates and governs his being.[4]

---

[3] Ibid., 239.
[4] Ratzinger, *Introduction to Christianity*, 59.

While contemplative or mystical spirituality has historically been the domain of monks and mystics, all Christian sojourners can benefit from the path, especially those seeking to heal broken relationships. Spiritual formation that highlights man's essence as an immortal soul enhances reconciliation. When people see the divine in the other, they show increased compassion. After experiencing a mystical state, they no longer seek to coerce or manipulate. They eschew deceptive practices, mind-altering pharmaceuticals, and coercive psychology.

Faith-based reconciliation can reshape a culture, one person at a time, by simultaneously nurturing spiritual truths and transforming worldviews that deny free will and divine relationship. Benedict explains how divine relationship is a path to transcendent knowledge:

> Belief in the biblical God expresses the conviction that the eternal mind produces a subjective mind that is called to apprehend itself as a declension of the former. Thus in a seemingly paradoxical mixture of awe and joy, human thinking finds itself "re-thinking" that which in reality had been divinely thought beforehand.[5]

In this paradigm, individual souls, endowed with the image and likeness of God, access the mind of God. Souls living in relationship with God gain an ability to know the Mind of God. Faith-based peacemaking is unique in

---

[5] de Gaál, *The Theology of Pope Benedict XVI*, 135.

that it recognizes that parties are souls infused with the ability to know divine consciousness.

In contrast, secular mediators work in darkness, possessing incomplete knowledge of reality. Though they might experience some success, such limited results are insufficient to hasten world peace. Faith-based peacemakers envision a loftier goal:

> The terminal point of earthly existence for the human being is not the absolutized condition of something belonging to this world, such as a classless society, designer children, economic efficiency, a healthy environment, or a racially pure nation, but rather the Sabbath rest granted by God alone.[6]

In summary, faith-based mediators bring about tangible change by infusing the culture with faith and reason.

Moral Relativism and Idealism

Some Christians argue that the subjective leads to moral relativism. They reject the idea of an idealistic path to peace: "An objection to subjective theories of truth is that they all lead to relativism. They all have the consequence that a statement may be true for me but not for you."[7]

---

6 Ibid., 71.
7 Alan Musgrave, *Common Sense, Science and Scepticism: A historical introduction to the theory of knowledge* (New York: Cambridge University Press, 1993), 252.

This observation should not be brushed aside, as a healthy fear of relativism is warranted, especially in light of Postmodernist claims that all beliefs are relative.[8]

Yet faulty Postmodernism should not preclude serious philosophical inquiry into the subjective reality brought forth by God, the Absolute Subject. Christian Idealism and Postmodernism differ. When we accept the subjective realm as the primary source of Creation, we do not necessarily accept moral relativism. This requires further explanation.

Those who battle moral relativism all too often dismiss all things subjective and elevate all things objective, but this signals confusion, as they do not really seek an objective solution to morality. When they have an opportunity to reflect, they realize they're not seeking the objective, but rather the Absolute. They've confused Objective with Absolute. Fundamental truth is not found in objects, in material conditions, but rather in the Absolute Subjectivity of God.

A passage from Benedict identifies one cause of this confusion:

> [M]an is fashioned in such a way that his eyes are only capable of seeing what is not God...thus for man God is and always will be the essentially

---

[8] In the late 20th century, postmodernist philosophy applied to literature and the interpretation of history, law, and culture prompted re-evaluation of Western values. The philosophy argued against universal values and declared each individual determined their own truth. Moral relativism began.

invisible, something lying outside his field of vision.[9]

When it comes to knowing the invisible, we stumble. We're disturbed by the idea that reality is shaped by invisible, subjective causes. The idea makes little or no sense to those steeped in materialism. And yet, for people of faith, it makes perfect sense to gaze beyond the transitory material realm to seek a transcendent Absolute.[10] Only then do they access fundamental reality.

In this search for the Absolute, they must reject the faulty premise that nothing exists beyond the material world. In this regard, Benedict assists our understanding:

> Things are, because they are thought. In the ancient and medieval view, all being is, therefore, what has been thought, the thought of the absolute spirit. Conversely, this means that since all being is thought, all being is meaningful, logos, truth.[11]

The preceding passage captures the focal point of faith and reason, the cornerstone of a theology of relationship: we live in a universe whose origin is the supernatural Logos, the Absolute Word. This is the source of all morality—the realm of Absolute Subjectivity. There is nothing objective about morality.

---

9 Ratzinger, *Introduction to Christianity*, 49.
10 A transcendent Absolute Subject refutes moral relativism. See details in following chapters.
11 Ratzinger, *Introduction to Christianity*, 59.

The primary obstacle blocking an understanding of subjectivity is our cultural adherence to the tenets of Materialism. We misuse the term "objective" to signify something lasting and solid, meaning material objects, but reflection confirms that material conditions are fleeting, ephemeral, transitory, and contingent on Mind for their existence.[12] That which lasts forever, Absolute or Eternal, is Subjective. All material conditions depend upon a subjective ground of being:

> In other words, faith means deciding for the view that thought and meaning do not just form a chance by-product of being; that, on the contrary, all being is a product of thought and, indeed, in its innermost structure is itself thought.[13]

Christian Idealism has the power to transform the culture with its powerful view of reality. Benedict sees the introduction of this worldview as a key step toward improving the world:

> Society is called to acknowledge the transitory nature of this world and accept its imperfections. This honesty allows society to consciously live the supernatural virtue of hope anchored in eternity. Human beings are then able to work to improve this world as a way to give expression to charity.[14]

---

12 See the proofs for the existence of God. St. Thomas Aquinas, *Summa Theologia*.
13 Ratzinger, *Introduction to Christianity*, 152.
14 de Gaál, *The Theology of Pope Benedict XVI*, 150.

Peacemakers call for a worldview conversion that incorporates Absolute Subjectivity. The view of reality that makes this possible is Christian Idealism—the only philosophy that recognizes the reality of grace, prayers, miracles, immortality, forgiveness, sacraments, the Real Presence, mystical union with Christ, and the Beatific Vision. This philosophy helps us understand why belief in the existence of the supernatural is not delusion or fantasy. The philosophy takes subjectivity beyond mere solipsism.[15]

Subjective awareness in the form of spiritual consciousness becomes the bridge to divine relationship. Spiritual consciousness, heightened by contemplative prayer, leads to knowledge of God. St. Francis of Assisi is a wonderful example of a contemplative whose insights bridged the weak and strong aspects of Christian Idealism. For this reason, the study of Franciscan spirituality is recommended for peacemakers.

Reflection

Aspiring peacemakers reflect on how the culture affects their views and the views of those to whom they minister. They become proficient in assessing party acceptance of harmful cultural views. They learn new ways to help disputants overcome the subtle but destructive cultural views that condemn them to bondage.

---

[15] Solipsism is the philosophical claim that the individual mind dictates reality. Knowledge of things external to one's mind is uncertain. Solipsism, a common critique of Idealism fails to take inter-subjectivity into account. The faults of solipsism are often used, incorrectly, to dismiss Idealism.

At first glance, managing worldviews seem daunting, as most cultures enforce the premises of Materialism. The culture engages in unrelenting efforts to enforce agreement with false views. Peacemakers face a challenge when they try to make a difference—they must first overcome doubt before attempting to help others through the quicksand of intractable conflict.

Peacemakers who hope to manage cultural worldviews prepare by engaging in deep reflection on the nature of reality. Before they attempt to help others, peacemakers attend retreats that foster spiritual formation. They assess how their views of reality mesh with their personal theology. They learn to defeat worldviews that undermine faith. Later, even as their ministry matures, they remain vigilant and periodically assess their personal views. They do not want bias to lead parties into dead ends.

Peacemakers identify worldviews that counter divine relationship and then transform them. In order to accomplish this transformative task, peacemakers encourage parties to engage in spiritual formation. Once parties have a clear view of reality, they are better able to engage the reconciliation process.

FIVE
God is Love

A pivotal accomplishment of faith-based reconciliation is the ability to heal divine relationship. A ministry that emerges from a sound "theology of relationship" celebrates mystical union with a living God, rather than ignoring or belittling it. The goal is to restore each individual's faith in and connection with a higher power at the same time we mend their personal relationships.

Unfortunately, the concept of divine relationship is met with skepticism or derision, not only among secularists but also among believers, many of whom greet the idea of an actual *relationship* with God with unvoiced skepticism.

Reconcilers must be able to confront doubts with calm assurance. They must kindle a party's desire to search for supernatural intimacy while simultaneously instructing them to see the divine spark in "the other." This process of spiritual re-formation may begin with an extended reflection on the phrase, "God is Love," a statement whose simplicity masks a complex and powerful theological principle, as laid out in Pope Benedict XVI's inaugural encyclical, *Deus Caritas Est*: *God Is Love.*[1]

God Is Love

The reflection begins with the first letter of John:

> "God is love, and he who abides in love abides in God, and God abides in him."[2]

This passage expresses the heart of the Christian faith, and captures a core premise of reconciliation ministry. If John's testimony is false, our peacemaking hopes are dashed. Therefore, his words deserve careful evaluation. Let us begin by shifting our focus from commandments to relationship, as captured in John's letter:

> Since God has first loved us (cf. 1 Jn 4:10), love is now no longer a mere "command"; it is the response to the gift of love with which God draws near to us.[3]

John establishes a central aspect of divine relationship—the give-and-take of divine love. Pilgrims do not chart their salvation journey with signposts comprised of rules and commands; rather, they turn to a different marker:

---

[1] Pope Benedict XVI, *God Is Love (Deus Caritas Est)* (San Francisco, California: Ignatius Press, 2009).
[2] 1 John 4:16.
[3] Pope Benedict XVI, *God Is Love*, 8.

> God himself is love. In this sense, love is indeed both the fundamental rule and the ultimate aim of life.[4]

The consequences of this statement are profound. If love is the "fundamental rule" rule of life, then the process of restoring divine relationship is not an abstract theological exercise that draws our attention to distant supernatural realms far removed from the consequences of our world. Rather, it is an intensely personal and highly practical way of re-orienting our lives toward that which matters most.

Divine love infuses and inspires our daily lives, providing hope and direction:

> Even from a purely human point of view, then, love is what we are looking for and is the goal toward which our lives are directed. But within its own framework and on its own terms it directs our view toward God and brings us to wait upon God.[5]

As Benedict explains so beautifully, our most basic need—to be loved—anchors our lives in the divine Ground of Being. Our thirst for love is quenched at a well that supplies limitless divine grace. Peacemakers draw from this well when they seek to reconcile warring parties. They

---

[4] Pope Benedict XVI, "March 23," *Benedictus: Day by Day with Pope Benedict XVI*, ed. Peter J. Cameron (San Francisco, California: Ignatius Press / Magnificat, 2006), 98.
[5] Ibid.

seek to quench disputants' thirst for the "fundamental rule and ultimate aim of life." They seek to reconcile parties with the essence of God:

> John wants to say that the essential constituent of God is love and hence, that all God's activity is born from love and impressed with love: all that God does, he does out of love and with love, even if we are not always immediately able to understand that this is love, true love.[6]

When reconcilers mediate "in the presence of the Holy Spirit," they invite the power of God's love into the process. They invite parties to listen with their hearts and connect with God's grace and mercy. They encourage the parties to mirror God's love by sharing reciprocal forgiveness. This exchange ignites a flame of affinity, the faint glimmer of which glows with a great warmth that infuses mediation with hope and lifts disputants out of darkness and despair.

This spirit-driven reconciliation resembles nuclear fission. Divine love acts as the fissionable fuel. As it increases, parties "...realize that a pure and generous love is the best witness to the God in whom we believe and by whom we are driven to love."[7] They understand the powerful role love plays in healing all relationships—not only divine relationship.

---

[6] Pope Benedict XVI, *The Apostles* (Huntington, Indiana: Our Sunday Visitor, 2007), 81.
[7] Benedict XVI, *God Is Love*, 82.

These discoveries lead us to conclude that while mediation techniques make *conflict resolution* possible, only the Holy Spirit's sacred presence guarantees *reconciliation*. Without love, technique adds nothing:

> Saint Paul, in his hymn to charity (cf 1 Cor 13), teaches us that it is always more than activity alone. 'If I give away all I have, and if I deliver my body to be burned, but do not have love, I gain nothing.'[8]

Students come to recognize that the premises of reconciliation parallel the lessons of scripture. This is good news. It means that our peacemaking analysis rests on solid footing. That being said, aspiring peacemakers may crave greater certainty. In order to assure them that they're walking the correct path, we need to drill deeper into revealed truth regarding divine love.

Love and Knowledge

Divine love is *the* critical ingredient for successful reconciliation. An absence of divine love lowers the odds of success to zero. But what does this love look like? Divine love is not trivial or sentimental; enhanced by knowledge and wisdom, it is powerful enough to overcome conflict, hostility, and war.

The contemporary cultural narrative, on the other hand, posits a dichotomy between love and knowledge. Those

---

8 Ibid.

rich in knowledge are assumed to be poorly equipped to love. And, conversely, lovers are idealized as naive fools, disconnected from intellect and reason. Lovers, according to the stereotype, divorce their minds so they might cling foolishly to their hearts' desires. In this narrative, love lacks substance. It is nothing more than an emotional by-product of neurochemical activity—untrustworthy at best, harmful and manipulative at worst.

Peacemakers cannot afford to operate on such flimsy foundations; instead, they must eschew cultural prejudices; they must challenge the narrative that love lacks reason. In order to grasp the link between love and knowledge, they might ask: What purpose does knowledge serve?

Reflection reveals the answer: Knowledge guides the exercise of free will. When we exercise free will, we typically seek to satisfy our needs and desires. Reason guides us as we draw close to that which we love; it helps us discern our decisions regarding what we should be, do, or have. To put it simply, love fuels desire, while knowledge directs our course. Love is the engine; wisdom is the rudder.

Smooth sailing is rare. Obstacles block the way. Lack of knowledge leads to social ineptness. Cursed with inadequate reason, a person's exercise of free will becomes clumsy. They fail to coordinate their intentions with the intentions of others; they stumble about and provoke conflict. Eventually, they must seek help mending their relationships. Love and knowledge work in tandem—not separately, as the contemporary narrative would have us believe. The bond becomes especially significant in light of the fact that:

> [E]ntering into relationship with both God and others sets the conditions for the emergence of the possibility of knowing at the deepest level.[9]

The idea that relationship brings about knowing at the deepest level is vital in peacemaking. This truism shapes a simple axiom: *relationships beget great love, which in turn begets great knowledge.*

Reconciliation delivers an ancillary benefit: *reconciled disputants understand life better.* Surprisingly, the restoration of relationship—especially divine relationship—broadens man's knowledge of life and his awareness of Creation. When a man shares the love of Christ, he automatically shares in treasured wisdom. Saint Bonaventure recognized the connection:

> In Christ are contained all the treasures of wisdom and knowledge of the hidden God, and He is the medium for this knowledge.[10]

Here we discover that great love opens doors to great knowledge. Benedict captures this synergy with the metaphor of taste:

---

9 Collins, *The Word Made Love*, 16.
10 Fr. Christopher Rengers, ed., *The 33 Doctors of the Church* (Rockford, Illinois: Tan Books and Publishers, 2000), 357.

> When it comes to the ultimate, important truths, you cannot judge by reason any more surely than you can tell whether an object is sweet or bitter by looking at it. You must taste it.[11]

We "taste" with the heart when we love one another, when we draw close to each other. Those who are unable to draw close to their neighbors are barred from knowing God and barred from knowing life in its fullest measure. Their alienation from divine love saddles them with an awareness deficit. Impaired relationship leads to impaired knowledge.

Atheists face a cruel dilemma. When they refuse to draw close to God, they undermine their understanding of life's basic principles and lock themselves out of the cosmic storehouse of wisdom. They commit a critical mental error when they assume they must know all about God before they can draw close to Him. They assume knowing precedes loving. The truth is often the reverse: love opens the door to wisdom.

This love-and-wisdom dynamic creates a dilemma: to know another we must draw close to them, but we cannot draw close unless we first love them. The reason is simple: we do not move close to those we dislike. Lacking affinity, we're repelled rather than attracted. In contrast, when we love, even modestly, we are drawn closer. A practical axiom emerges: love precedes knowledge of the other. In the case of the atheist, we find a worldview that dictates

---

[11] Ibid.

alienation from God. Unable and unwilling to love, the atheist is unable to draw close. He's barred from knowing God. Absent love for God, an atheist cannot know God. This lack of knowing reduces his ability to love, which further reduces his ability to know. A vicious downward spiral ensues.

It is easy to overlook the deficit-of-love dilemma faced by atheists. Many evangelists assume they can remedy the atheist's lack of faith with apologetics, but debate cannot remedy the problem. Atheists suffer a deficit of love, an inability to love, that is not cured by philosophical propositions.

On the other hand, prayerful contemplation can reveal the link between love and wisdom. For example, upon reflection, we come to realize that "blind faith" is a counterfeit idea. That's because faith is not an assumption about the unknown; it is not an imaginary datum used to fill blank spaces in our knowledge. Rather, it emerges from a loving relationship with a living God and infuses the intellect with knowledge. It is a spiritual movement of the heart *accompanied by* wisdom.

To put it another way, faith *is* knowledge of God. Both faith and wisdom, which arise from that relationship, are non-existent in the absence of a personal connection with the divine. Love and wisdom thus have a common ground. When a heart becomes infused with faith, blindness falls away and sight is restored.

When Christ's love pervades a soul's consciousness, that soul experiences mystical union, or being-in-love.

That soul is infused with mystical wisdom, a knowing of the deepest kind. The pinnacle of divine relationship, mystical union, thus adds clarity to the phrase "God is love." Benedict further explains:

> And the form, the life of Christ, is love; hence to believe is to conform to Christ and to enter into his love.[12]

This leads to a significant discovery: supernatural wisdom springs from being-in-love, not from rhetoric and debate. Great wisdom is not a product of philosophical propositions but rather emanates from intimate relationship with God—wisdom flows from the mystical union of being, loving, and knowing. This discovery explains the promise in scripture that we shall become "all in all" with a God who loves.[13]

One might say that, in our true nature, we exist in a triune state of being, loving, and knowing. A key axiom follows: *we know best that which we love best*. Benedict captures this idea in his marvelous description of Saint Francis:

> As the simplex and idiota, Francis knew more about God than all the learned men of his time—because he loved Him more.[14]

---

12 Pope Benedict XVI, *St. Paul*, 82.
13 John 17:21.
14 Joseph Ratzinger, *The Theology of History in St. Bonaventure*, trans. Zachary Hayes OFM (Chicago, Illinois: Franciscan Herald Press, 1971), 157.

Divine love—at first thought to be insubstantial, unreal, and fraught with delusion—turns out to be the deepest reality possible, the living water that nourishes all life.

Christ the Mediator

The phrase "Christ the Mediator," found in scripture, signals that a vital part of the divine plan is reconciliation. Christ reconciles humanity with God: Humanity rediscovers previously abandoned divine love. Christ, as a result of reconciling humankind with God, resurrects God's gift of joy:

> Jesus' farewell discourses in Saint John's Gospel present a theology of joy, which as it were illuminates the depth of this word. "I will see you again and your hearts will rejoice, and no one will take your joy from you" (16:22).[15]

Mediators would do well to follow the example of Christ the Mediator. They should acquire skills that prepare them to facilitate sacred mediation. They should learn to tap into their endowment of divine love and thus infuse the reconciliation process with love. Benedict has provided the rationale behind our ability:

> Love is possible, and we are able to practice it because we are created in the image of God.[16]

---

15 Joseph Ratzinger, *Jesus of Nazareth vol. 3: The Infancy Narratives*, trans. Philip J. Whitmore (New York: Image, 2012), 27.
16 Pope Benedict XVI, *God is Love*, 87.

This sacred endowment is the key to success or failure in mediation. If we dismiss the phrase, "endowed with the image and likeness" of God, we sever our connection to the living spring of divine love. We destroy our ministry, which calls on us to restore arid human landscapes devoid of spiritual truth.

This is why secular promises of worldly peace prove to be mirages. Those who hold a materialistic view may attempt to resolve protracted conflict; they may attempt to disentangle confusion and misunderstanding; they might offer strategies for achieving a negotiated settlement, but they do not restore divine love, and thus they fail to reconcile relationships. A deficit of love cripples true peacemaking. Only a source of unlimited love can remedy hostility and hate.

In contrast to secular mediation, Christ taught us that the peace we seek is not of this world: "The peace of Jesus is a peace that the world cannot give (cf. Jn 14:27)."[17] When peacemakers grasp this passage from scripture, they grasp the essential role played by the Holy Spirit:

> "The Spirit, in fact, is that interior power which harmonizes [believers'] hearts with Christ's Heart and moves them to love their brethren as Christ loved them." The Spirit immerses us in the very rhythm of divine life, which is a life of love, enabling us to share personally in relations between the Father and the Son.[18]

---

17 Pope Benedict XVI, *Jesus of Nazareth vol 3*, 78.
18 Pope Benedict XVI, *The Apostles*, 135.

This passage motivates us to "mediate in the presence of the Holy Spirit." We are motivated to reflect on sacred relationship, mystical union, and communion with and in Christ the Mediator.

Dialogue / Communio

Mediation conducted in the tradition of Christ the Mediator seeks to satisfy man's deepest hunger for peace. Though parties rarely articulate this innate desire, it is safe to assume they quietly long for spiritual tranquility and enduring happiness. Benedict explains:

> The ultimate goal, for all of us, is to become happy. But happiness is only to be found in togetherness, and togetherness is only to be found in the infinitude of love. Happiness is found only in the opening of self to the divine—that is, in divinization. [In which] the deepest longing of Creation will be realized: That God may be all in all. (1 Corinthians 15:28)[19]

Fostering togetherness is a core Christian practice: *when we make peace and deliver happiness, we practice Christianity; when we practice Christianity, we make peace and deliver happiness.* Peacemaking ministry does not stand apart from the faith as an isolated discipline; rather,

---

19 Joseph Ratzinger, *The Essential Pope Benedict XVI: His Central Writings and Speeches*, ed. John F. Thorton and Susan B. Varenne, (New York: Harper One, 2007), 313.

it forms a central component of Christian life. This overlap is found in the theological concept *God is love*:

> Caritas, care for the other, is not an additional sector of Christianity alongside worship; rather, it is rooted in it and forms part of it.[20]

Though I reference a Christian life, these fundamentals hold true in all times for all people. Reality or Creation is not split into a Christian universe and a non-Christian universe; rather, the principles of divine relationship are universal. All people seek to care for others and to be cared for by others; all desire togetherness. Thus, with confidence, we can proclaim:

> Life means communion, whereas the heart of death is the absence of relationship.[21]

If the absence of relationship is equivalent to death, then healing broken relationships is equivalent to restoring life. We can take the analysis a step further: *just as relationship is a vital sign of life, so dialogue is a vital sign of relationship.*

People who are unable to communicate fall out of relationship. As dialogue ceases, relationships fade. As relationships fade, people come to resemble the non-living.

---

20 Pope Benedict XVI, *Jesus of Nazareth vol. 2: Holy Week, From the Entrance into Jerusalem to the Resurrection* (San Francisco: Ignatius Press, 2011), 129.
21 Joseph Ratzinger, *Eschatology: Death and Eternal Life,* 2nd ed, trans. Michael Waldstein, (Washington, D.C.: The Catholic University of America Press, 1988), 82.

Dialogue is the breath of life for relationship; relationship is the breath of life for all people.

Reconcilers reestablish the dialogue that heals relationship, which, in turn, restores life. When mediators restore a party's communion with God, they restore a party's hope for eternal life. In other words, once a party's relationship with the divine is healed, that party gains new certainty that communion with God will continue beyond the life of their mortal body. Benedict describes the logic of this continuity of life:

> If on the one hand the physically still living and breathing human being can be 'dead' in a state of noncommunication, must it not also be true that the power of communion, of divine communion at any rate, is something stronger than physical dying? May there not be life beyond physical perishing?[22]

Sacred dialogue, which includes subtle forms of communication, such as prayer, breathes life into souls. Renewed divine relationship expands the scope of interests that parties negotiate. Their interests develop to include transcendent "goods."

In contrast to the renewal of sacred dialogue, when conflict escalates, it is common for dialogue to dwindle or cease altogether. Conflict destroys a willingness to communicate. Communication becomes sluggish and morose. Party vitality decreases, health declines. Alienation

---

22   Ibid.

spawns depression; relationships dissolve; joy evaporates. Mediators, facing the spiritual collapse of the parties, set out to restore life by reviving communication that leads to renewed relationship:

> A being is the more itself the more it is open, the more it is in relationship. And that in turn will lead us to realize that it is the man who makes himself open to all being, in its wholeness and in its Ground, and becomes thereby a "self," who is truly a person.[23]

Once communication is repaired, people regain a sense of wonder. The restoration can be remarkable, even miraculous. And yet this task can prove quite demanding on a mediator. Shortcuts are not helpful. Those who pursue the peace of Christ must painstakingly unearth timeless truths, such as the nature of divine love.

Divine Love

At the outset of the mediation process, we may find that parties have slipped out of alignment with the Will of God, bringing on an unrelenting deficit of love. They become enveloped in darkness after turning their backs on divine relationship. The spiritual landscape morphs into a virtual desert. Hellish conditions of alienation and loneliness arise:

---

23 Ibid., 155.

> If there were such a thing as a loneliness that could no longer be penetrated and transformed by the word of another; if a state of abandonment were to arise that was so deep that no "You" could reach into it any more, then we should have real, total loneliness and dreadfulness, what theology calls "hell".[24]

In the absence of authentic divine relationship, the joy and peace that accompany faith disappear. Communication dwindles. Relationships fall apart. Anger and suspicion replace love. Conflict becomes the norm.

Intuitively, we know it is not possible to love and fight at the same time. Our typical response is to address the fight in the hopes that love will grow as conflict diminishes, but sometimes we would do well to reverse the order in which we handle conflict. Faith-based mediators may find that an increase in divine love inspires affinity between quarreling parties. They teach basic courtesies that, when nurtured, grow into small deeds of kindness, which in turn cultivate great acts of charity. Little by little, love flourishes. "The fight" diminishes and the potential for peace improves. Finally, doors open and authentic love flows through the human heart.

This tells us that facilitating party alignment with the Will of God goes far beyond mere mediation technique. A party realignment with the Will of God inspires a spiritual pilgrimage in search of a healing elixir. The pilgrimage

---

24 Ratzinger, *Introduction to Christianity*, 300.

leads through the jungle of the fallen world. The journey leads to a path carved by divine love, a path that leads to mystical union.

Yet what happens to those who are cut off from the resources of divine relationship? Are peacemakers doomed to failure because so many parties lack faith? Will non-believers be stranded outside the circle of reconciliation? If so, might our dream of world peace be unrealistic?

In response to these questions, peacemakers must humbly admit that their risk of failure skyrockets with high-conflict individuals who reject the sacred in life. However, there is hope, as the ministry rests on solid universal truths. Initially disputants may lack faith, but when they come face-to-face with spiritual truths that dispel darkness, they experience a spiritual transformation.

Benedict observes:

> [V]ery many people, while not claiming to have the gift of faith, are nevertheless sincerely searching for the ultimate meaning and definitive truth of their lives and of the world. This search is an authentic "preamble" to the faith, because it guides people onto the path that leads to the mystery of God.[25]

This "authentic preamble to the faith" emboldens reconcilers to convene mediation even though a positive out-

---

25 Pope Benedict XVI, *Porta Fidei, Apostolic Letter "Motu Proprio Data" of the Supreme Pontiff Benedict XVI for the Indication of the Year of Faith* (Libreria Editrice Vaticana, 2011).

come is in doubt. They do not give up, but rather proceed in the hopes that closed doors will open and tentative steps toward faith will lead to an increase in wisdom and knowledge. Benedict's "authentic preamble" implies that success is not only possible, but nearly certain.

Though the percentage of disputants who lack a foundation in faith is high, we need not abandon the ministry. If we possess a robust desire for peace, we can bring even those who lack faith to the table. That said, it is important that mediators greet prospective parties with a reasoned introduction, as most disputants balk at platitude and empty sound bites. Any expression of naivete damages the effort:

> Peace convicts us of our lies. It brings us out of our comfortable indifference into the struggle and the pain of the truth. And it is only thus that true peace can come into being, in place of the apparent peace, beneath which lie hidden hypocrisy and all kinds of conflict... Truth is worth pain and even conflict. I may not just accept a lie in order to have quiet. For it is not the first duty of a citizen, or of a Christian, to seek quiet.[26]

A realistic assessment of the challenges that parties will face should be presented, but it should be imbued with optimism. Even though parties are embroiled in a noisy world, we invite them to participate in "divine listening." The invitation is extended because we know that

---

26 Pope Benedict XVI, "September 13," *Benedictus*, 280.

peace is an irrepressible yearning present in every heart. We speak to the desires of the human heart:

> We need to regain an awareness that we share a common destiny which is ultimately transcendent, so as to maximize our historical and cultural differences, not in opposition to, but in cooperation with, people belonging to other cultures. These simple truths are what make peace possible; they are easily understood whenever we listen to our own hearts with pure intentions.[27]

Though we must acknowledge that parties in conflict suffer from deficits of love, we set out to remedy those deficits, using mystical aspects of faith to soften hearts. We acknowledge the following axiom: *the practical is mystical and the mystical is practical*. We address worldly *and* supernatural concerns, leading troubled parties into previously undiscovered spiritual territory. Those who once suffered now find, quite unexpectedly, that the power of divine love lifts them up and the power of sanctifying grace realigns their free will with the Will of God.

Reflection

At this point, peacemakers can reflect deeply on the cornerstone concept of "God is Love," a phrase first written by John the Evangelist. They may want to explore the idea of synchronous loving, knowing, and being. They might

---

[27] Ibid., "October 15," 314.

want to understand how to invite the presence of the Holy Spirit and facilitate a turn toward God that restores a party's "being-in-love."

Peacemakers may take this opportunity to add to their library of conflict resolution materials with volumes on spiritual direction and pastoral counseling. They may also update any reality maps that chart the natural and supernatural realms. They would be well advised to improve their communication and counseling skills.

In addition, they'll want to formalize their own spiritual formation training, perhaps with the help of a personal spiritual director. They can assess and monitor their ability to help others by scheduling ongoing evaluation of their emotional, mental, and spiritual conditions.

Finally, peacemakers may wish to guard against becoming trapped in the gloom of the fallen world. Honest self-appraisal, conducted on a regular basis, can help them renew their ability to guide others to reconciliation.

SIX

Healing Relationships: Human and Divine

When peacemakers reconcile troubled and broken relationships and facilitate spiritual growth, they take on a sacred task. When they coach parties through the transition from worldly to heavenly concerns, they face challenges that Benedict foreshadowed:

> God is love. But love can also be hated when it challenges us to transcend ourselves. It is not a romantic "good feeling." Redemption is not "wellness," it is not about basking in self-indulgence; on the contrary it is a liberation from imprisonment in self-absorption.[1]

In the following sections, we will consider how peacemakers might launch parties on a spiritual pilgrimage.

---

1   Pope Benedict XVI, *Jesus of Nazareth vol. 3*, 86.

The Reconciliation Journey

In our model, the decision to make peace is not arbitrary or capricious. Rather, the decision emerges from the New Covenant in which Jesus advocates reconciliation with one's brothers and sisters, as in Matthew's gospel:

> "So if you are offering your gift at the altar, and there remember that your brother has something against you, leave your gift there before the altar and go; first be reconciled to your brother, and then come and offer your gift."[2]

Initially, after a person departs from the altar on a reconciliation journey, they may feel they walk alone. But they are *not* alone. When they go to meet their brother or sister, the Holy Spirit is their companion. As they go forth to heal human relationships, they simultaneously heal divine relationship. In contrast, if they fail to set forth to reconcile human relationships, they diminish divine relationship:

> You cannot come into God's presence unreconciled with your brother; anticipating him in the gesture of reconciliation, going out to meet him, is the prerequisite for true worship of God.[3]

Making peace is not a casual activity or frivolous en-

---

[2] Matthew 5:23.
[3] Joseph Ratzinger, *Jesus of Nazareth, vol. 1: From the Baptism in the Jordan to the Transfiguration*, trans. Adrian J. Walker (New York: Doubleday, 2008), 158.

deavor. Rather, it calms the turbulent seas of human relations and prepares men to stand before God. Jesus, who considered peacemaking vital, put forth a protocol:

> If your brother sins [against you], go and tell him his fault between you and him alone. If he listens to you, you have won over your brother. If he does not listen, take one or two others along with you, so that every fact may be established on the testimony of two or three witnesses. If he refuses to listen to them, tell the church. If he refuses to listen even to the church, then treat him as you would a Gentile or a tax collector.[4]

Jesus thus provided a framework upon which peacemakers construct conflict resolution systems. But, you might ask, why must we augment the core admonition with a formal system? The answer is obvious: Though we desire reconciliation, we ordinarily lack the necessary skills and proper procedures. We lack the discipline required to implement Jesus' framework. Our ineptness blocks our path. We hurdle this barrier of incompetence by designing a formal mediation protocol.

For example, in the second step put forth in Matthew's gospel, a disputant is instructed to bring two or three witnesses. However, if those witnesses are biased, the opposing party will reject their presence. They'll be greeted with skepticism that will lead to impasse.

Skill is thus required to execute this basic gospel in-

---

4 Matthew 18:15-17.

struction. In this example, the formal solution calls for selecting neutral witnesses—impartial elders or trained mediators. While Jesus provides the admonition, peacemakers must develop a structured process and apply their skill. Those who stumble blindly into peacemaking have little chance for success. Their attempts at mediation bear little fruit.

The steps of the Matthew 18 protocol follow a progression from conciliatory to judicial approaches. Peacemakers follow the same progression. Resolution efforts begin with conciliatory steps and then, only as needed, proceed to judicial verdicts, rulings, or edicts. Ideally, parties reconcile *before* a trial or hearing is convened. Yet too many disputants take the opposite route: they seek victory at trial and only later, when they fail, do they consider reconciliation. In a well-designed system, reconciliation efforts precede judicial solutions.

In addition, a conflict resolution protocol should not omit the presence and role of the Holy Spirit. At the same time, we should not invite the Spirit into anarchy; rather, we should provide a disciplined and structured process. Benedict, in his discourse on St. Paul, endorses such discipline:

> In fact, the Spirit who is the Love of the Father and the Son pours out his first gift, agape, into our hearts (cf. Rm 5:5); and to be fully expressed, agape, love, requires self-control.[5]

---

5   Pope Benedict XVI, *St. Paul*, 85.

A well-structured mediation process encourages the self-control needed for love to take root. When mediators provide guidelines and structure, they nurture safety and hope, which allows tender shoots of love to grow.

Healing and Negotiation

During settlement negotiations, faith-based mediators choreograph periods of healing. Since those suffering from personal turmoil struggle during negotiation, mediators plan "time-outs" that allow parties to pursue pastoral care. Healing breaks ensure that they negotiate while in sound emotional, mental, and spiritual health.

Mediators assist the party's spiritual healing by prompting them to reflect on God's grace and mercy. They discuss ways that grace and mercy affect our lives and they guide reflections intended to infuse parties with compassion. This softening of the heart bridges the divide between opponents and helps to bring the conflict to an amicable close.

Healing breaks confer an additional benefit on the mediation process. They renew our love for God. Mediators should remember a basic principle: relationships with our neighbors will be impaired if our relationship with God is impaired. Knowing that spiritual health is dependent on divine relationship, mediators prioritize reconciliation with God.

> [The person] draws life from being-in-relation, from receiving all as gift; he will always need the

gift of goodness, of forgiveness, but in receiving it he will always learn to pass the gift on to others.[6]

Peacemaking depends on mutual exchange, on reciprocity. The *principal of reciprocity* calls for parties to satisfy the interests of others at the same time they satisfy their interests. Reciprocity has also been expressed as the Golden Rule. The Our Father prayer advances the same idea: *we forgive as we have been forgiven*. All healthy relationships involve a reciprocal exchange of tangible and intangible value.

In keeping with the principle of reciprocity, mediators facilitate a mutual exploration of party interests. They help parties unearth interests and communicate them clearly, making sure that others truly understand their needs. This is necessary because typically parties are not aware of each other's interests. Usually, they have not listened closely to one another. And way too often they do not even know their own interests. Therefore, it is safe to assume parties can benefit from deep listening designed to foster reciprocal satisfaction.

All too often, however, underlying interests are overshadowed by negotiation positions. Each party vows, "This is where I stand. I will not move. Here are my demands; here are my claims. This is what I expect." The focus on positions leaves little room for negotiation or collaboration.

---

6   Ratzinger, *Jesus of Nazareth vol. 1*, 62.

A position usually states a narrow demand: "You must vacate by tomorrow." "I filed for divorce." "Pay today or forfeit your possessions." "Work the extra shift or you're fired." "Approve my promotion or find my replacement." When such demands lead to inevitable impasse, mediators convince disputants to shift gears and explore reciprocal interests. They facilitate a transition to listening mode:

> To listen means to know and to acknowledge another and to allow him to step into the realm of one's own "I." Thus, after the act of listening, I am another man, my own being enriched and deepened because it is united with the being of the other and, through it, with the being of the world... When we speak of dialogue in the proper sense, what we mean is an utterance wherein something of being itself, indeed, the person himself, becomes speech.[7]

Reconcilers all too often encounter human islands separated by angry seas of emotion. In order to calm the angry seas, they must nurture affinity, confident that love will surface, perhaps when least anticipated.

Mediation rarely advances smoothly at the beginning. Negotiation often runs aground when unhealed wounds bring about impasse. Parties balk, afraid that negotiation will not satisfy their true needs. At this point, mediators must restore confidence in the process; they must keep

---

[7] Pope Benedict XVI, "January 18," *Benedictus*, 31.

the dance going. As a general rule, they should balance time spent in negotiation with time spent in healing. Over time, as a result of healing, disputants move closer to one another with almost imperceptible moves.

Paradoxically, the give-and-take of negotiation itself becomes therapeutic. The process of exchanging value heals and strengthens relationship. Regardless of the substantive outcome, good-faith negotiation leaves parties feeling better about self and others. Even if a negotiated settlement cannot be reached, positive benefits have been delivered.

Facilitating collaborative negotiation requires considerable skill, including an ability to heal emotional or spiritual wounds. The ability to nurture an exchange of love becomes vital, as reconciliation success is only made possible because all people share a common source of love: God.

Benedict explains:

> Men are capable of reciprocal comprehension because, far from being wholly separate islands of being, they communicate in the same truth. The greater their inner contact with the one reality which unites them, namely, the truth, the greater their capacity to meet on common ground. Dialogue without this interior obedient listening to the truth would be nothing more than a discussion among the deaf.[8]

---

8 Ibid.

At this stage of preparation, it helps to have a definition of mediation consistent with a theology of relationship: *mediation is the art of restoring harmony by seeking unity in the presence of the Holy Spirit.*

> The presence of the Holy Spirit makes itself known in the manner of love. Love is the criterion of the Holy Spirit as against unholy spirits; indeed, it is the presence of the Holy Spirit himself and, in that sense, the presence of God.[9]

The "unholy spirits" mentioned in the preceding passage cause division, disunity and disharmony. They are present when mediation begins, but depart when the Holy Spirit rekindles divine love. With this in mind, reconcilers learn to pray and summon the presence of the Holy Spirit. Later, they may encourage parties to receive pastoral counseling, which leads to increased party awareness of the Holy Spirit, also known as the Advocate.

In contrast, in secular mediation, which is often associated with litigation, the focus is on "the deal." While some attention may be paid to healing, such efforts are secondary. The primary work focuses on negotiating party claims and demands. Negotiation may or may not result in agreement or settlement. Should a deal be struck, the outcome will not necessarily include a healing component. Parties may take the deal and walk, terminating existing relationships.

---

9   Ibid., 166.

A faith-based process, in contrast, prioritizes reconciliation. While the value of negotiating substantive issues is not discounted, spiritual transformation is also valued as a key component of enduring peace. Mediators pay attention to the party's relationship with a loving God—the supernatural component that guarantees lasting peace.

The Dual-Axis Model

Among the admonitions Jesus delivered, one stands above the rest: the great commandment, which calls for simultaneous reconciliation with God and with our brother:

> Love of God and love of neighbor have become one: in the least of the brethren we find Jesus himself, and in Jesus we find God.[10]

The New Covenant, put forth by Jesus, weaves a relationship between man and God, as St. Paul preached:

> Paul knows that in the twofold love of God and neighbor the whole of the Law is present and carried out. Thus in communion with Christ, in a faith that creates charity, the entire Law is fulfilled. We become just by entering into communion with Christ, who is Love.[11]

When we translate Paul's preaching into a dispute resolution protocol, the result is a "dual-axis model": the hor-

---

10 Pope Benedict XVI, *God is Love*, 40.
11 Ibid., 82.

izontal axis represents reconciliation with our neighbor; the vertical axis represents reconciliation with God. They are linked:

> Only my readiness to encounter my neighbor and to show him love makes me sensitive to God as well. Only if I serve my neighbor can my eyes be opened to what God does for me and how much he loves me.[12]

This New Covenant theology gives us a two-part axiom: *when we reconcile with our neighbor, our relationship with God improves; when we reconcile with God, our relationship with our neighbors improves.*

When we analyze the breakdown of relationship, we find the reverse is true: *diminishing our relationship with God diminishes our relationships with our neighbors; diminishing our relationships with neighbors diminishes our relationship with God.*

The dual-axis model is a powerful conceptual tool for planning mediation. For example, if a party has difficulty living peacefully with others, we can predict that reconciliation on the horizontal axis will grind to a halt. Faced with this situation, a mediator shifts attention to the vertical axis—to the party's relationship with God. Impasse on one axis calls for work on the other axis.

The shift to the vertical axis, to the relationship with God, includes party participation in spiritual direction,

---

[12] Ibid., 46.

pastoral counseling, retreats, contemplative prayer, and daily examination of consciousness. Mediators use many tools to enhance party awareness of divine love as they know that:

> [T]here is a certain relationship between love and the Divine: love promises infinity, eternity—a reality far greater and totally other than our everyday existence.[13]

Parties are encouraged to reach up toward God as God bends low to meet them. They begin to realize that their lives extend beyond worldly constraints. In theological terms:

> The sacramental 'mysticism,' grounded in God's condescension towards us, operates at a radically different level and lifts us to far greater heights than anything that any human mystical elevation could ever accomplish.[14]

The previous void of relationship is now filled with an I-Thou connection. After a party heals on the vertical axis, they unexpectedly experience success in reconciling with their fellow man. Reconciliation on one axis supports reconciliation on the other axis.

In a similar manner, when a party expresses hostility toward God, mediators shift attention to the horizontal

---

13   Ibid., 17.
14   Ibid., 36.

axis. They work on restoring human friendships; they choreograph charitable acts of mercy. They promote activities that restore human fellowship. The ancillary result is an unexpected improvement in their relationship with God.

This cause-and-effect link between the axes may seem mysterious, but it is simple to express: *repairing friendships simultaneously repairs our faith life; repairing our faith life simultaneously repairs our relationships.* Ideally, we heal on both axes simultaneously. When impasse threatens, mediators adroitly shift from one axis to the other. If they fail to make the shift, they may aggravate party intransigence—parties feel they're being pushed into an intractable barrier.

A party pushed up against a stiff barrier feels their mental and spiritual "spaces" being compressed. Movement becomes increasingly difficult. Mediation shuts down. In contrast, when mediators shift fluidly between axes, barriers are dislodged and impasses are overcome.

Divine Interests

During the convening stage, parties examine the needs and interests they hope to satisfy. They also contemplate how they might satisfy the other party's interests. Rarely, however, do parties consider God's interests. It does not even occur to them to ask what those interests might be. They assume God satisfies any interest he chooses—so they might as well ignore the question.

But our faith-based, collaborative assessment protocol dictates that we assess the interests of all parties. Skilled reconcilers turn to Benedict for help in envisioning God's interests:

> I must begin by no longer looking at myself, but by asking what he wants. I must begin by learning to love. That consists precisely in turning my gaze away from myself and toward him. With this attitude I no longer ask, What can I get for myself, but I simply let myself be guided by him, truly lose myself in Christ; when I abandon myself, let go of myself, then I see, yes, life is right at last, because otherwise I am far too narrow for myself. When, so to speak, I go outside, then it truly begins, then life attains its greatness.[15]

However, in most disputes, we find narrow party views that are limited and solely focused on self-interest. But, during mediation, parties must abandon this exclusive concern for self and instead seek mutual satisfaction. They must honor the principle of reciprocity; they must collaborate. A focus on mutual benefit automatically increases love:

> Love now becomes concern and care for the other. No longer is it self-seeking, a sinking in the intoxication of happiness; instead it seeks the good of the beloved: it becomes renunciation and it is ready, and even willing, for sacrifice.[16]

---

15 Pope Benedict XVI, "March 14," *Benedictus*, 89.
16 Pope Benedict XVI, "July 28," *Benedictus*, 231.

A collaborative process thus increases love, the cornerstone of reconciliation. Peacemaking is further augmented by exploring vertical axis concerns; for example, Christ's desire to love man and receive love in return. When parties are endowed with this sacred interest they develop a desire to satisfy others:

> Seeing with the eyes of Christ, I can give to others much more than their outward necessities; I can give them the look of love which they crave.[17]

This look of love is absent in secular approaches that exclude reconciliation with God. The omission generates adverse consequences:

> If I have no contact whatsoever with God in my life, then I cannot see in the other anything more than the other, and I am incapable of seeing in him the image of God.[18]

Secular processes tend to dim awareness of God's presence. They deny the divine endowment that dwells in the human heart. These omissions diminish the love available to the parties. In contrast, faith-based peacemakers remain mindful that the healing elixir of divine love makes reconciliation possible.

---

17 Ibid., 45.
18 Ibid.

Responses to Conflict

Conflict arises from blunted attempts to satisfy interests. When people find their satisfaction blocked, they engage in conflict behavior. During the reconciliation process, they're expected to balance competing demands. In workshops, when I have discussed the need to balance interests, I've often introduced a diagram of the habitual responses to conflict.[19]

This diagram has two axes. On the vertical axis we chart the need to satisfy self-interest; the desire or willingness to satisfy the other party is charted on the horizontal line. Habitual responses to conflict always combine self-interest with concern for the other.

For example, one who concentrates on satisfying another's interests *accommodates*. Those who focus on self-interest, *compete*. Others, those who seek to dodge all clashes and do not care if they satisfy anyone, engage in *avoidance*. With *compromise,* both parties experience partial satisfaction and partial disappointment.

People frequently assume that mediation promotes compromise, but that's not the case. In mediation, the preferred response is *collaboration*, an effort to satisfy all party interests to the greatest extent possible. Collaboration seeks mutual satisfaction.

While mediators prefer *collaboration*, there are times when other responses to conflict may be valid. The appro-

---

19   Thomas, Kenneth and Kilmann, Ralph, "The Thomas Kilmann Conflict Mode Instrument," see http:/kilmann.com/conflict.html.

priateness of the response depends on circumstances. For example, there are times when *avoidance* is optimum, as the financial or emotional costs of negotiation may simply be too great. In order to achieve the best outcome, parties should avoid habitual responses. Instead, they should spend time assessing the plusses and minuses of different responses, seeking an optimum response for each situation. They will want to remain mindful, rather than reactive or habitual. The diagram charting possible responses serves as tool for assessing any particular situation.

In a faith-based model, we can expand the options available. Parties evaluate their personal interests against the Will of God. We can call this approach *divine collaboration*.

Managing Intentions

Conflict arises when multiple parties exercise free will in a way that generates opposing intentions—conflict is the result. This can be illustrated using vector arrows to represent intentions.

In a fallen world, these arrows of intention point in a multitude of directions. Seen from a bird's-eye-view, they resemble a bumper-car ride. They head in random directions and occasionally point directly opposite one another. These head-to-head collisions represent conflict.

As an example, if a manager micro-manages employees but one of his workers prizes self-management, they will clash. They harbor opposing intentions. A young lady who absolutely must set a wedding date will clash with a boyfriend who intends to "wait and see." There is no limit to the number of potential clashes. In a fallen world—which unleashes random intentions—we can expect a pattern of colliding intentions.

Mediators redirect the parties' exercise of free will, seeking to reduce the frequency and severity of collisions. They must redirect the exercise of free will so intentions do not aim in opposite directions. Mediators resemble carnival ride attendants at the bumper-car concession—they disentangle collisions, re-aim the cars, and keep parties moving.

Mediators begin by encouraging small modifications that redirect the vector arrows. For example, they may advise the micromanaging boss to grant the employee increased autonomy over his work while also requesting progress reports. A series of mutual adjustments can be used to unstick colliding intentions that have become frozen in place.

In most instances, we find that parties do not know *how* to break the iron grip of the forces that have them pinned down; they lack full understanding of their situation. In order to regain freedom, they must grasp the nature of the clashing intentions and learn how to redirect their intentions.

Baseline Intention

The vector diagram illustrates an effective strategy for lessening conflict. We can imagine routing the bumper cars, the intention arrows, in one direction. With one-way traffic, collisions cease. In this case, we do not force the intention vectors to align with one another; rather we align them with a third factor, a boulevard or channel.

As an example, imagine a family sets out to plan a summer holiday. Each family member selects a different beach. They're on the verge of a major argument, but when they study the map carefully, they realize only one highway allows them to reach a vacation beach and return home in the allotted time. Facts outside of their control determine the outcome. Debate is pointless. The merits of each preferred destination become irrelevant. The group's decision must conform to reality. In this case, there is only one possible solution.

In most instances, however, there's more than one correct route. Parties are not channeled into accepting one decision. Nonetheless, the principle applies—if parties agree on a common path, they reduce conflict. Rather than fight over which party shall prevail, they measure their desires and interests against a neutral standard. They identify a baseline intention around which they can align their intentions.

Fortunately, a universal baseline exists: the Will of God. When parties align their individual wills with the baseline of divine will, opposition dissipates. They no longer wage a battle over whose intentions should prevail. Instead, they evaluate intentions according to how well they line up with divine will.

This simple idea is rich with theological consequences.

When we seek to align with divine will, we automatically shift attention from the mundane to the supernatural. We automatically draw closer to God with softened hearts that accept the grace of divine love, thus opening doors to St. Paul's knowledge of the heart.

After parties move closer to God, they are better able to draw closer to one another. The gap between them—physical, mental, emotional, and spiritual—shrinks. Drawing closer to one another, they come to know one another better. This paradigm shapes our reconciliation ministry: mediators nurture increased love. The initial increases are modest, but no matter how minor, increased affinity draws parties closer. The closer they become—physically, emotionally, psychologically, and spiritually—the more understanding they share.

As love deepens, wisdom increases. An upward spiral of love and unity lifts disputants higher and higher. A pattern emerges: *an increase of love brings greater closeness; increased closeness brings greater knowledge.*

Mediators choreograph this dance, supplying safety and hope. As parties heal, they hurt less. Relief and comfort generate a stillness of mind that allows wisdom to take root. Misunderstanding is replaced with epiphany. Light shines into darkness, illuminating paths to reconciliation.

This dynamic is fueled by the theological premise that God is Love. The Holy Spirit choreographs a dance of love that flows from God and then returns to God. This eternal loop of give-and-take is a fundamental component of a theology of relationship. For this reason, we study the dynamics of divine love and attempt to reconcile the relationship with God before attempting reconciliation between disputing parties.

Contemplative prayer, as practiced by Saint Francis of Assisi, reveals that *God pervades the universe with Being-in-Love*. In addition, they learn that all souls have the potential to experience mystical union, a "being-together-in-love." They discover that the Peace of Christ is woven into the fabric of the universe. A paradox arises: *divine love, though invisible, is more real than the visible world*.

In its essence, peacemaking removes adverse factors that impede, inhibit, or oppose supernatural Being-in-Love. It strips away the detritus of falsehood and restores divine love. Only when peacemaking is based on that which is most true is its success assured.

Ancillary Concerns — Ethics and Morality

An emphasis on love, often misperceived as sentimentality, might provoke criticism—some may fear the ministry values feeling good over principle. However, mediation guided by a theology of relationship does not abandon ethics and morality. Benedict clarifies:

> Ethics is not denied; it is freed from the constraints of moralism and set in the context of a relationship of love—of relationship to God.[20]

---

20 Ratzinger, *Jesus of Nazareth* vol. 1, 62.

Nonetheless, some critics fear that emotions will replace ethics and morals. They fear that ethical norms will be scuttled; they fear that love and dialogue are too flimsy to provide an adequate firewall against moral anarchy. They worry that a dialogical approach invites a culture to spin out of control.

Rather than ignore such critics, reconcilers should address their concerns. They might note that Benedict perceived a different threat—he feared we might mistake Jesus for a moralist:

> [T]he type of interpretation that makes Jesus a moralist, a teacher of an enlightened and individualistic morality, for all of its significant historical insights, remains theologically impoverished, and does not even come close to the real figure of Jesus.[21]

Saint Paul, in his letter to the Romans, explored the threat that moralism might trump love. Though Paul's letters offer valuable insights, many continue to struggle when it comes to making a full transition to a New Covenant viewpoint. Peacemakers may need to caution parties that:

> [R]educing Christianity to morality loses sight of the essence of Christ's message: the gift of a new friendship, the gift of communion with Jesus and thereby God.[22]

---

21 Ibid, 186.
22 Joseph Ratzinger, *The New Evangelization*.

A person may desire the moral certainty offered by a strict code; on the other hand, they may want to avoid an extreme form of moralism that stifles relationship. Confusion regarding moralism may be the result of clashing theologies: while one theology advances a New Covenant vision of loving relationship, another promotes the idea of a distant judge who keeps score of transgressions and adjudicates fates. Mediators will need to clarify their personal theology. They will need to grasp ethics and morality within the context of a dialogical theology:

> This is essential: the Christian ethic is not born from a system of commandments but is a consequence of our friendship with Christ. This friendship influences life; if it is true, it incarnates and fulfills itself in love for neighbor.[23]

Love for neighbor is not an easy ideal to achieve. People stumble. However, failure is typically not the result of poor theology; rather, the stumbling block is often a missing reconciliation protocol. It's a problem of practice rather than theology. Though they desire peace, they're missing the "know-how" needed to bring it about.

In ancient times, the faithful were diligent in monitoring adherence to commandments. With a New Covenant model, the faithful must diligently manage relationships. They require disciplined peacemaking, mediation, and reconciliation, practices that emerge organically from the New Covenant. They must know that:

---

23 Pope Benedict XVI, *St. Paul*, 88.

> The ascending movement of humanity in its union with Christ is answered by the descending movement of God's love in its self-gift to us.[24]

Reconcilers respect this supernatural movement of love and its stunning power in our lives:

> Man is a relational being. And if his most fundamental relationship is disturbed—his relationship with God—then nothing else can be truly in order.[25]

True ethics and morality emerge from a robust theology of relationship grounded in the theological premise that God is Love.

Reflection

After initial preparation, peacemakers set out to heal broken relationships that have become arid, relationships that no longer satisfy the thirst for love.

Peacemakers address the misalignment of man's will with divine will, a misalignment that created a spiritual desert in which divine love, the source of "living water," slows to a trickle.

In the midst of this fallen world, peacemakers orchestrate a restoration of divine love. They help parties align with the great commandment that calls on man to love

---

24 Joseph Ratzinger, *Eschatology*, 234.
25 Pope Benedict XVI, *Jesus of Nazareth vol. 3*, 44.

his neighbor as God has loved him. They parallel the great commandment with a dual-axis reconciliation model.

In further preparation, they reflect on the dynamic interplay between the axes. They learn how people can satisfy their interests at the same time they satisfy others' needs. They learn how to assess habitual responses to conflict. They gain skill in assessing and reducing biases.

Even as they practice their craft, mediators continue to assemble technique toolkits used to rescue parties from deficits of love. They accumulate techniques used for increasing affinity. Most importantly, they practice divine collaboration, the realigning of individual will with the Will of God.

They may discover that realignment with the Will of God alone has the power to restore divine love. When that living spring has been restored, the desert blooms into a garden paradise.

At this stage, as reconcilers complete their preparation and begin their practice, they will want to inventory personal doubts. They will want to grasp how they will set those doubts aside, find renewed courage, and continue to build on their strengths.

SEVEN

Fallen World: Realm of Disordered Will

Jesus taught men to honor thy Father's will, especially on that horrible night in the Garden of Gethsemane. Throughout scripture, frequent admonitions call for us to conform to the Will of God. In prayer, we implore God to help us know his will so that we might follow. Thus, the idea of aligning our free will with the Will of God is not new.

Perhaps we break new ground when we declare that "realignment of the will" is a central feature of reconciliation. Realignment protocol serves two purposes: it helps resolve conflict and it helps foster spiritual redemption:

> The only way he [Christ] can redeem man, who was created free, is by means of a free 'yes' to his will.[1]

When peacemakers initiate a process of Divine Collaboration, they realign party will with the Will of God, thereby tapping into salvation ministry.

---

[1] Pope Benedict XVI, *Jesus of Nazareth vol. 3,* 36.

The Will of God and Free Will

Typically, when warring parties arrive at mediation, they have not reflected on the question: *what is free will?* They have not contemplated the question of how free will works. Rather, they've become embroiled in a struggle of wills, pitting force against force. Suffering tunnel vision, they are focused on defeating their opponent at any price.

When parties first meet with a mediator, they usually disguise their desire to exercise raw power. Savvy mediators nonetheless discern the compulsive desire to crush their opponent's intention and will.

For example, in the legend of St. Francis and the Wolf, the townspeople of Gubbio,[2] who've been terrorized by a fierce wolf, summon Francis, the humble peacemaker, because "he talks to animals and to God." Soon after Francis arrives, however, they discard all talk of peace and beg Francis to slay the wolf.

Before peacemaking has even begun, the townspeople of Gubbio unmask a desire to terminate their opponent. This is common. However, Christianity, which informs our quest, eschews such raw power. Instead, faith teaches us that lasting peace cannot be achieved through force, coercion, or domination. Instead, peacemakers must employ faith and reason to guide the exercise of free will.

Benedict, in his discourse on personal freedom, supplies us with the rationale for honoring free will, a fundamental principle of existence:

---

[2] Stone, *Taming the Wolf: Peace through Faith*.

> Freedom belongs to the basic structure of creation, to the spiritual existence of man. We are not just laid out and determined according to a particular model. Freedom is there so that each one of us can shape his own life and, along with his own inner self, can in the end follow the path that best corresponds to his essential being. Freedom is a gift inherent in creation... Freedom means that of my own free will I take upon myself the potential of my being.[3]

Many people find Benedict's analysis inspiring. Others dislike the implication that they must eschew raw power and respect the innate freedom of their fellow man. Instead of dominating over their neighbor, they are called upon to collaborate in an effort to identify and satisfy mutual interests.

Collaboration, however, runs counter to man's normal inclination. Ordinarily, people marshal coercive power in an attempt to overwhelm the other party. In contrast, mediators encourage a temporary suspension of coercive power. They encourage parties to realign and redirect their exercise of free will.

Realignment Procedure

Conflict freezes opposing intentions in a collision of wills. Mediators seek to reduce the frequency of collisions and disentangle webs of conflict. When they take a faith-based

---

[3] Pope Benedict XVI, "March 16," *Benedictus*, 91.

approach, they introduce a common baseline intention—*the Will of God*. Aligning personal goals with a "neutral" intention frees each parties' will from the frozen embrace of conflict.

The preceding description makes realignment sound easy, but if we suggest too quickly that a party modify their intentions, we'll be greeted with steely skepticism: "*Are you kidding me?*" Parties, neither willing to bend to others' wishes nor to divine will, want their desires satisfied as swiftly as possible.

When mediators first ask a party to consider the wishes of others, the result is usually a skeptical query: "*Where are we going with this?*" Premature requests for collaboration trigger a fear of coercion. Any perceived threat to a party's self-determinism causes them to retreat. Therefore, such queries are non-starters.

As you may have observed, parties do not naturally think in a collaborative manner. Rather, they seek to impose their will, often in covert ways that skirt direct confrontation. Mediators counter such impulses. They convince parties to set aside coercive means, at least temporarily. They launch the peacemaking process with a temporary truce.

During the negotiated lull in hostility, mediators "set the table" by identifying intentions, interests, and needs that must be negotiated. They engage in *discovery*, a disciplined search to uncover "what happened." They listen carefully to narrative accounts and assess conflict drivers. They ask parties if they feel entitled to specific outcomes; they ask parties how their claims express a vision of justice. They assume an inquisitive demeanor as they sort through the rich tapestry of stories that arise during the course of negotiation.

As mediators listen, they often detect false assumptions. For example, parties may assume, incorrectly, that they possess the right *to be, do,* or *have* anything they desire. Or they may assume, incorrectly, that they possess the right to prevent others from *being, doing,* or *having* what they desire.

The mismatch between actual rights and falsely assumed rights may be due to a false sense of entitlement, a misguided view of justice, or plain narcissism. For example, a party might assume that simply because they showed up for work they deserve to be compensated, even though they failed to perform any actual work. They may assume the job is a right, that they cannot be fired. A manager may assume he possesses unlimited power over employees. He may issue arbitrary demands or harbor invalid expectations. Imbalances of this nature can be found in all aspects of life—faulty assumptions abound.

In such instances, when parties assume rights that do not exist, they may fight to obtain goods, freedoms, or status to which they're not entitled. They may assert false claims. When this occurs, peacemakers rein in unrealistic expectations using reality checks.

At other times, rather than claiming rights they do not possess, a party may overlook legitimate interests. Intangibles—such as love, respect, or trust—may remain unrecognized. Mediators encourage parties to mine interests in their search for intangibles. In spite of such efforts, valid interests often escape notice until they surface in the midst of intense negotiation.

Once "mining" begins, the interests surfaced will vary considerably. Some will be mundane, others spiritual. In a consumer culture, spiritual interests may be devalued. The faithful may be too embarrassed to speak up; they may assume they dare not share their faith concerns. Unfortunately, parties who fail to express their spiritual interests ultimately fail to satisfy their deepest needs.

Another factor that inhibits accurate assessment is the inability of parties to examine their hearts. Conversations regarding "matters of the heart" are rare. When people suffer an inability to discern or share their most essential needs, they soon become disillusioned. The needs that are overlooked are usually those of greatest value—from the perspective of an immortal soul.

As an example, St. Francis of Assisi believed that transcendent needs were more important than worldly needs. He routinely sacrificed mundane interests in order to satisfy his need to imitate Christ. The example of Francis suggests that a mediator might call on a spiritual director for assistance when parties are prepared to assess intangible and transcendent needs. Pastoral counseling may rehabilitate a party's ability to examine their heart. In the manual *Taming the Wolf*,[4] I encourage readers to routinely seek spiritual direction as they add overlooked transcendent needs to Maslow's secular "hierarchy of human needs."

---

4   Stone, *Taming the Wolf*.

During this phase, mediators proceed with caution, seeking to avoid faulty assessment. They know that parties commonly skip the time-intensive step of "visioning" interests; they know parties tend to avoid the difficult process of prioritizing concerns, separating primary needs from secondary needs. The "visioning" process, though time-consuming, ensures that parties avoid common errors that occur when they improvise at the negotiation table.

Expanded "visioning" is one way to increase the satisfaction achieved during the process.[5] Discovery steps—assessment, evaluation, and prioritization—may take time, but are worthwhile. Parties who "vision" interests are more successful in collaborative negotiation and are more likely to satisfy personal needs as well as the needs of others.

In the step that follows mining interests, the ante is raised: disputants share their interests and needs with one another. The act of sharing needs can be stressful, as parties frequently assume that their opponents will be unwilling to take their interests into account. Fear of rejection looms large. At this stage in the process, peacemakers help parties mitigate their fears.

In summary, during discovery, peacemakers seek to discover how each party exercised their free will. They want to know how opposing intentions became locked

---

5   Abraham H. Maslow, *Motivation and Personality*, 2nd ed (United Kingdom: Harper and Row, 1970): see also Abraham H. Maslow, *Toward a Psychology of Being*, (United States: John Wiley and Sons, 1968).

up, creating impasse. Peacemakers may mentally diagram these "vectors of intention" as a prelude to the realignment step.

A key principle guides a mediator's planning: when parties redirect their intentions so the "vectors" aim roughly in the same direction, the frequency and intensity of collisions diminishes.

Going "Below the Line"

Fisher and Ury of the Harvard Project on Negotiation, working in a secular context, championed "interest-based negotiation" in Getting to Yes.[6] They taught mediators to shift party focus from positions to interests.

A position is a stance or firm demand. For example, a distraught spouse might announce, "No more talk. Sign these divorce papers. Agree to the terms. Let's wrap it up. Now." That would be an expression of a position.

In contrast, a statement of one's interests is more flexible and expresses motivation. It answers the question, *why are you making this demand?* The upset spouse might wish to escape emotional pain. Rather than state an inflexible position, the spouse should express unmet interests, desires, and needs. When the motivation is known, solutions multiply.

Fisher and Ury argue that, when parties cling to positions, mediation success becomes unlikely, as a position

---

6   Roger Fisher and William Ury, *Getting to Yes* (New York: Penguin Books, 1981).

permits only one solution—a specific demand must be satisfied. If the other party will not capitulate or acquiesce, the conflict escalates. Peacemaking demands a more flexible approach.

Flexibility increases when mediators and parties "go below the line," shifting from positions to interests. After party motivations become increasingly clear, creativity blossoms, different ways to satisfy an interest surface. Scenarios for achieving satisfaction come to view and stalled negotiations spring to life.

Disputants typically arrive at mediation after having experienced multiple failed attempts to resolve their conflict. Prior efforts usually focused on positions rather than interests. After mediators shift the focus, the impasse unsticks. For this reason, peacemakers should become skilled in guiding parties "below the line."

Habitual Responses and Divine Collaboration

Typically, parties do not reflect on their exercise of free will when they're faced with conflict; rather, they default to habitual responses. As noted in a previous chapter, they most often respond to conflict with *avoidance, accommodation, competition, or compromise.*[7] We can analyze each response in terms of satisfaction: how is the party's effort to satisfy their self-interest balanced with their efforts to satisfy the interests of others?

---

7   See Kenneth Thomas, and Ralph Kilmann, "The Thomas Kilmann Conflict Mode Instrument," http:/kilmann.com/conflict.html.

For example, when parties *avoid* they make no attempt to satisfy their own self interest or the interests of others. They simply wish to escape from the conflict and suffer the least harm possible.

A party who *accommodates* places an emphasis on meeting the needs of the other party; he sacrifices his own satisfaction. When parties *compromise*, they share satisfaction and disappointment equally; each experiences partial satisfaction and partial disappointment. They "cut the pie in half." When parties *compete* they focus on self-interest and have little or no concern for satisfying others.

Mediators choreograph movement away from these habitual postures toward the ideal: *collaboration*, the creative search for mutual benefit, with both parties experiencing the greatest possible satisfaction.[8] In mediation circles, the value of collaboration is well established. With faith-based mediation we ratchet up the value of collaboration with a new feature: we add a shared baseline intention that functions much like a marked channel used to guide ships safely into harbor.

When parties align their personal intentions with a common baseline, they begin to head in the same general direction, which diminishes the frequency of collisions. This shared baseline intention is the Will of God. When parties align their personal free will with the Will of God, they engage in Divine Collaboration.

---

[8] For a complete description read Chapter 10 in Stone, *Taming the Wolf*.

For example, scripture reveals that God intends for us to love our neighbor. Parties who try to love one another thus seek to align with divine intention. This has a positive affect on negotiation outcomes. Divine collaboration works on three axes: *parties seek to satisfy their own interests, others' interests, and God's interests.*

Divine Collaboration and Spiritual Gifts

Divine Collaboration calls upon spiritual gifts, such as "knowing with the heart." Divine relationship supplies mystical intuition:

> Just as a person becomes certain of another's love without being able to subject it to the methods of scientific experiment, so in the contact between God and man there is certainty of a quite different kind from the certainty of objectivizing thought.[9]

This "different kind of certainty" emerges as divine love reshapes human will. Benedict teaches that such love precedes reason:

> We are able to give the assent of faith because the will—the heart—has been touched by God, "affected by him." Through being touched in this way, the will knows that even what is still not "clear" to the reason is true.[10]

---

9   Pope Benedict XVI, "January 22," *Benedictus*, 35.
10 Ibid.

Peacemakers also discover, firsthand, that divine love precedes reason. They observe that parties, those who are infused with divine love, reconcile *before* reason matures. They watch as parties whose hearts have been softened by the Holy Spirit move closer together *before* they comprehend possible solutions to the conflict. This leads to an axiom: *hearts infused with Spirit awaken before reason awakens.* Thus, peacemakers who wait for clarity of reason often risk overlooking the heart-based movement that takes place earlier.

Infused with Spirit, parties draw closer to one another—physically, emotionally, psychologically, and spiritually. They perceive more clearly, feel more deeply, and understand more accurately. After parties align with the Will of God, reason kicks in and confusion gives way to "ah-hah" moments. Parties discover that: "...entering into relationship with both God and others sets the conditions for the emergence of the possibility of knowing at the deepest level."[11]

Remarkable changes come about as a result of healing divine relationship. Being and knowing converge. Truth no longer concerns facts or data "out there"; rather, truth describes "being-in-love." Wisdom, we discover, does not arise from knowledge as much as from an infusion of divine love. Parties come to know best that which they love best, and the greatest possible love resides in Christ:

> And the form, the life of Christ, is love; hence to

---

[11] Christopher Collins, *The Word Made Love*, 16.

believe is to conform to Christ and to enter into his love. So it is that in the Letter to the Galatians, in which he primarily developed his teaching on justification, Saint Paul speaks of faith that works through love (cf. Gal 5:14).[12]

These principles shape a two-part axiom: 1) Knowledge and wisdom emerge from love, not computation; 2) Knowledge of God emerges from relationship, not from philosophical argument. Thus, Divine Collaboration produces the light of love that dispels shadows. After darkness is dispelled, previously hidden counter-intention comes to view. Parties view emotional, mental, and spiritual terrain with renewed clarity. They become willing, even eager, to realign their intentions and their subsequent dialogue takes on a more loving quality:

> Acknowledgment of the living God is one path towards love, and the 'yes' of our will to his will unites our intellect, will and sentiments in the all-embracing act of love.[13]

The story of the Good Samaritan captures divine love infusing man with love for neighbor:

> The Samaritan, the foreigner, makes himself the neighbor and shows me that I have to learn to be a neighbor deep within and that I already have the answer in myself. I have to become like

---

12 Benedict XVI, *St. Paul*, 82.
13 Pope Benedict XVI, *God is Love*, 43.

someone in love, someone whose heart is open to being shaken up by another's need. Then I find my neighbor, or—better—then I am found by him.[14]

Mary, the mother of Jesus, provides an additional example. Love dictates that she place God's interests above all else:

> Because of Mary's "yes," the union of God and humanity can take place. In Mary's fiat we see a kind of consummation of the dialogical relationship between God and humanity that had been unfolding since the beginning of human history.[15]

In stark contrast to Mary's example, others cling to self-interest. They descend into silence; their relationships deteriorate into hostility. This prompts us to listen the words of John the Evangelist:

> "If anyone says, 'I love God,' and hates his brother, he is a liar; for he who does not love his brother whom he has seen, cannot love God whom he has not seen" (1 Jn 4:20). ...Saint John's words should rather be interpreted to mean that love of neighbor is a path that leads to the encounter with God and that closing our eyes to our neighbor also blinds us to God.[16]

Divine Collaboration should be recognized as more

---

14 Joseph Ratzinger, *Jesus of Nazareth vol. 1*, 197.
15 Collins, *The Word Made Love*, 116.
16 Pope Benedict XVI, *Deus Caritas Est*, 41.

than a technique. It helps a party attain a state of being-in-love. Through the presence of the Holy Spirit, it fosters the love needed for peacemaking:

> [I]n God and with God, I love even the person whom I do not like or even know. This can only take place on the basis of an intimate encounter with God, an encounter which has become a communion of will, even affecting my feelings. ... Then I learn to look on this other person, not simply with my eyes and my feelings, but from the perspective of Jesus Christ.[17]

Divine Collaboration realigns wills, beginning with an experience of unity with the Holy Spirit:

> First, the dynamism of unification, in which men draw together by moving toward God, is a component of the new people of God as Jesus intends it. Second, the point of convergence of this new people is Christ; it becomes a people solely through his call and its response to his call and to his person.[18]

Previously, in the opening stages of reconciliation, peacemakers guided warring parties "below the line" to mine personal interests. Now, with Divine Collaboration, they lead parties even deeper "below the line" to unearth divine interests. When it comes to this deeper dive, sec-

---

17 Ibid., 45.
18 Joseph Ratzinger, *Called to Communion: Understanding the Church Today*, trans. Adrian Walker (San Francisco, California: Ignatius Press, 1991–1996), 23.

ular mediation falls short. While parties may resolve disputes, they ordinarily fail to heal wounded relationships. They may even formalize an *avoidance* strategy as part of the settlement, vowing never to see each other again.

Platforms for Peace

Though our focus must remain on the individual, briefly we will consider realignment as it applies to the society. John Paul Lederach, in his work, *The Moral Imagination*,[19] argues that formal peace accords often fail to ensure lasting peace because they lack adequate "platforms for change." These "platforms" are formal-yet-flexible dispute resolution protocols designed to prevent, manage, and resolve societal conflict. They're conflict resolution tools needed to reestablish civil society in a post-war period.

Violent conflicts that escalate into wars destroy civil society. They bring about heinous crimes against humanity that deliver unimaginable suffering and rend the fabric of human dignity. When wars end, through attrition or "victory," civil society must be reestablished. Relationships must be healed. Unfortunately, many peace accords do not include comprehensive plans for healing or for establishing enduring peace. The unhealed wounds of one war eventually foment another war.

A faith-based reconciliation paradigm offers a truly effective "platform for change." The protocol guides a so-

---

[19] John Paul Lederach, *The Moral Imagination: The Art and Soul of Building Peace* (New York: Oxford University Press, 2005).

ciety-wide realignment with the Will of God. A peaceful and prosperous civil society echoes the nature of divine relationship. Social policies based on supernatural truths are woven into the fabric of Creation to ensure lasting peace. In contrast, societies that ignore the supernatural aspects of life flounder and become belligerent players on the world stage.

The Catholic social doctrine concept of *subsidiarity*, which dictates that decisions be rendered at the level closest to the individual, provides a good base for effective policy. In this doctrine, policy decisions are negotiated by the smallest decision-making unit possible. For example, policy set at the village level produces better results for villagers; they fare better under policy set at the local level than with policy set by a powerful central government.

Face-to-face decision-making is a core principle of subsidiarity. This might be stated as follows: decisions should not be made by a remote governing body when they can be made at a local level. Decision-making power should reside with the individuals affected. This is established doctrine:

> Subsidiarity is among the most constant and characteristic directives of the Church's social doctrine and has been present since the first great social encyclical.[20]

---

20 Pontifical Council for Justice and Peace, *Compendium of the Social Doctrine of the Church*, (USCCB, 2005), 81. The referenced encyclical, *Rerum Novarum*, was written by Pope Leo XIII, 1892.

Subsidiarity, in essence, advocates citizen participation in governance:

> The characteristic implication of subsidiarity is participation..."[21] which becomes, "...a duty to be fulfilled consciously by all, with responsibility and with a view to the common good."[22]

The tenets of subsidiarity parallel the principles of collaborative negotiation. Both require individuals to engage in a search for mutual satisfaction. In the same way that mundane (secular) collaboration comes up short, mundane subsidiarity fails:

> No legislation, no system of rules or negotiation will ever succeed in persuading men and peoples to live in unity, brotherhood and peace; no line of reasoning will ever be able to surpass the appeal of love. Only love, in its quality as 'form of the virtues,' can animate and shape social interaction, moving it toward peace in the context of a world that is ever more complex.[23]

In summary, the doctrine of subsidiarity will come up short unless policy decisions emerge from Divine Collaboration and align with divine will. Policy must be infused with divine love. "Platforms for change" must be built on a foundation of divine interests.

---

21 *Compendium of the Social Doctrine of the Church*, 83.
22 Ibid.
23 Ibid., 91.

As we reconcile individual relationships, we also minister to entire nations. Individuals who realign their wills with divine will hasten the arrival of a new earth based in peace.

Reflection

Aspiring peacemakers should reflect on the nature of opposing intentions—the primary cause of conflict, division, suffering, and alienation. They will want to contemplate how alignment with a common baseline intention—the Will of God—can assist the reconciliation process. They will want to reflect on ways to foster and strengthen divine relationship.

Aspiring mediators should develop skill in helping disputants as they realign their free will. The typical disputant does not arrive at mediation with a passionate desire for spiritual communion; rather, they're deeply mired in the fallen world, caught up in turmoil and chaos. A peacemaker must learn how to guide them out of confusion.

Peacemakers will also want to reflect on the concept, "knowing and being converge in mystical unity." How will they encourage disputants to accept the grace of divine love? How will they nurture affinity sufficient to draw parties together—physically, emotionally, and psychologically?

Peacemakers will need to know how love lifts parties out of darkness. They will need to understand the dynamics of love and knowledge. How can increased affinity bring greater understanding? How does greater understanding increase affinity?

Peacemakers will also want to consider the following fundamental principle: when the exercise of free will is unimpaired and uncompromised, a person prefers unity to separation and chooses love over alienation.

In order to comprehend mankind's impulse toward division, they may want to reflect on Genesis: How was the Serpent able to seed envy, doubt, and pride? How did He "coach" souls into a dark matrix of intentions?

Throughout preceding chapters we've developed insight into peacemaking. At this point, does the reader feel emboldened? Or have the challenges generated worry or despair? If so, please set aside trepidation, as the following chapters will introduce powerful new tools you can use to overcome challenges.

EIGHT
Managing Disordered Will

When parties first begin to reconcile, they're not eager to grant their opponent's wishes. They're not ready to align with divine will. If a mediator suggests they realign their intentions, they balk.

So, instead, meditators ask the parties to imagine all the ways they might satisfy their needs. They show respect for party self-determinism and creativity. Later, after parties have become more confident in their decision-making, they'll be more eager to collaborate. After they acquire a collaborative mindset, they'll be open to realigning their intentions, but they'll also face a new challenge—managing their own disordered will.

Man's Failure to Hasten World Peace

Realignment protocol is powerful in its simplicity. However, simplicity might provoke skepticism. Can achieving world peace really be this easy? There is little doubt the realignment protocol is valid—it conforms to reason, scripture, and sound practice. But, if the model is accurate, why has world peace proven elusive?

Peace remains elusive because realignment of free will, while simple in theory, is difficult to implement. The concept is simple; the execution is terribly difficult. While people may know the desired outcome, they do not know how to achieve it. Realignment makes sense, but discerning intentions taxes our ability.

This difficulty was modeled prophetically by the failure of Adam and Eve. After being deceived by the Serpent, they failed to manage their free will. The account of the Garden prompts a question: *what is this free will that proves so difficult to manage?*

We know that free will allows a person to choose their path in life. They're free to craft a personal life narrative that fits their vision of themselves. Free will also presents a vital opportunity for a soul to enter into a loving relationship with God. Perhaps most of all, free will enables this reciprocal expression of love between man and God. This, in turn, opens the door to a life of spirituality.

However, once a soul crosses the threshold of the spiritual path, his perceptions, once clear, may become distorted. His will may be battered by negative impulses. The spiritual life, a choice born of free will, most often meets resistance.

Paradoxically, the more a person seeks spiritual joy, the greater opposition they face. St. Paul captured this plight in his letter to the Romans: though he knew what he wanted to do, he often did the opposite.[1] Paul's observation addresses one of many barriers people face as they seek to realign their will.

Go Slow to Go Fast

Disputants arrive at mediation with their free will under siege. Stimulus-response triggers, rather than thoughtful deliberation, drive their decisions. While they may display an "in-control" facade, mediators sense their discomfort.

At first, parties are reluctant to fully consider their opponent's wishes. This is no surprise—most likely, their unwillingness to satisfy others' wishes precipitated the conflict. By the time they arrive at mediation, they hold unyielding positions.

The same conflict dynamics apply to reconciliation with God. Parties, when asked to align with divine will, tend to balk at the "suspicious" request. Mediators must avoid the natural instinct to rush headlong into this roadblock. Instead, they should switch to a counter-intuitive approach: *to go fast, they must go slow.* They advance cautiously, taking small steps that explore the party's relationship with God. They engage in open-ended, non-threatening conversations about matters of the heart.

Mediators know that parties will defend their exercise of free will with great passion, so they avoid triggering party defenses. They often ask for permission before

---

[1] Romans 7.

posing questions. For example, "Would it be okay for us to discuss how you feel about trust?" In this way, they gently explore how a party might repair or build trust. After a period of non-threatening dialogue, hot-button issues may be raised. Gradually, questions touch on emotional issues that might have caused distrust between disputants. As the conversation deepens, mediators might introduce the following idea from theology:

> The human being does not trust God. Tempted by the serpent, he harbors suspicion that in the end, God takes something away from his life, that God is a rival who curtails our freedom and that we will be fully human only when we have cast him aside...[2]

These preliminary conversations launch the task of rebuilding trust with God. This may be counterintuitive. Ordinarily, when it comes to God, people do not think in terms of trust or distrust. They do not anticipate needing to reestablish trust, yet it is critical:

> The human being lives in the suspicion that God's love creates a dependence and that he must rid himself of this dependency if he is to be fully himself. Man does not want to receive his existence and the fullness of his life from God. He himself wants to obtain from the tree of knowledge the power to shape the world, to make himself a god,

---

[2] Pope Benedict XVI, "December 6," *Benedictus*, 369.

raising himself to God's level, and to overcome death and darkness with his own efforts.³

In this passage, Benedict sketches a compelling portrait of a person opposed to the Will of God. Their fear-based opposition becomes the soil in which evil takes root. Later, we will inspect the link between a person's fear and their opposition to God. At this time, we simply note that our chance of success plummets when we minister to parties stricken with fear. Benedict describes this type of personality:

> He does not want to rely on love that to him seems untrustworthy; he relies solely on his own knowledge since it confers power upon him. Rather than on love, he sets his sights on power, with which he desires to take his own life autonomously in hand. And in doing so, he trusts in deceit rather than in truth and thereby sinks with his life into emptiness, into death.⁴

Peacemakers encounter disputants who are alienated from the sacred in life. When this occurs, peacemakers assess and catalog spiritual afflictions. They evaluate how fear shapes the intentions that oppose the Will of God. When a peacemaker misjudges the nature of the fear that drives opposition, they lose control and become flustered, confused, disoriented.

---

3   Ibid.
4   Ibid.

During such times of confusion, a peacemaker can turn to Benedict's theology to clarify the origins of man's opposition to God. The theology becomes a valuable addition to a peacemaker's "repair toolkit."

Theology Guides Practice

The study of theology helps reconcilers discern a party's spiritual maturity; it enables them to better detect deception and misdirection. The study of theology enhances a mediator's pastoral demeanor and helps them map the human condition. Their pastoral demeanor is enhanced by their study of theology. When reconcilers encounter parties struggling to integrate mundane and supernatural concerns, their theology background proves especially valuable. And, when peacemaking efforts veer off the road into a ditch, the tow truck of theology is summoned.

In most instances, warring parties will claim that they're not lost nor confused. They will claim they're fully in control of their emotions and decisions. Reconcilers, however, find that the parties are disoriented; their struggles are not trivial. Benedict describes the situation:

> On the one side, there is an interior opening up of the human soul to God; but on the other side, there is the stronger attraction of our needs and our immediate experiences. Man is the battlefield where these two contend with each other. He is not capable of sloughing off God completely, nor does he have the strength to set out on the journey toward him. On his own, he is not capable of con-

structing a bridge that could establish a concrete relationship with this God.[5]

The preceding passage suggests a simple axiom: Without God's love, a party will have difficulty completing the reconciliation journey. A person stranded in an emotional desert devoid of love has only one escape route—a conversion from worldly illusions to the truth of a loving relationship with God. Their pilgrimage depends on one key variable—their exercise of free will must become infused with divine love.

Benedict explains the dynamics at play when someone rejects the gift of divine love:

> The gravitational pull of our own will constantly draws us away from God's will and turns us into mere "earth." But he accepts us, he draws us up to himself, into himself, and in communion with him we too learn God's will.[6]

Benedict clarifies the dynamics:

> The love-story between God and man consists in the very fact that this communion of will increases in a communion of thought and sentiment, and thus our will and God's will increasingly coincide: God's will is no longer for me an alien will, something imposed on me from without by the commandments, but it is now my own will, based

---

5 Ratzinger, *Christianity and the Crisis of Cultures*.
6 Ratzinger, *Jesus of Nazareth vol. 1*, 150.

on the realization that God is in fact more deeply present to me than I am to myself.[7]

Spiritual directors illuminate this paradoxical truth when they help parties discover God's presence. Their formal spiritual formation helps parties recognize the sacred nature of reality.

In contrast, parties who lack spiritual direction risk slipping into confusion and doubt about reality and their true nature. At first, they achieve minor advances but, later when they come under the spell of deception, they'll backslide and fall into spiritual traps. Often, mediators bridge the gap created by a lack of spiritual direction until the party secures a spiritual director.

When God's presence is missing in a party's life, fear will make frequent appearances. This is perhaps the most daunting obstacle blocking reconciliation. Fearful parties blindly attack the source of their fear. This impulse leads them into spiritual quicksand. The more they struggle, the quicker they sink. Parties caught in a trap respond with knee-jerk attacks against any and all perceived enemies. Their desperate reactions contradict core spiritual wisdom:

> Only when our will rests in the will of God does it become truly will and truly free.[8]

---

7 Pope Benedict XVI, *Deus Caritas Est*, 44.
8 Pope Benedict XVI, *The Spirit of the Liturgy*, trans. John Saward (San Francisco, California: Ignatius Press, 2000), 187.

Reconcilers offset the fear-based responses by providing safety and hope. They create a sanctuary where the presence of the Holy Spirit, even if temporary, reduces fear. They set the stage for an inquiry into the causes of fear.

Reconcilers begin by identifying past traumatic events that involve betrayal—times when deception promised freedom but delivered entrapment. A mediator cannot afford to underestimate the role of deception and betrayal as drivers of fear. Sometimes the roots of fear extend so deep that even minor setbacks cause parties to spiral out of control. Fear sweeps them up like panicked swimmers pulled out to sea by a deadly riptide. Thus, peacemakers must treat fear with respect at the same time they remain mindful of the scriptural admonishments, "be not afraid" and "fear not."

Peacemakers may seem to resemble action heroes as they battle fear and deception. They rescue deceived parties from spiritual traps designed to instill terror. They battle alongside disputants who struggle to realign their free will, knowing that:

> Where God's will is done, there is heaven, there earth becomes heaven.[9]

During this phase of the peacemaking journey, a party discovers, often during worship, that alignment with the Will of God brings release from fear.

---

9 Ibid., 176.

> Surrendering ourselves to the action of God, so that we in our turn may cooperate with him—that is what begins in the liturgy and is meant to unfold further beyond it.[10]

Worship—especially Holy Communion—infuses troubled sojourners with calm strength, with the power of tranquility.

In contrast, fearful souls lacking access to the liturgy draw apart from God and their fellow man. Living in fear, desperate and alone, they eventually wage a battle *against* the Will of God. They take a dark turn toward destructive nihilism; but, even then, they encounter dead ends, as the goal of nihilism—nothingness—proves unattainable. Their counterfeit destination delivers only suffering. Their destructive designs are smashed by a harsh reality: man cannot cancel or reverse God's creative act.

Benedict explains why a nihilistic philosophy fails to satisfy the human soul:

> The result of his sin is not pure nothingness. Like every other creature, man can only move within the ambit of creation. Just as he cannot bring forth being of himself, so neither can he hurl it back into sheer nothingness. What he can achieve in this regard is not the annulment of being, but lived self-contradiction, a self-negating possibility, namely "Sheol." The natural ordination towards the truth, towards God, which of itself

---

10   Ibid.

excludes nothingness, still endures, even when it is denied or forgotten.[11]

An ironic dilemma is revealed: those who seek to nullify God ultimately nullify their own existence. Nihilists, with their path to nothingness blocked, engineer a black hole of self-negation. They do not cease to exist—rather, they exist in darkness. Failing to discover an exit into non-existence, they cloak themselves in the blackness of pseudo-nihilism. They're swallowed up in a black hole of their own making. It is hard to imagine a more brutal trap.

These conditions spawn desperate psychopaths who target all creation with destructive intentions. When we plot their intentions on our vector-arrow diagram, they aim directly opposite the Will of God. God intends Being; they intend Non-Being. God intends love and unity; they intend hatred and division. These souls, who are frozen in existential fear, must be handled with care. They resemble kidnap victims strapped with spiritual bombs. Mediators must defuse the explosive devices before the reconciliation process can continue.

In the preceding discussion I have highlighted just a few of the "house of mirrors" barriers that must be overcome using the lessons of applied theology. In the next section, we will look closer at opposition to the Will of God.

---

11 Ratzinger, *Eschatology*, 156.

Fallen World Misalignment

When intentions oppose the Will of God, they create conflict scenarios with a good-versus-evil dimension. It is fair to say that evil intentions are those that oppose the Will of God, those that bring suffering. Benedict, in the language of theology, addresses the ills they cause:

> Enmity with God is the source of all that poisons man; overcoming this enmity is the basic condition for peace in the world. Only the man who is reconciled with God can also be reconciled and in harmony with himself, and only the man who is reconciled with God and with himself can establish peace around him and throughout the world.[12]

This idea—that enmity toward God poisons the peace—provides us with a tool for predicting the probable success of peacemaking. We evaluate divine relationships; we seek to detect sources of hostility toward God—any underlying emotional state that threatens to block divine collaboration. When mediators detect animosity, they craft a plan to heal the mental, emotional, or spiritual factors that poison divine relationship. In particular, they will want to know what went wrong. What destroyed the party's relationship with God?

The Genesis narrative of Adam and Eve in the Garden supplies us with a good example of a relationship dam-

---

12 Ratzinger, *Jesus of Nazareth vol. 1*, 85.

aged by evil intentions. In Paradise, their individual wills were perfectly aligned with the Will of God. All was good; harmony and unity prevailed. Then everything changed. The Serpent's shady "counseling" disrupted the alignment. Under the influence of the Deceiver, Adam and Eve exercised their free will unwisely: they veered off in their own direction, rejecting unity with God. The Genesis paradigm repeats whenever man turns away from God:

> At the heart of all temptations, as we see here, is the act of pushing God aside because we perceive him as secondary, if not actually superfluous and annoying, in comparison with all the apparently far more urgent matters that fill our lives.[13]

When we vector diagram the exercise of free will, the resulting graphic illustrates the common cause of conflict in the world. Mankind's intentions point in all directions:

> [W]hen one's own will and desire is the decisive criterion, schism is a foregone conclusion, because there are multiple and opposing varieties of taste.[14]

Benedict's words echo the vector diagram lesson: human intentions are scattered, aimed in a multitude of directions. The diagram illustrates the conflict that occurs

---

13   Ibid., 28.
14   Joseph Ratzinger, *Called to Communion: Understanding the Church Today*, trans. Adrian Walker, in particular see Epilogue (San Francisco, California: Ignatius Press, 1991–1996), 37.

when the Church veers out of alignment with divine will and steers toward worldly intentions:

> The more we ourselves do in the Church, the more uninhabitable she becomes, because everything human is limited and is in opposition to other human realities.[15]

But, we must ask once again, if the problem is clear, why does man continue to suffer? In addition to man's lack of competence, the power of deception and the darkness of doubt cause a person's resolve to fade:

> Temptation does not begin with the denial of God and a fall into outright atheism. The serpent does not deny God; it starts out, rather, with an apparently reasonable request for information, which in reality, however, contains an insinuation that provokes the human being and lures him or her from trust to mistrust: "Did God say, 'You shall not eat of any tree in the garden?' (Gen 3:1) The first thing is not the denial of God but rather doubt about his covenant, about the community of faith, prayer, the commandments—all of which are the context for living God's covenant.[16]

Spiritual drift exacts terrible consequences. Benedict, with a touch of sarcasm, describes the dilemma:

> There is indeed a great deal of enlightenment

---

15 Ibid.
16 Ratzinger, *The Essential Pope Benedict XVI*, 262.

when one doubts the covenant, experiences mistrust, demands freedom, and renounces obedience to the covenant as a straitjacket that prevents one from enjoying the real promises of life. It is so easy to convince people that this covenant is not a gift, but rather an expression of envy of humankind and that it is robbing human beings of their freedom and the most precious things of life. With this doubt, people are well on their way to building their own worlds.[17]

Deception foments doubt, which clouds the course of free will. A person's choices—like metal filings scattered in a magnetic field—are pushed, pulled, and dragged out of alignment by deception and doubt. Here we find an explanation for Paul's observation that a man is prone to doing that which he does not want to do: disturbed oppositional forces twist and distort his intentions. Benedict goes a step further and notes, with irony, that people who exercise free will in order to assert human or worldly power may inadvertently cast themselves into slavery:

> They do not free themselves, but place themselves in opposition to the truth. And that means that they are destroying themselves and the world.[18]

Patterns inaugurated in the Garden repeat in the present. The common factor tying the present to the Biblical past is human departure from alignment with base-

---

17   Ibid.
18   Ibid., 264.

line divine will. Once free will slips loose and becomes unmoored from its divine baseline, intentions veer out of alignment and collide, setting destructive conflict in motion.

Charting Fallen World Misalignment

When we study theology, we find scripture passages that describe conflict. In these passages, the "wages of sin" parallel the consequences of conflict. Both end in soul-crushing alienation. When Benedict describes people who turn away from God, he also (inadvertently) describes the mindset of the typical disputant:

> They consider their dependence on God's creative love to be an imposition from without. But that is what slavery is, and from slavery one must free oneself. Thus human beings themselves want to be God. When they try this, everything is thrown topsy-turvy. The relationship of human beings to themselves is altered, as well as their relationships to others. The other is a hindrance, a rival, a threat to the person who wants to be God.[19]

Benedict accurately captures observations of human behavior. The match between theology and direct observation confirms that we've found the proper approach for mediation. The description we find in scripture applies to our disputants:

---

19 Ibid.

> The relationship with the other becomes one of mutual recrimination and struggle, as is masterfully shown in Genesis 3:8-13, which presents God's conversation with Adam and Eve. Finally, the relation to the world is altered in such a way as to become one of destruction and exploitation. Human beings who consider dependence on the highest love as slavery and who try to deny the truth about themselves, which is their creatureliness, do not free themselves; they destroy truth and love.[20]

Deductions drawn from theology match the deductions drawn from mediator observations. When people destroy their relationship with God, they also destroy the truth and love they need to reconcile conflict.

In addition, we find a parallel between conflict behavior and scripture's description of sin: souls afflicted with sin turn away from the truth; they separate themselves from God and fellow humans; they obfuscate; they advance falsehoods. Those caught up in sin bear a striking resemblance to those caught up in a conflict. In both instances, they descend into alienation that resembles living death.[21]

Sorrow brought on by sin also mirrors the kind of despair generated by conflict. An understanding of sin thus provides greater understanding of conflict, as they share common coordinates in "spiritual space." When we understand conflict, we better understand sin. For example,

---

20 Ibid.
21 Ibid.

the concept of original sin meshes perfectly with the concept of misaligned intentions. Benedict sets the stage when he describes common misunderstandings regarding original sin:

> The account tells us that sin begets sin, and that, therefore, all the sins of history are interlinked. Theology refers to this state of affairs by the certainly misleading and imprecise term original sin. What does this mean? Nothing seems to us today to be stranger or, indeed, more absurd than to insist upon original sin, since, according to our way of thinking, guilt can only be something very personal, and God does not run a concentration camp in which one's relatives are imprisoned, because he is a liberating God of love who calls each one by name. What does original sin mean, then, when we interpret it correctly?[22]

Thus, we should not be surprised when we find original sin widely rejected and ridiculed. However, with the realignment-of-wills model, clarity is restored. When we look closely, we realize original sin is simply the misalignment of free will—the same misalignment that generates conflict! The classic definition of sin—"missing the mark"—echoes the concept of a misaligned exercise of free will. The errant intentions "miss the mark."

---

22   Ibid., 265.

The Mystical Paradigm

The Biblical account of Adam and Eve turns out to be much more than an intriguing tale of ancient times. Rather, it is a mystical lesson that extols alignment with God's Will and tells us that men and women cannot be coerced into aligning their wills; rather, they must be invited to seek alignment. This is commonly called conversion.

Exploring these ideas further, we discover the sacred gift of free will ties in with the Christian view of freedom:

> But if the logos of all being, the being that upholds and encompasses everything, is consciousness, freedom, and love, then it follows automatically that the supreme factor in the world is not cosmic necessity but freedom. The implications of this are very extensive. For this leads to the conclusion that freedom is evidently the necessary structure of the world.[23]

Free will, in this view, is a building block of Creation. When a person accepts the gift of free will, he incurs a sacred obligation—a duty to discern consequences. Peacemakers assist with the discernment of choice and consequence; they map the "intentional space" in which free will is exercised. They encourage discernment through reflection on divine relationship:

> Jesus is the one, in Ratzinger's Christological anthropology, who simultaneously shows humanity

---

23 Pope Benedict XVI, *Introduction to Christianity*, 159.

what a human response to the longing for the "absolute You" looks like and how the absolute "I" speaks in turn to humanity, which longs to be drawn out of the experience of loneliness into relationship.[24]

Prodigal souls, stranded in exile, long for home; they eagerly anticipate the journey from loneliness into a renewed loving relationship with God. Secular mediators fail to address such existential loneliness. Faith-based mediators, on the other hand, assess the party's *ontological condition*—the emotional, mental, and spiritual landscapes that make up a party's true state of being. They chart the terrain so they might guide the pilgrimage.

Disputants typically lack a sacred compass with which to track the "coordinates of faith." Instead, they wander aimlessly in a spiritual desert until, stricken with despair, they perish. A soul who wishes to avoid this fate will enlist a spiritual director, someone who can function as a human GPS, identifying sacramental signs that point to invisible truths.

Ultimately, each individual must construct a "reality map" that charts the condition of his body, mind, soul and relationships. The map includes invisible causes and conditions:

> Similar to Plato, he [Ratzinger] perceives tangible reality in confrontation with invisible substances, which are actually the more real entities. For the

---

[24] Collins, *The Word Made Love*.

Christian-modified Platonist that Ratzinger is, this means tangible reality is approached by way of the faith.[25]

An approach "by way of faith" offers a stark contrast to the approach of philosophical naturalism. When such materialists omit fundamental truths, they operate detached from reality. They lead parties on a heroic but tragic effort to orient themselves to reality; in the final analysis, however, all roads mapped with errors of materialism are dead ends. Souls traveling these dark paths lose sight of their final destination; frustrated and angry, they provoke a high percentage of the world's conflicts. How far off the valid path do they wander? Theologian Frank Sheed opines:

> God's will is the sole reason for our existence; be wrong about His will and we are inescapably wrong about the reason for our existence; be wrong about that, and what can we be right about?[26]

In the final analysis, when peacemaking is derailed, it is almost always due to a lack of supernatural awareness. Materialists lack a proper foundation from which to negotiate peace, as their tenets are detached from comprehensive reality. Their flawed decisions make peace diffi-

---

25 de Gaál, *The Theology of Pope Benedict XVI*, 152.
26 Frank J. Sheed, *Theology and Sanity* (San Francisco: Ignatius Press, 1993), 50.

cult or impossible. Conversations with materialists prove challenging:

> [Y]ou cannot discuss the purpose of life with a man who denies the existence of God. You cannot profoundly collaborate in human affairs, in sociology, say, or education, with a man who denies the existence of God. You cannot simply agree to omit God from the collaboration for the sake of argument, any more than you could agree to omit the sun from navigation.[27]

People of faith enjoy an advantage when it comes to reconciliation and peace, as all aspects of reality come together in the Church:

> [T]he Church is the dynamic process of horizontal and vertical unification. It is vertical unification, which brings about the union of man with the triune love of God, thus also integrating man in and with himself.[28]

Peacemaking requires a sane exercise of free will, which is possible only when one has discerned the Will of God. Only the process of realignment with divine will can tame the disordered free will of a party embroiled in conflict. Only after a party realigns with Truth, will they find peace. This view is not popular in today's secular culture; nonetheless, it's an observable truth.

---

27 Ibid., 51.
28 Ratzinger, *Called to Communion*, 76.

Reflection

Aspiring peacemakers learn how to help parties realign their free will, beginning with a reflection on how the Holy Spirit makes this transformation possible. They learn to infuse the peace process with divine love while they synchronize intentions. They learn to enhance party self-determinism, while promoting safety and hope.

Each peacemaker must develop a personal approach to helping parties discover that God's love is real and accessible. In preparation for this task, they inventory personal skills they'll need as spiritual directors. They must reflect on how they'll assist parties to seek transcendent reality through mystical union.

In addition, they come to know Christ as the ultimate mediator who will reconcile humanity with God. They reflect on the importance Jesus placed on following his Father's will. They ask what they must do in order to foster divine collaboration.

Students of peacemaking travel challenging territory. They work intimately with the powerful supernatural aspects of life; they'll experience trepidation, but they must overcome doubt and constantly evaluate their state of readiness. After engaging in such personal evaluation, they recommit, over and over, to their study of peacemaking ministry, knowing there is much to learn.

NINE

The Will of God

The fallen world resembles an overgrown jungle where little light enters. There appears to be no way forward and no retreat. At times, life in this jungle may play out like a horror film scenario. Nonetheless, even in the midst of tribulation, light may unexpectedly break through the jungle canopy, illuminating an escape route, a path to freedom. This unexpected "good news" typically appears at the moment humans align their will with divine will. At that moment, a path to peace appears, as if by magic, a path seemingly cleared by supernatural hands.

For this reason, we will turn to the supernatural lessons that Jesus taught in word and deed, in which he stresses alignment with the Will of God. This theme appears frequently in the Gospel:

> The Gospel of John places particular emphasis on the fact that Jesus unites his own will totally with the Father's will.[1]

---
1   Ratzinger, *Jesus of Nazareth vol.1*, 341.

Assessing the Will of God

Negotiating with one's brother may seem difficult, but not nearly as daunting as making peace with God. Most people would wonder if it even makes sense to speak of God's interests. After all, how could we possibly discern those desires? Jesus was in a unique position to know the Father's will—a Trinitarian position. In stark contrast to Jesus, most people suffer doubt, confusion, and mystery when it comes to God's will.

However, discernment is possible for one reason: *man is endowed with the image and likeness of God*. A soul, created in the image and likeness of God, inherits spiritual consciousness, which opens a conduit to knowledge of divine will. St. Bonaventure was correct when he said God reveals his interests through relationship, not in treatises or rule compilations. Benedict explains:

> Whereas it had been common in Catholic theology in the early part of the twentieth century to think of revelation primarily as the objective data given by God to humanity, for Bonaventure revelation is primarily the more foundational act by which God reveals what had previously been hidden; it is not the "objectified result of this act."[2]

Bonaventure imparts an important truth: *we come to know divine will by entering into relationship*. Though inspired Scripture reveals the Word, we also encounter the

---

2 Collins, *The Word Made Love*, 24.

Living Word in prayerful relationship, best captured in the phrase, "the Holy Spirit at work in our lives."

Only from the perspective gained once one has 'gone behind' the positive sources of Scripture and tradition to revelation itself does it become possible to begin to see the unfolding of the Word in salvation history.[3]

The Holy Spirit's supernatural advocacy is one aspect of divine relationship. Without such inspiration and infused revelation, realignment of wills would be impossible. The spiritual guidance that flows from divine relationship is *real*. This sacramental dialogue forms the cornerstone of Benedict's theology:

> There is simplicity at the core of Ratzinger's articulation of the Christian mystery. God speaks. Humanity listens…or not. To the degree that humanity does listen to the Word spoken by God, it opens up to the possibility of responding to the Word, thereby fulfilling what it means to be truly human. In this speaking and listening a relationship is established, a transformation occurs, a story is told.[4]

In spite of this encouraging reality, peacemakers encounter parties who take a firm stance in opposition to God, rejecting supernatural reality. They can expect to come upon those who distort, diminish, or invalidate humanity's sacred endowment of the image of God.

---

3   Ibid., 39.
4   Ibid., 171.

This barrier to reconciliation must be cleared away before spiritual sight, which is vital for peace, can be restored. Once a disputing party's spiritual consciousness resonates with divine consciousness, the process of realignment accelerates.

Nonetheless, peacemakers should not become overly discouraged when they encounter a party's antipathy toward God. They should know that the Holy Spirit is capable of breathing new inspiration into hardened hearts. Though a party may be temporarily blind to the Spirit's presence, ultimately their sacred endowment—the image and likeness of God, which infuses them with latent spiritual consciousness—will become a conduit for supernatural grace. As a result, we can have confidence that even fleeting epiphanies will help a party discern divine will.

Discernment and Love

Parties engaging in discernment begin by reflecting on divine nature. During contemplation, they often find themselves infused with divine love:

> Acknowledgment of the living God is one path towards love, and the "yes" of our will to his will unites our intellect, will and sentiment in the all-embracing act of love.[5]

When a person softens their heart and contemplates

---

5   Pope Benedict XVI, *God Is Love*.

the nature of God, they are often swept up—supernaturally—into alignment with the Will of God. This infusion of divine love predisposes them to collaborate with their brethren in a search for peace. Slowly, they begin to embrace the other:

> Love now becomes concern and care for the other. No longer is it self-seeking, a sinking intoxication of happiness; instead it seeks the good of the beloved: it becomes renunciation, and it is ready, and even willing, for sacrifice.[6]

Oppositional stances dissipate, allowing parties to become more flexible. Previously rigid intentions become more malleable. Though peacemakers rarely craft a perfect realignment of intentions, they are able to facilitate a transformation that reduces conflict.

Discerning Divine Will—Perspectives

When a peacemaker first asks a party to evaluate their personal interests in light of the Will of God, they may encounter protest: *how could I even hope to know the Will of God?* There's no single answer. Discernment is not a rote task.

As a general rule, however, inflexible approaches are ineffective. Rather, a mediator must work "in the moment," adjusting their style for specific clients and unique conflicts. They observe each party's ability to discern divine

---

6 Ibid., 21.

will, then design an approach that proceeds at the appropriate pace.

The following discussion should prompt reflection. How can we discern divine will? How can we help others discern divine will? The discussion may be brief, but mediators can use the reflections to develop skills and processes that will help them define a personal approach to assisting parties.

This bare-bones survey of discernment methods starts with a simple mention of the most powerful and direct approach—contemplative prayer as found in the spirituality of Saint Francis and St. Bonaventure; in the Carmelite tradition of St. John of the Cross; in St. Ignatius' examination of consciousness; in the teachings of the Desert Fathers; and in the writings of the mystics throughout history. In later sections and chapters devoted to mystical union with Christ, we will revisit this option. For now, however, we will consider options suitable for those who have not yet developed proficiency in mystical practices.

A common discernment option not to be overlooked is regular celebration of the Blessed Sacrament, known as the Eucharist. During the celebration of the Mass, worshippers find communion with the Holy Spirit. Enveloped by the Real Presence that softens their hearts with sanctifying grace, they are able to intuit divine providence at work in their lives. In the Blessed Sacrament they encounter the Living God. Lifted out of worldliness, they comingle with the supernatural. This encounter takes place in transcendent time:

> As Ratzinger [Benedict XVI] elaborates in his *The Spirit of the Liturgy*, the Church's time in the Eucharist integrates the past, present, and future that "touches eternity."[7]

Worshippers transcend ordinary time and are infused with divine love, which nurtures prayerful listening. With their hearts and minds open to the Holy Spirit, they are better able to intuit how God intends for them to love:

> The Spirit, in fact, is that interior power which harmonizes their hearts with Christ's heart and moves them to love their brethren as Christ loved them, when he bent down to wash the feet of the disciples (cf. Jn 13:1-13) and above all when he gave his life for us (cf. Jn 13:1; 15:13).[8]

Ideally, during the period of reconciliation, parties alternate between mediation sessions and celebration of the Blessed Sacrament. Breaks are scheduled between mediation sessions to allow parties to attend Mass, where they can reflect on their conflict in a worship setting. Though one might assume these breaks create unnecessary delays, worship enhances discernment and thus accelerates reconciliation.

In yet another approach to discernment of will, disputants mine settlement criteria from Scripture. If their personal intentions do not violate the tenets of sacred texts,

---

7 de Gaál, *The Theology of Pope Benedict XVI*, 246.
8 Pope Benedict XVI, *God Is Love*, 49.

those intentions might align with the Will of God. In this task, they employ a disciplined and contemplative reading of Scripture called *Lectio Divina*. This technique uses the written Word to condition the heart. Saint Bonaventure recognized the potential results:

> For Bonaventure scripture and revelation produce the *visio intellectualis* (spirit-filled vision) of the human *mens* (mind), illuminated by God.[9]

A similar technique involves comparing scriptural narratives with the present-time conflict narrative, looking for parallel themes. Or a party may reflect on the life of a Biblical figure, and seek inspiration from their example. They may reflect on how Jesus mentored his disciples, how he taught them to resolve conflict. In all these approaches, Scripture is integrated with conflict scenarios in an effort to augment discernment. Paul's letters to the early Christians, for example, comprise an invaluable guide for discerning divine intention.

An additional discernment strategy adopts the Beatitudes—the guidelines of the New Covenant—as baseline criteria for evaluating party intentions. Or a party might study the lives of saints, searching for criteria they can use to guide their decisions.

The wisdom of the early Church Fathers—the stories of their tribulations—can be harvested for practical insights. Papal documents—encyclicals, exhortations, decrees, and

---

[9] de Gaál, *The Theology of Pope Benedict XVI*, 69.

homilies—form a library that can be tapped for insight into divine will. Or parties may turn to the Catechism, which documents "what we believe." In most cases, parties will want to consult all these sources to build certainty when it comes to discerning God's will.

Spiritual direction accelerates discernment. A spiritual director, a priest or retreat master, may design a spiritual formation plan compatible with each party's intellectual and spiritual abilities. A good spiritual director knows that lessons a party cannot apply will be a waste of time, even if those lessons are filled with uncanny wisdom.

Ideally, a spiritual director will possess insight into the specific conflict so they might prudently design a targeted formation program. When the party returns to mediation after pastoral counseling, they will bring fresh insights and a renewed passion for peace.

In rare instances, however, a spiritual director might sabotage reconciliation. Inept spiritual directors who move too slowly may keep a conflict in play. The rapid pace of spiritual transformation that takes place in mediation may be intolerable to those accustomed to a slower pace of change. For this reason, mediators will want to work with only the most qualified spiritual directors.

It is vital that parties steady and focus their minds during discernment. Consider the following analogy: two inflatable rafts float in a hot tub. Pressurized air from the Jacuzzi jets buffets the rafts, causing them to spin about and collide. When the same rafts are launched in a mountain creek, they travel downstream in a single direction with minimal collisions. In reconciliation, the flow of the creek is the Will of God. Parties enjoy a smooth journey to peace when their will is aligned with the Will of God.

Perpetual Pentecost

In the New Testament account of Pentecost, the Disciples become aware of the Will of God in a dramatic manner.[10] Reading their account may inspire in us a desire for a perpetual Pentecost—a desire for a never-ending stream of revelation from the Holy Spirit that forms a spirit-driven Church:

> Saint Luke's depiction of Pentecost: vehement wind and fire of the Holy Ghost establish the Church. The origin of the Church is not the decision of men; she is not the product of human willing but a creature of the Spirit of God.[11]

Parties who lose sight of the markers identifying the Will of God can also turn to their Church community for help. They may solicit help in resetting their course beyond worldly concerns. This type of assistance was prevalent in the early church:

> The image of Pentecost presented in the Acts of the Apostles shows the interplay of plurality and unity and in this sense teaches us to perceive the distinctive character of the Holy Spirit as opposed

---

10 See Acts of the Apostles, Chapter 2.
11 Ratzinger, *Called to Communion*, 43.

to the spirit of the world. The spirit of the world subjugates, the Holy Spirit opens.[12]

Mediators who echo the work of the Apostles frequently rescue parties from soulless conformity to worldly powers. In stark contrast, disputants who lack such aid and assistance are at risk of drowning in rough seas. They need a life raft—a theology of relationship—that lifts them above crushing forces that divide the world. Benedict describes their predicament:

> Man's will to power, symbolized in Babel, aims at the goal of uniformity, because its interest is domination and subjection; it is precisely in this way that it brings forth hatred and division.[13]

It is up to mediators to escort parties past the traps of enforced conformity and past ubiquitous invitations to hate. Unfortunately, even drowning men refuse a lifeline. When they are cornered by fear, with their ego defenses on high alert, they may fiercely reject divine collaboration. Such parties need a period of contemplation, during which they can reorient themselves by further inspecting their interests and desires. After they take a deeper look, they often discover that they suffer from distorted perceptions and intentions. They may find themselves wrestling with ego and pride, two traits that block collaboration. In Scripture, we find another view of collaboration:

---

12 Ibid.
13 Ibid.

> For Jesus' "I" is by no means a self-willed ego revolving around itself alone. "Whoever does the will of my Father in heaven is my brother, and sister, and mother"(Mk. 3:34): Jesus' "I" incarnates the Son's communion of will with the Father.[14]

"Communion of will" acts as the fuel that energizes collaboration. When such communion is missing, we find hostility and impasse. Disputants lacking this powerful affinity feel imprisoned in a cell constructed from their opponent's counter-intentions. They assume their escape will be similar to a prison break, requiring the use of explosive force. Jesus taught a counter-intuitive path:

> As Son, Jesus brings a new freedom: not the freedom of someone with no obligations, but the freedom of someone totally united with the Father's will, someone who helps mankind to attain the freedom of inner oneness with God.[15]

Realignment produces an inner movement of the spirit, a reorientation of the soul away from materialism and self-concern, toward divine truth and love of neighbor. This allows spiritual captives to break free from their prison cells. Mystical union with the Father's will becomes the primary instrument of peace and freedom; it allows parties to release the knots of bondage that keep them trapped in a fallen world. A party who remains

---

14   Pope Benedict XVI, *Jesus of Nazareth vol. 1*, 117.
15   Pope Benedict XVI. *Jesus of Nazareth vol. 3*, 2012.

alienated, on the other hand, rapidly descends into the quicksand of conflict.

Suffering with Others, Empathy

The mediator's primary process goal is peace through collaboration. Division is healed when wills and intentions are brought into alignment, when consensus is facilitated. Initially, however, parties harbor a fear of opening their hearts to the wounds and/or aspirations of the other. Their typical "battle plan" does not include embracing another's suffering or dreams. Yet Christ taught us that "suffering with others" brings peace and unity, even in extreme encounters with evil:

> [Jesus] goes down in the role of one whose suffering-with-others is a transforming suffering that turns the underworld around, knocking down and flinging open the gates of the abyss. His Baptism is a descent into the house of the evil one, combat with the "strong man" (cf. Lk 11:22).[16]

The conflicts men typically encounter are not as profound as Jesus' descent into the nether regions; nonetheless, "suffering with others" does matter. Empathy is the key factor in successful collaboration and may even invoke a touch of irony: all too often, parties sift through the wreckage of past misdeeds only to discover they caused the suffering that now demands their empathy. Paradox-

---
16 Pope Benedict XVI. *Jesus of Nazareth vol. 1*, 20.

ically, they must now experience the suffering they once caused another.

Empathy possesses another unique quality worth noting: a display of empathy invites the other party to reciprocate. Empathy is rarely a one-way street. Peacemakers usually "prime the pump" by injecting empathy into the process, modeling behavior they hope will be copied.

However, some parties are repulsed by the thought of showing empathy for another's suffering. Why should my opponent's suffering be my concern? they wonder. In spite of such misgivings, there is good reason for them to show concern: *empathy releases their opponent's fear and hostility*. Without a show of empathy, fear remains frozen in place; hostility percolates. Empathy, on the other hand, functions as a solvent, dissolving antipathy.

A word of caution: *empathy is not sympathy*. Empathy is a solvent, dissolving conflict; sympathy acts like glue. With sympathy a person collapses into another's suffering and becomes ensnared. Sympathy binds one false self to another false self. Empathy is different: a person with empathy views from the perspective of unbound divine self. With empathy they see the pain "as it is" when exposed to the light. Empathy does not precipitate a collapse into the shadow reality of a false self. In contrast, sympathy drags a party into the shadows where visibility is low.

When reconcilers demonstrate empathy by "suffering with" another, they simultaneously remove veils of falsehood. Their empathy illuminates the bondage that must be released in order for suffering to end. They refuse to become trapped in the sticky tethers of the false self.

An analogy may clarify the difference between empathy and sympathy. Imagine you stand on the deck of a ship at sea and happen to witness a man fall overboard. With empathy you grasp the drowning man's plight, including his panic and fear, yet you remain clear-headed. You toss him a life jacket and a rescue line.

Sympathy, in contrast, would inspire you to jump overboard and wrap your arms around the man. In a panic, he would cling to you with adrenalin-enhanced strength. No longer able to swim, you would both sink beneath the waves and perish. Sympathy draws you into the other's dire situation in a way that scuttles your ability to render aid.

Empathy is vital during collaboration as, when parties share compassion, they disentangle false selves. They jettison chains binding them to conflict. Parties, even at an early stage in mediation, intuit that they both contributed, in some measure, to the conflict. They begin to realize they have co-authored their tribulation. It is empathy that nurtures this epiphany of shared causation. Empathy nurtures this epiphany of shared causation and fosters a deeper knowledge of "what happened."

Perhaps the most powerful function of empathy, often overlooked, is allowing parties to share their passion for escape from bondage. When they share their stories of suffering, they also share dreams of freedom and release from duress. Collaboration ultimately becomes a search for mutual freedom. In order to free ourselves, we must free others.

Reconciliation and The Good News

Everyone fears losing free will. We cling steadfastly to our desires and resent any suggestion that we give up our freedom to be, do, or have what we want. Few appreciate the paradox: parties who surrender to the Will of God and realign their intentions with divine intention experience greater freedom, not less. For people of faith, realignment with God's will does not involve coerced adherence to commandments, but rather releases one into a state of unfettered joy:

> God's will is not a law imposed...from without. It is "joy"...the law is simply Gospel, good news, because he reads it with a personal, loving openness to God and in this way learns to understand and live it from deep within.[17]

Realignment of will requires discipline and wisdom, which are often in short supply. We know that love nurtures wisdom, however, in the midst of conflict, love has become scarce. Yet reason for hope remains: divine love is never exhausted and never totally out of reach. Though love dwindles during a conflict, parties always have the option of accessing divine love by turning with an open heart to God:

---

17 Pope Benedict XVI, *Jesus of Nazareth vol. 3*.

> It remains true that we could not love if we were not first loved by God. God's grace always precedes us, embraces us and carries us. But it also remains true that man is called to love in return, he does not remain an unwilling tool of God's omnipotence: he can love in return or he can refuse God's love.[18]

Divine love awaits man's assent. Spiritually arid conditions are not the result of a deficit of divine love, as God's presence remains constant. Rather, the desert arises as a result of a drought of "Amen" responses to divine love. The human ability to love ebbs and flows, and the human heart is subject to hardening.

Therefore, reconcilers must harness disputants' hearts to divine love. This process is guided by theological axioms, such as "God is love." Another axiom states God freely extends his grace. A third acknowledges that man is free to accept God's grace and return his love.

Softening hearts with divine love puts the principle of reciprocity into play. God first extends and then receives love in return; in reverse, man first receives and then returns divine love. The reciprocal exchange of love becomes the medium through which divine will infuses human will. Divine love softens hearts and renders them sufficiently malleable to be conformed to the Will of God.

The principle of reciprocity deserves additional reflection: all souls endowed with free will exist in relation-

---

18 Ibid., 76.

ship to God; all souls are therefore inherently capable of a response to God's presence; all souls possess a trace of divinity that fuels an inclination to align with the Will of God. Thus, for an immortal soul, God is never entirely "other." There is reciprocity of Being; there is relationship. Mediators must learn to choreograph these supernatural dynamics that make realignment of wills possible.

Faith Community and Reconciliation

The Church is more than a worldly institution; it is part of the Body of Christ. This mystical body encompasses all souls living in relationship with Christ, both the faithful of this world, and the communion of saints in the next world. As a result, each person's actions affect the health of the group. As individuals undergo spiritual formation, they simultaneously transform the Body of Christ.

In spite of this interdependence, the church does not always experience unity. Misaligned intentions fuel conflict: in this sense the Church always faces an immense task of reconciliation; she is not a Church if she does not bring together those who—from the point of view of their sensibilities—do not suit one another and have no sympathy for one another.[19]

Those who learn to discern the Will of God also come to understand their own participation in the Body of Christ. They realize that they foreclose their access to re-

---

19 Pope Benedict XVI, *Called to Communion*, 78.

vealed truth the moment they abandon divine relationship:

> A community that is its own author is no longer an image of the dialogical mystery of revelation and of the gift of grace that always comes from without and can be attained only in receiving.[20]

One can even argue that accurate discernment of divine will is a driver of conversion within the Church:

> Indeed, the essence of conversion lies precisely in the fact that I cease to pursue a path of my own that safeguards my interests and conforms to my taste but that I put myself in his hands and become his, a member of the Body, the Church.[21]

Divine collaboration based on the example of Christ the Mediator can be a primary driver of world peace. He acts as our primary mentor, rescuing souls trapped in the fallen world and reconciling them with God. In this way, faith-based mediation, more than mere technique, is best demonstrated by the example of Christ surrendering to his Father's will:

> [B]eing like God, this similarity to God, is being a Son, and hence it is totally relational. "I do nothing on my own authority" (John 8:28)[22]

---

20 Ibid., 120.
21 Ibid.
22 Ratzinger, *The Essential Pope Benedict XVI*, ed. John F. Thorton and Susan B. Vareene, 266.

Benedict further clarifies this concept:

> The Son, who is by nature relationship and relatedness, reestablishes relationships. His arms, spread out on the cross, are an open invitation to relationship, which is continually offered to us. The cross, the place of his obedience, is the true tree of life.[23]

When Christ reconciles humanity with the Father, submission to a "higher power" no longer poses a threat. From this perspective, Divine Collaboration does not mean one must abandon self-determinism. Instead, the infusion of divine love sets the stage for world peace:

> It means to accept the love of God, which is our truth—that dependence on God which is no more an imposition from without than is the Son's sonship. It is precisely this dependence that is freedom, because it is truth and love.[24]

Christ models the reconciliation that is inherent in supernatural relationship; the Trinity is its ultimate expression:

> ...we saw that Jesus is wholly "relational," that his whole being is nothing other than relation to the Father.[25]

---

23 Ibid.
24 Ibid.
25 Pope Benedict XVI, *Jesus of Nazareth vol. 1*, 348.

A peacemaking process that began as a method of fostering consensus takes an unexpected turn when we realize that a Trinitarian relationship showcases perfect alignment of wills, which remains a primary goal of peacemaking.

Reflection

Peacemakers will want to reflect on the Biblical account of Adam and Eve, who rejected the Will of God. In this ancient mystical narrative, humanity turns away from divine love and jettisons the elixir that protects all souls from harm. The result is a deficit of love that destroys mankind's immunity to evil intentions. The supernatural solvent that dissolves conflict was left behind when they exited the Garden.

Peacemakers will want to contemplate what they must do to restore divine love, the ultimate elixir, to the lives of the disputants.

Aspiring reconcilers will also want to inventory approaches to discerning divine will. Those active in a faith tradition will inventory the texts and materials used to guide discernment—the homilies, catechism, retreat materials, and spiritual formation guides. The inventory should be comprised of formation tools that can be applied with competence and ease by the individual mediator. Tools that can be applied with certainty should be placed ahead of those that are more difficult to use.

Later, the peacemaker can develop more sophisticated approaches that require additional skill. Many of these tools will be useful during spiritual direction, spiritual formation retreats, and relationship skills workshops.

Peacemakers will also want to study Scripture passages that present the idea of Christ the Mediator, a model for their ministry. They will want to reflect on passages that describe the manner in which Jesus reconciles humanity with the Father.

At this point in the journey, the ministry climbs to a new level on the path to peace. Peacemakers may wonder if they can scale such a steep incline, and they may worry that the altitude will prove daunting. If so, they should continue reading, as we will explore additional tools that aid in the climb.

TEN
The False Self

Peacemakers discover, without fail, that all parties embroiled in conflict have assumed a false identity. Their true nature has been masked, veiled behind a false self, an ego identity. At the outset, when peacemakers first take up a conflict, they will always observe two or more false selves locked in battle. The following axiom applies: *conflict is the result of a hostile entanglement of two or more false selves.*

This axiom sheds light on a primary peacemaking task—stripping away ego-identity false selves. Reconcilers guide parties through a process of chiseling away false-self constructs. As the old deposits are chipped away, parties often look back and find they have behaved as Paul described in Romans:

> For I do not do the good I want, but I do the evil I do not want. Now if I do what I do not want it is no longer I who do it, but sin that dwells in me. So, then I discover the principle that when I want to do right, evil is at hand.[1]

---

1 Romans 7:15.

Peacemakers must become familiar with the false-self paradigm in order to rescue parties from the tyranny of false-self intentions.

The False-Self Paradigm

Standard secular mediation does not address the dilemma of the false self. In contrast, faith-based mediators seek to strip away counterfeit ego identities. If a person is not being himself, he cannot make sound decisions.

Consider the following example: Mary is out of sorts. She's not herself. Acting in the role of a false self, a proxy self, she confronts Bob with a hostile tone. Bob, his ego defenses triggered, confronts Mary with his own manufactured identity; he calls up an identity that he summons when he must "fight back." They both act as false selves locked in conflict. Their false selves "stand in" as proxy warriors.

Mary, in response to Bob's defensive stance, becomes even more determined to satisfy the dictates of her false self: she must *be, do,* or *have* something that her ego identity demands.

In return, Bob's defensive false self dictates that he must prevent Mary from *being, doing,* or *having* what she desires. His false self becomes invested in stopping Mary. He soon buys into the idea that he cannot win if Mary prevails in satisfying her wishes. This leads to the classic "win-lose scenario." Someone must lose for another to win.

False-self personas that dictate party intentions are

clusters of desires and intentions. These personality clusters are not rooted in the immortal soul or divine self; rather, they're comprised of arbitrary intentions subject to unexpected change. They manifest a random or chaotic quality.

During reconciliation, the false-self phenomenon brings about impasse. The process grinds to a halt; it seems there's no way to resolve the conflict. When this happens, mediators are in need of a peacemaking protocol sufficiently powerful to disentangle the warring parties. The influence of the false selves must be defused and removed. In this example, a mediator should help Mary:

1. Shed destructive ego traits;
2. Jettison false-self identity;
3. Downgrade desires from "I must have" to "I prefer;"
4. Replace destructive ego traits with divine-self traits;
5. Initiate conciliatory moves;
6. Navigate past Bob's false-self traits;
7. Soften Bob's heart with "I-Thou" moments;
8. Acknowledge Bob's reciprocation.

These positive movements toward reconciliation come naturally for an immortal soul. A party that dumps their false self begins to come into line with their divine nature. In summary, they:

1. Move beyond false-self boundaries;
2. Identify false-self desires;

3. Align with their true nature;
4. Slip past the defensive walls of another's ego self;
5. Adopt a conciliatory demeanor;
6. Soften hearts with divine love;
7. Open doors to "I–Thou" encounters;
8. Nurture unity.

These transformative actions move a party on the path from false self to divine self.

False Self Spawns Misaligned Intentions

The phenomenon of false self gives rise to a core principle: *when a false self hijacks a soul's exercise of free will, it is very likely that conflict will arise.*

When a false self takes over the reins, the person's intentions no longer align with divine will. This should not come as a surprise since the false self is an aggregate of misaligned intentions. Only those intentions consistent with divine self will align with the Will of God. False-self intentions do not align. Thus, mediators who facilitate realignment should also facilitate a transition from false self to divine self.

In addition, those who transition from false self to divine self find that their perceptions improve. When they cease clinging to ego self, they're better able to perceive the divine within others. Saint Francis possessed this sacred sight—a gift that imbued him with a love so deep that his mere presence often brought healing.

Francis managed to subdue the false self. But how was

he able to do so? The answer probably lies in his passion for imitating Christ in all things. His heart became so deeply infused with divine love that his humble gaze conveyed Christ's love. Friar Murray Bodo labeled this beneficent gaze "the Face of a Franciscan."[2] Benedict presented a similar idea in his inaugural encyclical:

> Seeing with the eyes of Christ, I can give to others much more than their outward necessities; I can give them the look of love which they crave.[3]

Fostering a loving gaze that recognizes the divine in all creatures is fundamental to peacemaking. However, before mediators or disputants can help others see "through the eyes of Christ," they must remove the clay from their eyes and discard the false-self traits that obscure their vision. In other word, mediators must secure their freedom from bondage to a counterfeit identity.

False-Self Personality

Most warring parties have never known their true or essential nature. If they once caught a fleeting glimpse of their true nature in a rare moment, it is likely they have forgotten their epiphany. Ewert Cousins, writing about Franciscan spirituality, describes this failing:

---

[2] Murray Bodo, O.F.M., *The Threefold Way of Saint Francis,* (New York: Paulist Press, 2000), 7.
[3] Pope Benedict XVI, *God is Love*, 45.

> The only problem is that we have forgotten ourselves, our true selves where we find the remembrance, knowledge, and the love of God. We use our faculties only to remember to know, and love the things of this world. So, without memory we have forgotten our true self; with our intellect we reflect wrongly on ourselves; and with our love we love the wrong things.[4]

James Finley, inspired by Trappist monk Thomas Merton, described false-self barriers preventing alignment with the Will of God:

> Once the false self gives birth to its own dark gossamer existence as cut off from God, it begins to function as its own God by passing final decisions and judgments upon everything under the sun. A whole system of formulas, laws and ideologies is created to form not only one's relationship to others but to God as well. Both self and God become equated with the definitions given to them. Both God and self become cogs in a smoothly running system of self-creation.[5]

In this dark existence, ego traits coalesce into proxy "personalities" that take on lives of their own. These false selves become internal dictators demanding allegiance.

---

[4] Ewert Cousins, *The Gethsemani Encounter: A Dialogue on the Spiritual Life by Buddhist and Christian Monastics,* ed. Donald W. Mitchell and James Wiseman O.S.B. (New York: Continuum), 172.

[5] James Finley, *Merton's Palace of Nowhere* (Notre Dame, Indiana: Ave Maria Press, 1978), 69.

Upon closer inspection, we discover that each false self is, in fact, made up of multiple packages or matrices of traits—counterfeit "I's" that encase a soul. Benedict recognized the bondage created:

> [I]n this world, marked by sin, the gravitational pull of our lives is weighted by the chains of the "I" and the "self."[6]

False-self personalities ensnare parties in illusory selves. The divine self finds itself surrounded by a cast of foreign characters; this does not differ greatly from the phenomenon of possession. The more victims struggle, the more they sink, as if trapped in spiritual quicksand. They rarely escape the false-self trap without the help of a peacemaker or a spiritual director.

With the right guidance, trapped souls can sculpt away the dust, dross, and detritus of the false self to set free their true nature. Escape from the false-self matrix restores the soul's freedom, allowing the soul to seek union with Christ. Benedict, in *Called to Communion*, reflects on the process:

> Reform is ever-renewed ablatio—removal, whose purpose is to allow the *nobilis forma*, the countenance of the bride, and with it the Bridegroom himself, the living Lord, to appear.[7]

---

6   Joseph Ratzinger, *Jesus of Nazareth vol. 1*, 193.
7   Ratzinger, *Called to Communion*, 142.

Disputants, mentored by reconcilers, chip away falsehoods, and lay bare truths. We turn to the metaphor of a sculptor:

> Saint Bonaventure...explains the path by which man truly becomes himself with the help of the likeness of the sculptor. The sculptor, says the great Franciscan theologian, does not make anything, rather his work is "ablatio"—the removal of what is not really part of the sculpture. In this way, that is, by means of *ablatio*, the *nobilis forma*—the noble form—takes shape.[8]

Bonaventure's metaphor reminds us that people require assistance in order to procure their release from the burden of ego identity:

> In the same way, continues Bonaventure, man, in order that God's image may shine radiantly in him, must first and foremost receive the purification whereby the divine Sculptor frees him from that dross that conceals the authentic figure of his being, making him appear to be nothing more than a stone block, whereas the divine form dwells in him.[9]

Indeed, when fragile ego mechanisms seize up, disputants soon resemble "stone blocks." Barricaded within the fortress of the false self, they find it difficult to summon

---

8 Ibid., 141.
9 Ibid.

the resources needed to escape as the mundane world offers no workable tools. Though prisoners desperately chip away at dungeon walls, they cannot make good their escape—absent transcendent help. They must summon the assistance of the supernatural sculptor.

Sadly, however, souls ensnared in ego traps do not entertain hope for divinely aided rescue. Walls built to protect ego impair their vision; they blindly assume no help exists outside the prison cell. They soon sink into despair.

Benedict describes the dilemma of the ego self:

> Today the concept of subject is gradually unraveling; it is becoming evident that the "I" locked securely in itself does not exist but that various influences pass in and out of us. At the same time there is a renewed understanding that the "I" is constituted in relation to the "thou" and that the two mutually interpenetrate.[10]

Benedict delivers a valuable insight: *true "I" exists in relationship with God*. Only divine self, living in a relationship with God, enjoys true freedom. This idea marks a major departure from modern beliefs. It can be quite upsetting to those encased in a false-self identity. The consequences for those who lack relationship with the divine are significant:

> If I have no contact whatsoever with God in my life, then I cannot see in the other anything more

---

10   Ratzinger, *Called to Communion*.

than the other, and I am incapable of seeing in him the image of God.[11]

The inability to see the divine in the other limits the potential success of divine collaboration. But there's good news: as spiritual blindness is illusory and self-inflicted, the relationship with God never actually ceases. In spite of temporal events, the underlying relationship remains intact, even though "dust" or "clay" may obscure a soul's vision. However, when the person is ready, grace will restore their sight. Furthermore, a soul lifted from the darkness into the light gains an improved ability to discern divine self:

> Where man as a whole comes into play, he transcends himself; an act of the whole self is at the same time always an opening to others, hence, an act of being together with others. What is more, we cannot perform this act without touching our deepest ground, the living God who is present in the depths of our existence as its sustaining foundation.[12]

Benedict warns against "going it alone" without guidance. Attempts to unbind the false self with worldly tools prove futile. For example, the discipline of psychology devises personality measurement instruments that fail to account for a person's spiritual component. For this reason, those measurements will always be faulty—they will be

---

11 Pope Benedict XVI, *God Is Love*.
12 Pope Benedict XVI, "April 17," *Benedictus*, 124.

images seen from a distance through a glass darkly. They exclude or omit mankind's supernatural essence.

One such personality instrument, popular in many seminaries, is the Myers Briggs.[13] The personality test, unfortunately, fails to capture the traits of divine self, and instead maps only false-self traits. Of course, given that the discipline of psychology is limited by the tenets of naturalism, it can be expected to measure only ego identity and not the nature of a soul. Benedict describes the gap to be closed:

> The functional truth about man has been discovered. But the truth about man himself—who he is, where he comes from, what he should do, what is right, what is wrong—this unfortunately cannot be read in the same way. Hand-in-hand with growing knowledge of functional truth there seems to be an increasing blindness toward "truth" itself—toward the question of our real identity and purpose.[14]

Reconcilers and pastoral counselors require an instrument that measures spiritual aspects, qualities, or traits. We can hope that, in the near future, seminary directors of formation will develop instruments designed to measure the complete person.

---

13 For more on the Myers Briggs instrument: https://en.wikipedia.org/wiki/Myers%E2%80%93Briggs_Type_Indicator.
14 Pope Benedict XVI, *Jesus of Nazareth vol. 2*, 193.

Discerning the False Self

It is an error to assume that all false-self traits will appear nasty and brutish; it is an error to assume such traits will be infused with the demeanor of a wounded wolf. Rather, a person trapped in a false-self persona may smile like a saint and display the manners of the royal court. They may exhibit polish and erudition and they may attain social or political rank. In spite of their worldly status, false selves will never possess the qualities of divine self and will never align with the Will of God.

As an example, consider a common false-self compulsion—to be liked or admired. This compulsion may strip a party of integrity, negating their ability to render unpopular ethical decisions. Instead, they *must* be liked at any cost. A person overcome with a compulsion to be liked dares not upset anyone—which means they cannot defend unpopular truths. Popularity trumps morality; virtue signaling trumps discipleship. The agenda is set by the compulsions, desires, and whims of the false self.

Those who cling to a false self often display a thin veneer of social grace while harboring evil intentions. They show one face to the world, but another face appears in the mirror. For example, a false self that craves applause and status may sympathetically idealize and champion "the poor," while knowing that poverty does not assure alignment with the Will of God:

> Purely material poverty does not bring salvation, though of course those who are disadvantaged in this world may count on God's goodness in a

particular way. But the heart of those who have nothing can be hardened, poisoned, evil—interiorly full of greed for material things, forgetful of God, covetous of external possessions.[15]

The examples are endless. Mediators should know that false-self traits are innumerable and complex. Therefore, rather than compiling an endless list of false-self characteristics, mediators should simplify the process and focus on traits that transcend false self. This narrows the analysis to the smaller set of transcendent traits.

A thought experiment may help: Does divine self differ from false self in the same way that Paradise differs from the fallen world? Does the Holy Spirit touch Paradise and divine self in an analogous manner?

> The garden is an image of the world that bears the imprint of the Spirit, for a world that came into existence in accordance with the will of the Creator. ...we see that the world, which was created to be at one with its Lord, is not a threat but a gift, a sign of the saving and unifying goodness of God.[16]

But most people, confused and defiant, fail to see this imprint of the Spirit when it comes to divine self. Man does not recognize that he is endowed with the image of God. Instead, he clings desperately to created objects for

---

15 Ratzinger, *Jesus of Nazareth vol. 1*, 76.
16 Ratzinger, *The Essential Pope Benedict XVI*, 261.

his identity. He shuts down awareness of his divinely endowed nature and seeks an identity tied to material forms.

This all makes sense to most people as, in the view of the fallen world, the material world is primary. Materialists believe Creation magically brought about its own existence. Perhaps it appeared through spontaneous quantum combustion, as one famous scientist (incorrectly) speculated. In the materialist perspective, the material world is worshipped as Cause; material idols replace God.

Peacemakers, however, will need to use caution when facilitating the process of dumping such falsehoods. Souls trapped in a false-self mindset will covet, hoard, and defend material existence with tenacity. A peacemaker seeking to remedy false worldviews faces a stiff challenge.

A false-self personality lives for form and flesh rather than spirit. They view fellow humans as competitors, or even potential assassins. As a result of being exiled from their spiritual home, a false self is overcome with negative feelings, emotions and, most of all, fears. Finding an exit from struggles seems impossible, inconceivable even. If a sadistic villain set out to design a maze that would defeat all attempts at escape, he could do no better than this fallen world. All other traps pale in comparison.

Nonetheless, in spite of their exile, souls retain lingering traces, remnants, of the "divine within." When a person accepts divine grace, this latent spiritual imprint is resurrected. Once a person is infused with grace, they glimpse their true self, and the epiphany ignites a passion for escape from bondage.

This rebirth of spiritual freedom spawns a fragile willingness to extend love to others. Previously, a person might have seriously doubted they could be rescued. The emotional, mental, and psychological bonds of the false self weighed on them; the trap appeared ironclad, precluding escape. They might have even asked, how can escape to freedom even be an option?

Benedict hints at a way out:

> Love is possible, and we are able to practice it because we are created in the image of God. To experience love and in this way to cause the light of God to enter into the world – this is the invitation I would like to extend.[17]

Benedict suggests that it is this forgotten blessing that ultimately sets one free. The image and likeness of God imprints souls with a latent supernatural recall of their spiritual home. The image of God "within" emits light needed to disperse the shadows cast by a false self. Divine endowment lights the path to salvation and peace.

However, most people, prior to rekindling the latent image of God within, fill their mental space, their mental galleries, with portraits of false identities. They collect masks to be worn for various occasions. During reconciliation, disputants rifle through these mental warehouses searching for an appropriate ego portrait. They search for old character roles they can play to dominate in the present

---

17 Pope Benedict XVI. *God Is Love.*

conflict. Mediators must convince parties to abandon this folly; instead, parties are coached to compile an inventory of spiritual traits that reflect their true nature. Mediators thus facilitate the party's contemplation of the traits of an immortal soul, the traits of divine self.

Divine Self—Image of God

Throughout recorded history, mankind has endeavored to grasp human nature. However, current efforts—especially the efforts of psychology—appear misguided and futile. In spite of mammoth data collections, their search for man's true nature nets little progress. In fact, their effort seems to generate disinformation rather than truth. This failure stems from an unwillingness to acknowledge man's essential nature as an immortal soul. Scientists, too often chained to pillars of philosophical materialism, avoid truly insightful questions. The resulting vacuum of real answers forces us to turn to theology for answers:

> The human being is created in God's image and likeness. In the human being God enters into his creation; the human being is directly related to God. ...Each is willed by God, and each is God's image. Precisely in this consists the deeper and greater unity of humankind—that each of us, each individual human being, realizes the *one* project of God and has his or her origin in the same creative idea of God.[18]

---

18 Ratzinger, "October 6," *Benedictus*, 305.

Peacemakers, seeking to establish a baseline understanding of divine self, must turn to theology:

> The "image of God" in man is not, of course, something that we can photograph or see with a merely photographic kind of perception. We can indeed see it, but only with the new seeing of faith. We can see it, just as we can see the goodness in a man, his honesty, interior truth, humility, love—everything, in fact, that gives him a certain likeness to God. But if we are to do this, we must learn a new kind of seeing, and that is what the Eucharist is for.[19]

Benedict's "new kind of seeing" calls for enhanced perceptual tools: *we must view with spiritual eyes in order to perceive man's spiritual nature.* Science, which denies God's existence and dismisses the supernatural, negates spiritual perception. Science may possess sophisticated instruments, but none can measure phenomena beyond the natural world; thus, when it comes to supernatural phenomena, science falls silent or presents a stunted version of reality.

In contrast, Benedict's theology honors a basic axiom: in order to truly grasp a soul's divine endowment, we must seek to understand God. When God speaks and reveals himself, he reveals not just his wisdom and his goodness but his very self; therefore, revelation penetrates to the

---

19 Pope Benedict XVI, *The Spirit of the Liturgy*, 83.

very core of humanity that was created by the same Word of God.[20]

Though a path to understanding human nature exists, people alienated from their divine origins turn away; they confine their inquiry to the tenets of naturalism, a faulty philosophy, dooming their work to countless dead ends. The tools of natural science prove inadequate for understanding human nature. Spiritual means are required. In this regard, those blessed with the ability to perceive supernatural presence have an advantage:

> In someone in whom God is present through and through, there is naturally a much stronger presence of God, a greater inner closeness, than in the case of someone who has completely distanced himself from God.[21]

In the study of theology we learn that real knowledge of the supernatural emerges from mystical relationship with Truth; it arises from relationship with a living God. Materialists reject such a relationship; thus, by default, they reject all knowledge of the supernatural.

As we can see, materialistic science limits its inquiry from the outset. Prior to engaging in observations, materialist scientists erect arbitrary boundaries that limit the types of phenomena they're allowed observe. These arbitrary limits render science blind. Naturalistic scientists resemble travel writers on assignment wearing blinders;

---

20 Collins, *The Word Made Love*, 44.
21 Pope Benedict XVI, "March 26," *Benedictus*, 101.

their flawed accounts are riddled with omissions. In a similar manner, flawed methodology renders science blind to spiritual phenomena. This, in turn, sabotages their versions of reality.

We find this same theme in Scripture. Saint Paul preached that wisdom is contingent on a relationship with God. In his view, mystical unity with Christ dissolves the illusory construct of the false self, revealing divine self:

> Ratzinger sees St. Paul's experience as paradigmatic of this new subjectivity, recalling the apostle's declaration of his new identity: "yet I live, no longer I, but Christ lives in me" (Gal 2:20). This was not only Paul's experience; it is the fundamental experience of all Christians and involves a dying of the old "I" that "ceases to be an autonomous subject standing in itself.[22]

If we conclude the analysis at this point, we will have failed to provide a meaningful description of divine self. However, in the next section, we will begin such a description, which we will continue in later chapters.

Body-Soul Duality

Divine self is immortal. Divine self is resurrected into the Heavenly Kingdom. Divine self is Spirit, not flesh. These truths are straightforward—but a materialistic culture insists man is merely and solely a biological entity, an

---

22 Collins, *The Word Made Love*, 58.

animal. Unfortunately, in many quarters, the faith community suffers the same confusion due to centuries of theological drift. This confusion can easily sabotage the peacemaking ministry. Therefore, it is incumbent on reconcilers to clarify, in their own minds, the difference between flesh and spirit.

Contemporary theologians have added to the confusion, asserting that body and soul are one and dodging the question of differences or duality. At the same time, they grudgingly admit that some type of duality exists. Then they quickly brush duality aside, implying that it can be ignored. After making this dubious assertion, they turn the conversation to bodily concerns—to matters of the flesh, seemingly unwilling to explore the real nature of a soul. This "body and soul are one" assertion in many cases can be traced back to Scholasticism. Benedict offers a note of partial agreement, but then clarifies the matter. We start with the initial point of agreement:

> Christian faith...has always considered man a unity in duality, a reality in which spirit and matter compenetrate, and in which each is brought to a new nobility.[23]

However, Benedict then takes up the logical question that naturally follows:

> Is it not, then, much simpler to see the distin-

---

[23] Pope Benedict XVI, *God Is Love*, 20.

guishing mark of man in the fact that he has a spiritual, immortal soul?[24]

This query is consistent with his prior reflections:

> "[H]aving a spiritual soul" means precisely being willed, known, and loved by God in a special way; it means being a creature called by God to an eternal dialogue and therefore capable for its own part of knowing God.[25]

As we can begin to see, knowledge of God is not a function of a temporal and transitory flesh body. Rather, when we contemplate the phrase "eternal dialogue," we are reflecting on an aspect of immortality. Only souls imbued with spiritual consciousness can access such knowledge of God. Mystics, for example, engage in contemplative prayer to access their living relationship with God. They are able to observe that which remains hidden for most people.

Peacemakers will need to ask what it means to anticipate immortality. Does expectation of post-mortem existence create a stronger desire to reconcile in this life? How do current decisions affect the afterlife? Is there a connection between what we do now and our post-mortem existence? Do consequences extend beyond this mortal life? When we begin to inquire into this expanded time frame, we capture the perspective of an immortal soul.

---

24 Ratzinger, *Introduction to Christianity*, 355.
25 Ibid.

Immortality is a central tenet and promise of Christianity, a promise grounded in body-soul duality. In order to understand this promise, peacemakers should pose questions: what does post-mortem continuity of consciousness mean? If a soul possesses eternal life, isn't our essence as a soul much more important than our temporary flesh body? John the Evangelist certainly thought so:

> There, in John, it says, just after the real presence of the flesh and blood of Jesus in the Eucharist has been sharply emphasized: "It is the spirit that gives life, the flesh is of no avail."[26]

From a Christian viewpoint, that which is most real in our lives lies beyond the purely physical realm. A passage from *Introduction to Christianity* adds clarity:

> Let us start from [Corinthians 15] verse 50, which seems to me to be a sort of key to the whole: "I tell you this, brethren: flesh and blood cannot inherit the kingdom of God, nor does the perishable inherit the imperishable." It seems to me that the sentence occupies much the same position in this text as verse 63 occupies in the Eucharistic chapter 5 of St. John's Gospel: for these two seemingly widely separated texts are much more closely related than is apparent at first sight.[27]

What is the lesson Scripture conveys? *We should avoid collapsing body and soul into a single identity; we should*

---

26 Ibid., 356.
27 Ibid.

honor the inherent duality of body and soul. Both Saint Paul and Saint John view the perishable flesh body in an inferior position; it is the soul that inherits the Kingdom. We can safely conclude that all attempts to grasp man's true nature, his divine self, must consider the qualities of an immortal soul.

Nonetheless, in spite of this logic, supported by Scripture, mention of duality is frequently met with a "yeah, but..." argument that goes as follows: but the body is resurrected and, if the flesh body is resurrected, we might as well consider the body equivalent to the soul. In this view, immortality does not grant the soul elevated status—as the flesh body is presumed to enjoy an equivalent fate. However, this extremely flawed understanding of scripture contradicts Paul and John's letters (and John's gospel), which impart a very different understanding:

> English cannot fully convey the enigmatic character of the biblical Greek. In Greek the word soma means something like "body," but at the same time it also means "the self." And this soma can be sarx, that is, "body" in the earthly, historical, and thus chemical, physical, sense; but it can also be "breath"—according to the dictionary, it would then have to be translated "spirit"; in reality this means that the self, which now appears in a body that can be conceived in chemico-physical terms, can, again, appear definitively in the guise of a transphysical reality.[28]

---

28   Ibid., 357.

Benedict thus clarifies the translations that have caused confusion. Whereas many people of faith imagined they possessed a valid scriptural understanding of the flesh body's fate, those views have been in error. We return to scripture to find a deeper understanding consistent with spiritual reality:

> In Paul's language "body" and "spirit" are not opposites; the opposites are called "physical body" and "spiritual body." We do not need to try here to pursue complicated historical and philosophical problems posed by this. One thing at any rate may be fairly clear: both John (6:63) and Paul (1 Cor 15:50) state with all possible emphasis that the "resurrection of the flesh," the "resurrection of the body," is not a "resurrection of physical bodies."[29]

The preceding explanation dispels common confusion. Paul and John prevent us from making the mistake of collapsing spirit and flesh. Paul clearly states spirit and flesh stand apart, and thus creates a logical framework for understanding divine self:

> To recapitulate, Paul teaches, not the resurrection of physical bodies, but the resurrection of persons, and this not in the return of the "fleshly body"; that is, the biological structure, an idea he expressly describes as impossible ["The perishable cannot become imperishable"], but in the

---

29 Ibid.

different form of the life of the resurrection, as shown in the risen Lord.[30]

Paul is not alone in advancing this view:

> John distinguishes between bios and zoé—between biological life (bios) and the fullness of life (zoé) that is itself a source and so is not subject to the dying and becoming that mark the whole of creation.[31]

Gospel accounts of Jesus' words support Paul's preaching. Jesus says: "It is the spirit that gives life, the flesh is of no avail" (Jn 6:63). This may remind us of Saint Paul's words: "The first man Adam became a living being; the last Adam became a life-giving spirit."[32]

In *Eschatology*, Benedict returned duality to its rightful place.[33] He slammed the brakes on Scholasticism, a theology tainted by Aristotelian Realism, a philosophy that rendered the Church susceptible to faulty views. Scholasticism hastened the cultural slide toward "body only" materialism that became prevalent in the late nineteenth and early twentieth centuries. In his critique of flawed views of resurrection, Benedict quite simply noted:

> The idea of the soul is meant to convey nothing

---

30 Ibid.
31 Ratzinger, *Jesus of Nazareth vol. 1*, 241.
32 1 Cor 15:45.
33 Ratzinger, *Eschatology*.

other than...the continuing reality of the person in separation from his or her body.[34]

The core concept can be stated quite simply: *the divine self separates from the body to enjoy post-mortem consciousness and immortal existence.* Benedict explains, from a biblical perspective, that an immortal soul temporarily pervades a perishable body. He explains how a concept associated with Greek philosophy, when integrated with Christianity, reveals deeper truths:

> [I]t is also perfectly possible to develop the idea out of the body-soul schema, whose importance, perhaps even indispensability, lies in the fact that it emphasizes this essential character of human immortality. But it must also be continually put back in the biblical perspective and corrected by it in order to remain serviceable to the view of man's future opened up by faith.[35]

Benedict dispels confusion built up over centuries by returning to the Patristic age in which scripture was read in a spiritual context:

> We have already seen that the true meaning of Scripture is found only when it is understood spiritually. He who does not understand Scripture spiritually does not understand it at all.[36]

---

[34] Ibid., 109.
[35] Ratzinger, *Introduction to Christianity*, 353.
[36] Ratzinger, *The Theology of History in St. Bonaventure*, 77.

He invites reflection on theology, which was common in the early church:

> [T]he word "soul" had already become a key word for Christian believing and praying in the patristic age. In that age, it gave expression to the certainty that the human I would endure undestroyed, in continuity, beyond death. Thus a picture of what it is to be a human grew up for which the "immortality of the soul" and the "resurrection from the dead" were not opposites, but rather complementary affirmations of the single, albeit-phased, hope of which Christians were certain.[37]

Benedict moves us to seek a deeper comprehension of spirit and leads us away from an attachment to flesh. This movement toward the spiritual does not herald a new age of Manichean hatred of the body. (Manichean rejection of all things physical cannot possibly be a part of reconciliation ministry, as it blocks satisfaction of interests.) Nonetheless, a mention of body-soul duality often triggers critics who hurl accusations that one is engaging in Manichean Gnosticism, but, in reality, such critiques only testify to widespread confusion regarding duality.

In contrast, faith-based peacemakers will come to see body-soul duality as an accurate picture of reality. It is a truth that helps parties correctly discern their real interests, their deepest needs. If parties fail to recognize the spiritual truth inherent in the dualistic model, they

---

[37] Ratzinger, *Eschatology*, 246.

will also fail to find valid criteria to guide their exercise of free will. They will overlook needs most relevant to an immortal soul. Benedict notes that, from a dualistic perspective, a proper relationship between body and soul is one in which the soul disciplines the exercise of free will (*emphasis added*):

> Man's fundamental affective disposition actually depends on just this unity of body and soul and on man's acceptance of being both body and spirit. *This means he places his body under the discipline of the spirit*, yet does not isolate intellect or will. Rather, he accepts himself as coming from God, and thereby also acknowledges and lives out the bodiliness of his existence as an enrichment for the spirit.[38]

The preceding passage offers reconcilers insight into managing the dynamic relationship between body and soul. Disputants typically do not arrive at mediation with a transcendent mindset. Instead, they must be coached to view conflict through a spiritual lens, until they experience a common epiphany: *the greatest possible satisfaction is spiritual satisfaction.*

Party claims designed to satisfy only ego self—claims based on narrow, worldly self-interest—often preclude restoration of healthy relationships. With faith-based reconciliation we add a new component, spiritual transformation. With spiritual formation, parties sculpt away

---

38 Ratzinger, *Jesus of Nazareth vol. 1*, 93.

false-self traits that impair perception and inhibit love. In a step-by-step process, parties are coached to gradually release their iron grip on ego concerns. They then experience being lifted up by the emerging "I–Thou" relationship:

> The "I" ceases to be an autonomous subject standing in itself. It is snatched away from itself and fitted into a new subject. The "I" is not simply submerged, but it must really release its grip on itself in order then to receive itself anew in and together with a greater "I."[39]

Saint Paul, in a Letter to the Galatians, preached that conversion is:

> [T]he surrender of the old isolated subjectivity of the "I" in order to find oneself within the unity of a new subject, which bursts the limits of the "I," thus making possible contact with the ground of all reality.[40]

Paul describes a conversion nearly identical to the spiritual transformation sought in reconciliation ministry. Disputants come to know that man's true nature—an "I" endowed with the likeness and image of God—is firmly anchored in divine relationship:

---

[39] Ratzinger, Cardinal Joseph, *The Nature and Mission of Theology* (San Francisco, California: Igantius Press, 1993).
[40] Pope Benedict XVI, "January 25," *Benedictus*, 39.

> To be the image of God implies relationality. It is the dynamic that sets the human being in motion toward the totally Other. Hence it means the capacity for relationship; it is the human capacity for God. Human beings are, as a consequence, most profoundly human when they step out of themselves and become capable of addressing God on familiar terms.[41]

This I–Thou conversion experience, grounded in spiritual relationship, is the cornerstone of reconciliation. Faith-based reconciliation transcends biology and the world of material conditions. For additional insights, Benedict turned to Plato, who influenced early Christians:

> For Plato, what is important is that justice is truth and so reality. The truth of justice is more real than mere biological life or individual self-assertion. In comparison with justice and truth, mere biological existence appears as outright unreality, a shadow cast by the real, whereas the person who lives by justice lives by the really real.[42]

This view has particular relevance for mediation, as parties in conflict seek justice and truth. They seek an accurate perception of a higher reality, which will enable them to disentangle from conflict. When mediators help parties differentiate reality from unreality, they help uncover truths that lead to justice.

---

41 Ibid., "February 1st," 46.
42 Ratzinger, *Eschatology*, 78.

During this task, mediators, functioning as spiritual directors, clarify transcendent reality with a special focus on connection and relationship. They help clarify the causal relations between soul and body. They know the disputants they are counseling are immortal spirits. They know that when they assess conflict they're assessing many levels of reality. And just because they address supernatural aspects of life does not mean they flee the world:

> The recognition of the living power of truth, which includes the thought of immortality, is not part of a philosophy of flight from the world...[43]

Idealistic duality—found in the works of Plato or Plotinus—assigns man's biological existence a lesser position, but does not advocate for a nihilistic flight into nothingness. Rather, it provides a framework for assessing truth and reality:

> If we try to capture the core of Plato's discovery we can formulate it by saying that man, to survive biologically, must be more than *bios*. He must be able to die into a more authentic life than this. The certainty that self-abandonment for the sake of truth is self-abandonment to reality and not a step into the night of nothingness is a necessary condition for justice.[44]

---

43 Ibid., 79.
44 Ibid.

A peacemaker who embraces body-soul duality in his search for world peace launches a spiritual pilgrimage designed for saints and mystics.

Praxis and Ministry

Though we've barely scratched the surface when it comes to the dramatic rescue of souls from false-self traps, we have explored basic principles that guide our practice. In the following excerpt, Benedict summarizes the process of separating divine self from false self (*emphasis added*):

> In general, we can reduce what is happening to the formula: *one must know oneself as one really is if one is to know God.* The primordial experience of all experiences is that man himself is the place in which and through which he experiences God... The woman stands face to face with herself. It is no longer a question now of *something* but of the depths of the I itself and, consequently, of the radical poverty that *is* man's I-myself.[45]

This two-sided formula—know the truth of self in order to know God, and know the truth of God to know self—is at once practical *and* spiritual. Thus, our practical ministry is bolstered with a deeply spiritual addition.

Reflection

Peacemakers will want to study the false-self construct.

---

45 Pope Benedict XVI, "March 11th," *Benedictus*, 86.

They will want to recognize ego traits that obfuscate divine nature. They will need to appreciate that all conflict is rooted in an underlying entanglement of false selves. And mediators will want to inventory the skills they will need to deconstruct ego trait clusters—so they might disentangle false selves caught in conflict.

Aspiring peacemakers will want to understand why psychology's approach to cataloging ego traits will never produce a true picture of man's nature—as such personality traits are invalid data points when it comes to divine self.

Instead, peacemakers should isolate divine qualities. They should first subtract traits or qualities that are *not* part of a soul's sacred endowment. They should reflect on the concept of the image and likeness of God in an effort to better understand the concept of divine endowment.

Peacemakers will also want to combine their personal spiritual formation with their reconciliation training. Personal experience gained during spiritual formation will prepare them to introduce body-soul duality during the realignment-of-wills phase of mediation. They will also want to attain certainty that an immortal soul's interests take precedence over the interests of a flesh body.

As a result of reading this chapter, aspiring peacemakers may have found that the path to peace is steeper than at first imagined. They may better appreciate the value of advanced spiritual formation, which will motivate them to seek spiritual direction as part of their training.

However, an aspiring peacemaker may begin to

wonder if they have what it takes to become a master reconciler. Soon the call to the vocation will grow stronger and stronger and there will be no turning back.

ELEVEN

I and Thou

Parties caught up in a conflict discover increased freedom—freedom of the heart—after they discard the false self. They renew their desire for divine relationship. Some seek to reach the pinnacle of reconciliation—the I-and-Thou encounter.

I-Thou and Divine Self

Parties that undergo spiritual transformation glimpse the image of God that lies hidden in their opponents. They're able to reach out to others, even if their reach is tentative. Benedict sees this move toward "the other" as being equivalent to a move toward God:

> [W]e advance gradually toward him, and the buried memory of God, which is written on the heart of every man, awakens more and more to life in the depths of our own being.[1]

---

1   Joseph Cardinal Ratzinger, *Christianity and the Crisis of Cultures,* trans. Brian

Once a man heals divine relationship, he finds it is natural to extend conciliatory gestures to his fellow man. Healing divine relationship naturally augments the healing of human relationships.

Paradoxically, the affinity that a party extends to others softens his own heart. A person perceiving the "divine within" the other becomes aware of the "divine within" the other. The experience of an I-and-Thou encounter summons divine self out of the depths to the surface. We might argue that people discover their true essence through the I-Thou encounter:

> The human person is fulfilled only when entering into the human-divine, I-Thou dialogue.[2]

The I-and-Thou encounter illuminates a subtle but important truth:

> The way I look at the other is decisive for my own humanity.[3]

When peacemakers nurture divine relationship, they transcend mere technique. They parallel steps on the path to salvation. Benedict recognized the bridge between reconciliation of relationships and salvation:

> The desire for immortality does not arise from the fundamentally unsatisfying enclosed existence of

---

McNeil (San Francisco: Ignatius Press, 2005), 115.
2   Collins, *The Word Made Love*, 66.
3   Ratzinger, *Christianity and the Crisis of Cultures*, 69.

the isolated self, but from the experience of love, of communion, of the Thou. It issues from that call which the Thou makes upon the I, and which the I returns. The discovery of life entails going beyond the I, leaving it behind.[4]

In other words, the act of reconciliation with our neighbor draws us out of our narrow, self-centered existence and brings us into the light of God's love. Once again, the road to peace intersects the road to faith. Many aspiring peacemakers travel these two paths in tandem. They repair the divine I-and-Thou relationship *and* seek spiritual salvation. Others choose not to reconcile; instead, they harden their hearts and turn their backs on their opponents:

> I can treat him quite simply like a thing, forgetting my dignity and his, forgetting that both he and I are made in the image and likeness of God.[5]

Peacemakers do not employ force and coercion to overcome a party's negative choices; rather, their approach should honor party self-determinism. They read the signs warning that parties are unable to proceed. They recognize that participants may be encumbered with false-self views that inhibit their progress, that it's difficult for most disputants to visualize a conciliatory path when glancing at their opponents. Rather:

---

4 Ratzinger, *Eschatology*, 94.
5 Ratzinger, *Christianity and the Crisis of Cultures*, 69.

What first meets the eye is only the image of Adam, the image of man, who, though not totally corrupt, is nonetheless fallen. We see the crust of dust and filth that has overlaid the image.[6]

Parties are likely to balk, unwilling to inch closer to adversaries they've come to dislike. Yet hope exists. Although, at first, warring parties may appear unlikely to reconcile, all souls possess a latent longing for reconciliation:

> [W]e all stand in need of the true sculptor who removes what distorts the image; we are in need of forgiveness, which is the heart of all true reform.[7]

Though an I-and-Thou encounter may seem unlikely, the potential for divine relationship never entirely evaporates. The potential remains hidden and becomes a latent catalyst that will eventually trigger a sacrifice of false self. One day, a new "I" will emerge:

> Paul describes this process, whereby the first "I" dissolves and wakes up in a larger "I", as a "rebirth". In this new "I", in which liberating faith immerses me, I do not, however, discover that I am united only to Jesus: I am united likewise to all those who have walked along the same path.[8]

---

[6] Ratzinger, *Called to Communion*, 148.
[7] Ibid.
[8] Ratzinger, *Christianity and the Crisis of Cultures*, 114.

This rebirth of a larger "I" imbues a party with gentle strength that fuels the emergence of a conciliatory demeanor; parties become more willing to move toward each other with a show of affinity. As hearts become increasingly filled with divine love, the I-Thou encounter unfolds, paralleling the spiritual journey that Saint Paul imagined:

> To the extent that he freely cooperates, man's thoughts and affections, mentality and conduct are slowly purified and transformed, on a journey that is never completely finished in this life. "Faith working through love" (Gal 5:6) becomes a new criterion of understanding and action that changes the whole of man's life (cf. Rom 12:2; Col 3:9-10; Eph 4:20-29; 2 Cor 5:17).[9]

Souls become immersed in a superheated crucible in which contemplative prayer fuels reconciliation. Newly purified souls move away from discarded shells of the false-self ego. Souls wrapped in God's grace don the "spiritual armor" made up of divine traits. Benedict describes the transformed being that emerges from healed relationships:

> A being is the more itself the more it is open, the more it is in relationship. And that in turn will lead us to realize that it is the man who makes himself open to all being, in its wholeness and in

---

9 Pope Benedict XVI, *Porta Fidei*.

its Ground, and becomes thereby a "self," who is truly a person.[10]

The "self who is truly a person" in this passage refers to divine self that's been resurrected through adoration and imitation of Christ. This self is open to receiving sacred gifts; it is a self that perceives the divine reality that Jesus views:

> Jesus, he who knows God directly, sees him. This is why he is the true mediator between God and man. His human act of seeing the divine reality is the source of light for all men.[11]

Souls that view through the eyes of Christ turn their gaze upon the world to perceive truths that redefine self and other. These changes, modest at first, become significant. Previously, when disputants stared across the table, they lacked warmth and they experienced only their opponent's harsh doubt:

> Indeed, it is hardly the case that we always and immediately see in the other the "noble form", the image of God that is inscribed in him.[12]

But, when parties see through the eyes of Christ, "seeing" becomes a mystical form of "sculpting." The divine sculptor, summoned by prayer, assists as parties

---

10 Ratzinger, *Eschatology*, 155.
11 Ratzinger, *Christianity and the Crisis of Cultures*, 107.
12 Ibid.

chip away at falsehoods. The Holy Spirit infuses these apprentice sculptors, the warring parties, with divine grace, love, and forgiveness. Seeing with the eyes of Christ, they begin to sculpt away their opponents' false-self burdens through a mystical connection.

Priests, not surprisingly, excel at this dynamic, as they have drawn close to Christ the Mediator while celebrating the sacraments. In their priestly formation, they acquired supernatural reconciliation skills, as Benedict describes:

> The ministry of the Word requires that the priest share in the kenosis of Christ, in his "increasing and decreasing." The fact that the priest does not speak about himself, but bears the message of another, certainly does not mean that he is not personally involved, but precisely the opposite: it is a giving-away-of-the-self in Christ that takes up the path of his Easter mystery and leads to a true finding-of-the-self, and communion with him who is the Word of God in person. This paschal structure of the "not-self," which turns out to be the "true self" after all, shows, in the last analysis, that the ministry of the Word reaches beyond all "functions" to penetrate the priest's very being, and pre-supposes that the priesthood is a sacrament.[13]

This beautiful passage highlights a key concept: *the true self appears to the uninitiated to be no self at all.* And, conversely, the self once assumed to be real turns out to

---

13   Ratzinger, *The Essential Pope Benedict XVI*, 310.

be illusion. These radical changes turn the world on its head. At first, the change can be difficult.

For example, after a soul amputates false-self traits, that soul may feel they have forfeited their identity. As they discard ego constructs, they fear nothing will remain. They feel they're being uncreated; however, the only things being surgically removed are untruths. As such, falsehoods are excised, positive changes occur. The soul, in collaboration with the master sculptor, unleashes divine qualities that make an I-and-Thou encounter possible.

I-Thou and the Dual Axes

Keeping the I-Thou encounter in mind, we now revisit the dual-axis model. The horizontal axis represents reconciliation with our fellow man, while the vertical axis represents reconciliation with God. When we improve relationship on one axis, relationship on the other automatically improves. As an example, Benedict describes the decision to love:

> When I decide to look him in the face, I am deciding on conversion, I am resolving to let the other address his appeal to me, to go beyond the confines of my own self and to make space for him.[14]

In the next stage, after opening their hearts to their

---

14 Ratzinger, *Christianity and the Crisis of Cultures*, 66.

brothers or sisters, parties rise on the vertical axis. They enter into an I-Thou encounter that reveals divine self:

> Paul expresses this happening in quite drastic terms: the old image sinks into nothingness, a new being has arisen (2 Cor5:17)—it is no longer I who live but Christ who lives in me (Gal 2:20).[15]

This preliminary glimpse of mystical union illuminates the nature of the healing paradigm: a conciliatory move toward one's brother heals relationship, which automatically activates reconciliation with God:

> I am wrested from my isolation and incorporated into the communion of a new subject; my 'I' is inserted into the 'I' of Christ and consequently joined to the 'I' of all my brothers.[16]

This dual-axis healing explodes like a tiny mustard seed.[17] Small gestures of kindness—seeds of affinity—leverage major change. The small seeds of love that parties share grow into willingness to draw closer. Parties work to know one another better. Benedict reflects on the underlying dynamics:

> Love is the fire that purifies and unifies intellect,

---

15 Ratzinger, *Called to Communion*, 153.
16 Leachman, James G. *The Liturgical Subject: Subject, Subjectivity, and the Human Person in Contemporary Liturgical Discussion and Critique* (Notre Dame, Indiana: University of Notre Dame Press, 2009).
17 Mustard seed parable references: Matthew 13:31; Matthew 17:20; Mark 4:30-31; Luke 13: 18-19.

will, and emotion, thereby making man one with himself, inasmuch as it makes him one in God's eyes. Thus, man is able to serve the uniting of those who are divided.[18]

Benedict unintentionally describes a mediator—one who unites the divided by restoring the unity inherent in man's spiritual nature:

> Human beings have their selves not only in themselves but also outside of themselves: they live in those whom they love and those who love them and to whom they are present. Human beings are relational, and they possess their lives—themselves—only by way of relationship. Alone I am not myself, but only in and with you am I myself. To be truly a human being means to be related in love, to be of and for.[19]

A network of relationships—an inter-subjective matrix—connects mankind and God. This spiritual "power grid" distributes supernatural grace, infusing the natural realm. This interplay between faith and observable reality was witnessed in the ministry of Jesus:

> [T]he prayer recalls the cry addressed to the Lord who was sleeping in the disciples' storm-tossed boat as it was close to sinking. When his powerful word had calmed the storm, he rebuked the disciples for their little faith (cf. Mt 8:26 et par.). He

---

18 Ratzinger. *Jesus of Nazareth vol. 1*, 95.
19 Ratzinger, *The Essential Pope Benedict XVI*, 265.

wanted to say: it was your faith that was sleeping. He will say the same thing to us. Our faith too is often asleep. Let us ask him, then, to wake us from the sleep of a faith grown tired, and to restore to that faith the power to move mountains—that is, to order justly the affairs of the world.[20]

The story of Jesus rebuking sleepy disciples in the Garden of Gethsemane also serves as notice: *if we hope to participate in divine creation, we must awaken.* Those who slumber and those who are withdrawn remain unaware of divine gifts they have inherited. Those who remain drowsy collapse and become isolated, dead nodes in the relationship matrix. In contrast, those who awaken break loose from false-self prisons and become free to energize the matrix. They reconcile with God, receive their bounty of divine love, and share that love with others.

Reconcilers who operate on both axes simultaneously are the maintenance crew for the living relationship matrix, the spiritual "infrastructure" through which the supernatural impinges on this world.

I-Thou Realized

Reconcilers free the spiritually downtrodden from dungeons of the false self. They awaken those who sleep, rescue the weak-willed from ego traps, and nurture

---

[20] Pope Benedict XVI, *Address of His Holiness Benedict XVI on the Occassion of Christmas Greetings to the Roman Curia, Monday, December 20, 2010* (Libreria Editrice Vaticana, 2010).

the exchange of affinity. They help disputants navigate treacherous straits where interpersonal relations often run aground. They impart counterintuitive truths and shed light on spiritual paradoxes, such as the following:

> [L]ove does admittedly run counter to self-seeking—it is an exodus out of oneself, and yet this is precisely the way in which man comes to himself.[21]

Peacemakers coach lessons that contradict worldly logic. They guide souls past malevolent deception designed to ignite fear, and past emerging fear that motivates the construction of ego defenses. They help souls avoid the allure of the fallen world, a world that promotes the fabrication of counterfeit identities. They help parties map out explosive falsehoods that create mental minefields on the path to salvation.

In their ministry, peacemakers uncover a key truth: *divine self exists, not in isolation, but by virtue of relationship.* This counter-intuitive idea—that "I" exist by virtue of my being in relationship—demolishes the concept of rugged individualism. We are all dependent on relationship.

Parties to a dispute do not always welcome the good news. Relationships are rife with danger. Most people do not want to be bruised and battered by their fellow man. Their desire to be self-reliant and avoid risk leads them

---

21 Ratzinger, *Jesus of Nazareth* vol. 1, 99.

to build ego defenses and install barriers that constrain relationships.

Ironically, however, when a party jettisons relationships out of fear, their ego hardens. Self-protection proves self-defeating—in spite of defenses, fear increases. In contrast, lowering one's defenses and welcoming loving relationships delivers the calm of the true "I":

> Only the yes that comes to me from a you makes it possible for me to say yes to myself in and through this you. The I realizes itself through a you. It is true, moreover, that only when we have accepted ourselves can we address a genuine yes to anyone else.[22]

This genuine "yes" to relationship is a sacred act that draws on God's grace. The opposite—an intention to destroy relationship—is equivalent to sin. Benedict recognizes this equivalence:

> But sin means the damaging or destruction of relationality. Sin is a rejection of relationality because it wants to make the human being a god. Sin is loss of relationship, a disturbance of relationship, and, therefore, it is not restricted to the individual.[23]

This analysis will upset narcissists who discount the value of relationship in favor of self-interest. Nonetheless,

---

22 Pope Benedict XVI, "February 27th," *Benedictus*, 72.
23 Ratzinger, *The Essential Pope Benedict XVI*, 265.

viewing sin as equivalent to destroying relationships inspires a valuable analysis of transgressions:

> When I destroy a relationship, then this event—sin—touches the other person involved in the relationship. Consequently sin is always an offense that touches others, that alters the world and damages it.[24]

This analysis adds meaning to the phrase "fallen world." Peacemakers do not find themselves surrounded by heavenly intentions and sweet sentiment. Instead, they face a malfunctioning network, a damaged relationship matrix:

> [W]hen the network of human relationships is damaged from the very beginning, then every human being enters into a world that is marked by relational damage. At the very moment when a person begins human existence, which is a good, he or she is confronted by a sin-damaged world. Each of us enters into a situation in which relationality has been hurt. Consequently each person is from the start, damaged in relationships and does not engage in them as he or she ought. Sin pursues the human being, and he or she capitulates to it.[25]

Following Benedict's logic, we see the assumption of a false-self identity as a prelude to sin. Slipping into false-self identities inhibits relationship, which is equivalent to

---

24 Ibid.
25 Ibid.

sin. This is why the sin of pride—the cornerstone of an ego self—is considered the greatest sin, as pride destroys relationship. It is for this reason that we find gospel admonitions warning against pride and recommending humility.

If we adopt this nuanced view of sin, we can see how peacemakers who free combatants from hostile entanglement in conflict, are actually working to dismantle sin. Surprisingly, conflict resolution targets sin and spiritual alienation. At first, mediation seemed a worldly endeavor, but then turns out to be much more than anticipated.

Reflection

Peacemakers build bridges that lead disputants to I-and-Thou encounters. Before bridge construction begins, the ground must be cleared. Damaged structures, such as false selves, must be torn down. Parties must sculpt away ego traits and an accumulation of falsehoods. With this in mind, peacemakers need to acquire skill in removing counterfeit traits. They must become demolition experts, deconstructing spiritual barriers and clearing away damaged egos.

This subtractive or destructive phase of reconciliation prepares the building site where we will use divine qualities to construct bridges of relationship. Later, after parties unburden, they will move into a tentative embrace. Infused with divine love, they will navigate newly constructed bridges to connect with one another, heart to heart. Crossing this bridge becomes a spiritual pilgrimage.

During the crossing, parties discover the sacred endowment of divine love previously hidden behind false selves.

Aspiring reconcilers learn to ignite flames of divine love that fuel the I-Thou encounter. They become masters at fostering unity with the Holy Spirit. They take part in spiritual formation, which prepares them to build reconciliation bridges out of divine love. Along the way, they learn to inventory spiritual direction tools they can use to soften hardened hearts and awaken the sleeping.

Peacemakers also gain expertise in repairing construction flaws, an expertise they'll need when construction hits a snag or a worn bridge requires repair. When a bridge shows signs of weakening, they serve as repairmen.

The task of building bridges that lead to I-and-Thou encounters should not be undertaken lightly. It may be one of the biggest challenges a peacemaker faces.

TWELVE

The Problem of Evil

Aspiring peacemakers soon gain the skill needed to move beyond mere platitudes and make a difference in people's lives. And yet, we must wonder: *Do they truly appreciate the challenges that lie ahead? Have they failed to grasp the staggering opposition that evil will bring their way?*

The latter seems to be the case. Students of peacemaking typically overlook the destructive role played by the devious Serpent, the pivotal character in the Garden of Eden narrative.[1] In that mystical account, the Serpent precipitates a Fallen World—the very world a reconciler must overcome to restore peace.

As the Genesis account opens, we find Adam and Eve residing in Paradise, aligned with the Will of God. If nothing had changed, they would have remained in such heavenly conditions for eternity. But things did change. The Serpent's wily deception and malicious manipulation caused the first couple to slip and fall:

---

1 Genesis 3.

> In the Book of Wisdom we read, "God created man incorruptible, and to the image of his own likeness he made him. But, by the envy of the devil, death came into the world" (2:23-24); and in the Apocalypse we read of "that old serpent, who is called the devil and Satan, who seduceth the whole world" (12:9).[2]

The Serpent we meet in Genesis (and later in Revelation) is the prototype, the archetype, of what we will call the *destructive hidden influence*—which turns out to be the greatest single barrier to reconciliation. With reptilian guile, the Serpent—also known as Satan, the Devil, the Deceiver, or the Evil One—slyly enters opposition to the Will of God into the world. His deception creates a Fallen World. A world previously in alignment with divine will shatters into discord.

In the Garden narrative, the Serpent cajoles and manipulates Adam and Eve into abandoning their alignment with God's Will. Operating as a *destructive hidden influence*, the Serpent manipulates mankind into opposing God. His actions and the ensuing results fully warrant the label "evil."

Defining Evil

We turn to the previously introduced vector diagram to illustrate evil intentions. We can visualize evil intentions

---

2 Sheed, *Theology and Sanity*, 204.

as force fields pointing directly opposite divine intention. These intentions clash directly with the Will of God. For example, the Will of God says, "Love one another," while the counter intention says, "Hate and destroy one another."

Peacemakers need to explore how these evil intentions affect mankind, and how they precipitated a Fallen World filled with strife and conflict. They must learn to manage and overcome such evil intentions; their ability to hasten the advent of world peace rests on such wisdom.

Evil Intentions, The Dynamics of Opposition

The Serpent's destructive hidden influence exerts hypnotic control over the fallen world. Humans are buffeted with a constant stream of evil intentions until, eventually, they grow weary and fall under the Serpent's spell. Free will is ripped from their lives; they are tossed about topsy-turvy, much as the disciples were tossed about in their fishing boat by the storm—until Jesus calmed the seas.

This fallen world turmoil warrants additional description. First, imagine a hypothetical intentional space *not* affected by the Serpent or his minions. In such a space, which lacks destructive hidden influences, a soul's free will, all on its own, has a tendency to wobble unsteadily. This unsteady or wobbly intention generates departures from perfect alignment with divine will. Yet the misalignment is only minor, a minuscule deviation compared to the total misalignment caused by the Serpent's supernatural opposition to God.

While people suffering minor misaligned intentions will stumble into clashes, all on their own, such conflicts are relatively easy to resolve. The misalignment is not sufficiently askew to produce major conflict. It produces glancing blows against the Will of God rather than head-on collisions. In stark contrast to man's weak and errant intentions, the evil intentions of supernatural destructive hidden influences generate violent opposition to the Will of God. Men of weak resolve are swept up in this force field of evil intention; they, too, begin to thwart the Will of God. A good example of a period when humans, on a massive scale, were overtaken with evil intentions can be found in the horrific wars and genocide of the 20th Century.

This discussion leads to a key working definition: *evil is the distortion of man's free will by deceptive and destructive hidden influences that actively oppose the Will of God.*

Assessing Destructive Hidden Influences

When peacemakers overlook destructive hidden influences, their mediation efforts cease to make sense. They're left wondering: *What could possibly be wrong with mankind? What am I missing?* They become befuddled and lose their edge. When they overlook the destructive hidden influence, their peacemaking skills come up short; reconciliation proves elusive and conflicts persist. For this reason, they must seek to identify the destructive hidden influence during conflict assessment. They must track and chart all influences—overt and covert, visible and hidden, natural and supernatural—affecting the parties.

Reconcilers must study the destructive hidden influence, starting with the mystical and prophetic events in the Garden, in order to avoid errors of omission during assessment. While the Biblical narrative is neither historic nor scientific, it delivers spiritual truths of immense value when it comes to understanding conflict. They are universal truths: they play a role in every conflict.

Reflection on the Adam and Eve narrative surfaces a key axiom: *destructive hidden influences opposing divine will are the primary cause of all major conflict.* A second related axiom emerges: *those who harbor disguised opposition to the Will of God will attempt to sabotage reconciliation efforts.*

Peacemakers will want to build a foundation on these two axioms. They will want to learn to identify the opposition to peacemaking that comes from covert agents who engage in deception, guile, and trickery. They will want to make a practice of identifying the players in a conflict that manifest the Serpent prototype.

An inadequate assessment—one that fails to identify hidden influences—guarantees failure. Faulty assessments allow opposition to the Will of God to simmer beneath the surface until that opposition erupts and derails reconciliation. Benedict, writing in *Jesus of Nazareth*, offers a warning:

> Enmity with God is the source of all that poisons man; overcoming this enmity is the basic condi-

tion for peace in the world. Only the man who is reconciled with God can also be reconciled and in harmony with himself, and only the man who is reconciled with God and with himself can establish peace around him and throughout the world.[3]

Enmity with God was not found in Paradise; it did not exist in the Garden. Such opposition was not in the nature of Adam and Eve—who were formed in the image and likeness of God. It was only *after* the Serpent deliberately choreographed a misalignment of wills that opposition took shape and conflict arose.

The Serpent's oppositional pattern, which has been imprinted on all history, sabotages Mankind's efforts to bring about world peace. Failure to identify the Serpent's dynamic pattern has sabotaged all previous attempts to secure world peace. Today's peacemakers must grasp the nature of such evil; their assessments must identify deceptive agents driving conflict—the destructive hidden influences.

Broken Relationships—Evidence of Destructive Hidden Influences

A deeper analysis of the problem of evil might begin with a study of Benedict's theology of relationship, best captured in *Deus Caritas Est*.[4] In his papal encyclical, he argues that God's primary purpose is to restore loving re-

---

[3] Ratzinger, *Jesus of Nazareth vol. 1*, 85.
[4] Pope Benedict XVI, *God is Love*.

lationship with the world—to pervade all creation and infuse all souls with divine love. His primary purpose is to pervade all creation and infuse all souls with divine love. Thus, when peacemakers reconcile broken relationships and restore loving relationships, they are forwarding this divine purpose. This analysis adds new meaning to the words: "Blessed are the peacemakers."[5]

However, peacemakers who seek to further divine purpose will encounter brutal opposition. Destructive hidden influences that embody the Serpent's dark legacy will wreak havoc. They'll spread lies, create confusion, and cause people to lose control of their free will. They'll lure victims into opposing divine intention and rejecting divine love, the supernatural glue that binds all relationships. In addition, the Serpent's minions will actively target mediation—as they cannot tolerate people achieving the joy of reconciliation.

The full-out assault on peacemaking is logical in a Biblical sense: Christ the Mediator reconciles Man and God; this thwarts the Serpent's compulsive desire to destroy divine relationship. The Serpent is heavily invested in halting the healing that comes from mediation, and the dark souls caught up in his paradigm follow his lead. The Serpent targets mediation for destruction.

How do the Serpent and his minions block reconciliation? They convince disputants that they're at risk if they dare realign with the Will of God. They warn parties that

---

[5] Matthew 5:9.

they will be forced to sacrifice their precious ego identity, their fallen-world self. They will be stripped of their ego and "unique" personality. Fear of ego loss makes the person cling even more tenaciously to false self. Loss of their fallen-world identity seems too great a sacrifice.

However, souls who realign with the Will of God do not sacrifice their true identity, they do not sacrifice their true nature as divine self. They only sacrifice the false self, the accumulation of dross and detritus that encumbers a soul. Their fear of losing something valuable proves counterfactual:

> Belonging to God has nothing to do with destruction or non-being: *it is rather a way of being*. It means emerging from the state of separation, of apparent autonomy, of existing only for oneself and in oneself.[6]

Benedict's words are prophetic: realignment with divine will is not going to destroy true self. But those who cling ferociously to the false self will not listen. Having been deceived, like Adam and Eve, they must protect the finite ego at all costs. They thoroughly identify with their false self and will not let go. In addition, they've been convinced, by the Serpent's legacy of deception, that they owe others nothing. They have no need for relationships; rather, they're free to focus exclusively on their false-self needs.

---

[6] Pope Benedict XVI, *The Spirit of the Liturgy*, 28.

Men and women who live under the control of a hidden influence have no desire to restore divine relationship. The price they expect to pay—the sacrifice of ego identity—seems steep. Convinced the sacrifice is too costly, they turn away, unaware that this sacrifice (paradoxically) brings gain rather than loss. When a person sacrifices false self they gain knowledge of their true nature as an immortal soul endowed with the likeness of God. The real gain far outweighs the imagined loss. They are being asked to sacrifice that which has little or no value for that which has the greatest possible value. Through sacrifice they gain the never-ending bounty of immortality:

> [T]he Christian understanding of the possibility of human immortality is grounded in the fact that we exist from the very beginning in the mind of God.[7]

The preceding discussion might be summarized as follows: destructive hidden influences sabotage divine relationship, which leads to the destruction of human relationships. Destructive hidden influences operate under the Serpent's paradigm; they find the truth of immortality a high-value target. They know that a person who fears losing ego self can be easily manipulated. They also know that a person who is certain they're immortal is very difficult to manipulate. Thus, in order to maintain control and carry out their manipulative scheme, they must convince

---

7 Collins, *The Word Made Love*, 160.

people that they're not immortal. These influences have a stake in discrediting Christianity's central promise.

The preceding analysis warns peacemakers to proceed with caution and remain vigilant. Destructive hidden influences will seek to sabotage mediation by escalating party fears. If they succeed, the probability that an I-Thou encounter will take place plummets; the potential for mystical union fades.

Unpacking Deception

Fortunately, peacemakers seeking to unpack deception can turn to Benedict as a mentor. In his theology, they will encounter basic theological truths that expose many layers of deception. One such truth is the idea that existence emerges from the Mind of God:

> [I]n this one description of human existence being sustained from within the mind, the memory of God, Benedict gives the grounding for both the origins and the "end" of human existence.[8]

His work inspires a powerful axiom: *if the beginning and end of our existence is found in the Mind of God, our deepest understanding of self must emerge out of our relationship with God.*

This truth shines light on a fundamental reality that helps reconcilers better minister to disillusioned souls who need help understanding their essential nature. Rec-

---

8 Ibid.

oncilers armed with this existential truth—our existence and awareness emerge from the Mind of God—are better able to counter lies advanced by nihilistic and atheistic destructive hidden influences.

We can state the axiom in a slightly different manner: *when a person realizes they are an immortal soul, their recognition of divine relationship is restored.* Benedict explains this core concept:

> The "we" of humanity that possesses the potential for eternal life does so based on the fact that our very existence is within God and in relation to God.[9]

The nature of a soul's spiritual consciousness, which emerges from the Mind of God, attests to the veracity of Christ's promise of immortality. When parties reawaken to their true nature through advanced spiritual formation practices, they rediscover the promise of immortality in a personal way. Reawakened, they toss aside the Serpent's Big Lie—the false claim that humans are solely biological entities destined for annihilation. Personal mystical revelation validates their immortality, demolishing Satan's dark prophecy of nihilism.

Managing Destructive Hidden Influences

Destructive hidden influences mostly operate out of

---

[9] Ibid.

sight—erecting barriers to peace through the use of gossip, character assassination, innuendo, deception, and false accusations. Mediators must defuse these covert attacks if they hope to reconcile the warring parties. However, rather than sorting through the countless ways discord can be sowed, they focus on the basic structure of such attacks. This is the same principle in play when we skipped cataloging endless lists of false-self traits. Now we skip compiling endless lists of covert tactics and, instead, we learn the basic pattern of the attacks. The details matter less when we know the pattern and can predict the opponent's next move.

For example, consider the following feature of the pattern: *parties under the influence of a destructive hidden influence arrive at mediation in a heightened state of distrust and fear.* Gossip and rumor have heightened fear and insecurity—the party has been influenced to take up a defensive posture within a self-constructed mental fortress. The specific trigger that begets their fear is less important than the pattern of fear-based ego defense.

Consider another basic element in the pattern: *a party's immediate opponent, the person seated across the table, is usually not the sole factor determining their defensive mindset.* Rather, an offstage destructive actor has prompted the defensive mindset. They have most likely whispered warnings of impending harm that trigger the fear-based defense. Thus, the actual person driving the conflict is not even in the room! This pattern of an offstage actor escalating party fear occurs across all manner of conflicts without regard to the subject matter.

Mediators who recognize these patterns are better able to assess the party's underlying fears. They know what to look for, which allows them to examine actual party interests without going down dead-end paths. They zero in and discern the party's true needs and interests, separating them from the counterfeit needs and interests injected by covert agents.

Knowing the underlying patterns, they're prepared to conduct sophisticated reality checks that expose "things that just don't fit." This includes illogical views, contradictory statements, and outright falsehoods. They look for twisted views of reality and troubling thoughts that defy logic. These are all clues that a destructive hidden influence has altered the party's mental condition.

A previously mentioned clue that a destructive hidden influence is at work, manufacturing distrust, discord, and discontent, is a pattern of broken relationships. When mediators notice a party has trouble maintaining rewarding relationships, they know it is likely that a hidden influence is actively seeding and driving the breakdown of relationships. Someone is actively and continually impairing the party's dealings with others. A thorough investigation will usually expose the behind-the-scenes culprit ruining the party's life.

Identifying the Culprit

So how does a peacemaker identify a destructive hidden

influence? Some wrongdoers may seem mundane and almost harmless, like Aunt Betty the gossip. Others may be supernatural or even demonic. They can be frightening. A destructive influence may play a significant role in the party's life—they may be a co-worker, acquaintance, family member, or "friend." Other influences may be more distant and less "mundane." Supernatural evil influences, for example, escape notice and may be detected only with the tools of spiritual warfare.

In most instances, mundane and supernatural destructive influences work in tandem. It is rarely one or the other. Their influence interlocks. Let's consider a hypothetical example with a fictional person we will call Sally. Her life is going along just fine but then she dabbles in the occult and becomes encumbered with a dark influence that renders her constantly fearful and insecure.

She feels that she must not allow anyone to discover her weakness. She imagines that if others discover her fear, they will take advantage of her. Anyone who recognizes her vulnerability has the potential to become a dangerous enemy who will prey on her weakness. She absolutely must not allow anyone to gain an advantage. She feels driven to eliminate all potential threats, even before concrete events transpire.

Fear and insecurity transform Sally into a destructive hidden influence—a covert agent using misdirection, deception, and detraction to destabilize others. Her subterfuge goes undetected; acquaintances and co-workers simply sense that the world around her has become disturbed for some unknown reason. Danger is "in the air." But they are unaware of what is actually transpiring.

This example concerns common or "routine" discord. The example is fairly mundane—compared to situations in which the fearful person possesses power. If the person who feels threatened possesses significant power—financial, political, bureaucratic, judicial, legal, military, police, or corporate power—they can do great harm to those they imagine pose a threat. A person plagued with great insecurity, yet possessing great power, is potentially a very dangerous destructive hidden influence.

Destructive hidden influences that possess power destroy lives or entire societies. The barbaric wars of the 20th century are a good example. The great injustices that wound Mankind are their doing. A true social justice warrior must recognize and manage the destructive hidden-influence paradigm. Radical political ideologies, common among "social justice warriors," do not bring peace or justice. Rather, an effective warrior avoids radical ideologies and instead addresses the pernicious dynamics of evil influences.

Returning to our analysis of Sally's example, we look deeper and realize that the original destructive hidden influence that overwhelmed Sally was the demonic entity she invited, perhaps unwittingly, into her life. The original destructive hidden influence overwhelmed her with fear and transformed her into a destructive hidden influence.

This contagion of destructive evil intentions lies behind tyranny, despotism, and genocide. The impulse toward nihilistic evil is first seeded at a supernatural level and then echoes into worldly conditions, with the pattern being duplicated, over and over. All the destructive hidden influences that a mediator will identify in conflict assessment originate in the shadows of supernatural destructive influences. The Serpent's paradigm repeats itself, creating an interlocking hierarchy of covert agents who manifest the pattern.

Mediators who recognize the pattern can easily detect hidden influences who oppose the Will of God, particularly those who closely align with the Serpent's original evil intention. A well-trained mediator should be able to distinguish between such actors. Most hidden influences, troubled by their inability to escape Fallen World conditions, have merely succumbed to a contagion of evil. Others, like the Serpent, willfully and consciously attack divine relationship on a large scale, generating widespread suffering. Peacemakers who can render such actors harmless will hasten the advent of world peace.

As we dig deeper into the art of peacemaking, we come to appreciate the role of applied theology. We begin to see theologians as partners. We may also discover that some lack a key skill—the ability to identify sources of evil intentions. They may *discuss* the idea, but they rarely *practice* the discipline.

Divine Relationship in Crisis

When a person's relationship with God breaks down, they're beset with a constant and pervasive anxiety. This anxiety leads them to wrestle with a nagging impulse, a latent desire, to heal their relationship with God. The open wound gives rise to a natural impulse to seek healing. That which has been torn asunder cries out to come back together, as souls possess an inherent impulse toward unity. However, the person typically does not understand and cannot articulate this urge to journey "homeward" to the sacred in life.

Unfortunately, it is precisely at this moment of alienation that the destructive hidden influence intervenes and tramples the nascent healing impulse. The urge to heal gives way to resentment and hostility, doubt and uncertainty. The impulse to seek unity runs into a wall of evil intentions that oppose the Will of God and thwart movement toward God. During such moments the Serpent's paradigm is at its most destructive. When doubt casts a shadow on divine relationship, the Serpent swings into divisive action.

Once a soul falls under the spell of a destructive hidden influence, it becomes unmoored from its true spiritual nature. It becomes untethered from divine love and wanders in shadowy regions where worldly conflict rages. By the time mediation begins, they have become disoriented. They're in bad shape. The path to unity has all but disappeared.

During subsequent mediation sessions, reconcilers gently guide troubled parties out of the shadows. A rescue-and-repair action rekindles the party's desire to encounter the sacred. The urge to embrace healing returns and tips the scale toward renewal of divine relationship.

Renewal Blunted — Nihilism

On their peacemaking journey, mediators may encounter a particular kind of difficult case, namely nihilists who crave non-existence. Those who hold such views face a brutal conundrum: they are inherently immortal; therefore, their efforts to achieve non-being are doomed to failure. An immortal soul, by definition, exists eternally. Thus, any effort to "not exist" must fail.

In their attempts at "not being," nihilists hit a barrier: They achieve only the blackness of unconsciousness. They continue to live, but only in a state of reduced awareness, a dark, semi-conscious existence as a false self. Many are haunted by a vague sense of having reached a dead-end; they feel "there's no exit, no escape" from pain, fear, and suffering. This feeling of entrapment provokes a destructive rage; it generates a desire to destroy, to reduce creation to zero. Some go so far as to target their fellow man. In short, this craving to "make nothing of everything" fuels a stream of destructive impulses.

The actions of enraged nihilists are often covert. Nevertheless, they can cause considerable harm. When mediating between two disputing parties, a peacemaker should always be aware of the role such third parties play in the conflict. In many cases, these hidden influences have targeted the disputants in an effort to undermine their interests, relationships, happiness, salvation—even their lives. Even when peacemakers fail to locate the source of the turmoil, they can almost always see the emotional carnage left in their wake.

The Serpent's Pattern

Upon reflection, we find that all conflict is simply a by-product of enraged destructive hidden influences. Conflict is a standard feature of a fallen world; it is the unavoidable result of the Serpent's evil intentions, intentions that oppose divine will. The supernatural roots of all conflict come to our attention when we tap divine wisdom in the study of applied theology.

However, most parties embroiled in conflict (as well as most mediators) are oblivious to the Serpent's paradigm. They're blind to the presence of destructive hidden influences, blind to the hierarchy of destructive influences. They fail to recognize deception and manipulation, gossip, innuendo, character assassination, and deception. They have not detected the hidden actor or actors who have a stake in ruining their relationships. They do not know what to think when they find their interests blunted by misdirection, deception, and cloaks of invisibility.

Though the odds are against them, parties can be liberated from destructive influences—with the help of a faith-based mediator. They can be coached and taught how to uncover covert influences that fuel hostility. They can be made aware of the contagious nature of evil intentions and learn how quickly they can become infected with evil impulses once a destructive hidden influence gains control.

Even mediators may fail to detect the influences in play. Covert destructive actors can be overlooked during assessment. A conflict driver hidden behind a cloak of invisibility is nearly impossible to assess with standard methods. However, truly skilled mediators learn to detect clues and recognize telltale patterns. They become detectives who "pull strings" and expose behind-the-scenes agents.

For example, one commonly overlooked clue that a party's free will has been co-opted is strong antipathy toward virtues. The party expresses hostility toward "right behavior." This antipathy is usually expressed with illogical arguments that read like prepared scripts. The anti-virtue diatribes appear to be out of character; the language seems borrowed; the arguments are rote and unreasoned. Skilled mediators question the views expressed: Did they actually originate with the party? Or have they been implanted or enforced by a destructive hidden influence?

Another common clue arouses mediator suspicion: *destructive influences discourage souls from receiving or sharing divine love.* Falsehoods, misdirection, detraction, distortion, gossip, doubt, and fear are used to dampen the party's desire to be loved and to love others. The stunted ability to share love, in even the most basic manner, signals that a destructive hidden influence is crushing the party's spiritual essence. They're being cajoled or coerced into assuming a false-self identity. That trait which should be most natural—the ability to share love—goes missing.

The astute mediator knows that a deceptive agent will try to weaken their victim's free will; they will use deception to create confusion and uncertainty. For this reason, the mediator looks for clues that signal duplicity. He or she also looks for signs of diminished mental capacity—conditions that weaken a party's will and makes them an easy target. The mediator is on constant alert for a loss of free will. The mediator wants to know if a destructive influence controls a party's intentions.

Further clues emerge. When a party loses their ability to exercise free will, they also lose their ability to defend their faith. A mediator may observe that a party remains silent when atheists claim that immortality is delusional; or they meekly accept euphemisms that equate humans with computing bio-robots. These are clues the party no longer operates from the viewpoint of a divine self. Once they are no longer certain they're an immortal soul, they'll cease perceiving the "divine within" the other. They'll see their fellow man as little more than a herd animal. These clues reveal that a party is viewing the world through the distorted lens of a destructive influence.

Knowing these patterns becomes crucial. Peacemakers who are not aware a party is being crushed by a destructive hidden influence may become discouraged and frustrated with the lack of progress. They may terminate mediation without realizing their struggle is with the party's false self, which has been triggered into play by a destructive hidden influence. In contrast, a faith-based mediator who knows the Serpent's pattern engages in a campaign designed to restore divine relationship that has fallen into crisis.

Disguises

Destructive hidden influences appear in many forms: espionage agents covertly foment war; social activists gnaw at the moral pillars of society; rogue bankers profit from war; propaganda specialists empower tyrants; psychopaths use guile to seize corporate power; gossips protect their "turf"; black sheep secretly fuel family turmoil; drug dealers promise pleasure, yet deliver enslavement; media outlets disseminate disinformation; judges disguise tyranny as justice; dissidents sabotage faith; heretics distort sacred teachings. Destructive hidden influences can be found in these guises and many others, using underhanded methods to bring discord and suffering.

In addition to worldly covert agents, supernatural influences that we might label "demons" goad vulnerable men and women to commit insane acts that harm others. This type of influence is unrecognized in secular mediation and rarely addressed even in faith-based mediation; yet it remains a very real factor with very real consequences. In either situation, whether the influence is mundane or supernatural, all foment discord, distrust, and antipathy—and *all reject God's love*. Their influence shares one common goal: *destroy divine relationship.*

At the very least, these influences impede mediation, bringing about impasse. For this reason, reconcilers facing a stalled mediation must revive the process by identifying the destructive hidden influence at work.

In order to accomplish this task, a mediator might mimic Columbo, the bumbling television detective who disarmed villains with naive questions, coaxing his villains into carelessly exposing their crimes. His clever tactics, based on common sense and logic, exposed criminal deception. Mediators can also play detective; they can flush hidden actors out of hiding. With bumbling moves, they can lure villains out of the shadows. Playing detective, they can uncover fresh evidence that weakens the grip of deception and exposes agents who are determined to hijack party free will.

After a mediator unmasks the disguises of evil, the parties view the conflict in dramatically revised terms. People they once considered enemies (due to lies, gossip, and character assassination) become potential friends. The barrier of impasse is overcome. Dreams of peace are rebooted and the parties experience renewed awareness of the Holy Spirit's presence:

> In asking to be liberated from the power of evil, we are ultimately asking for God's Kingdom, for union with his will, and for the sanctification of his name.[10]

Naive observers assume mediators work solely with parties seated before them; they assume all key players appear on stage in plain sight. But this is not accurate.

---

10 Ratzinger, *Jesus of Nazareth vol. 1*, 167.

Disguised agents fomenting conflict from offstage must be located and disarmed. Masks must be ripped off the deceptive villains of the conflict drama.

Victims of Hidden Influences

Some personalities are particularly susceptible to the effects of hidden influences: those who cling to false-self identities; those who have lost control of their free will as a result of sickness or injury; and individuals impaired by substance abuse. All become easy targets for predators.

Those who suffer from such conditions can reduce risk by diligently aligning their personal interests with divine will. Properly aligning intentions steadies the rough seas of life. Meanwhile, divine assistance frees people to don spiritual armor so they can battle destructive influences that seek to erode peace and subvert free will.

The path to peace and freedom is fraught with danger, heartache, and disappointment. Many turn back before reaching the first waystation. When people first decide to regain control over their own errant free will, they are met with supernatural forces that buffet them into fallen world bondage. The embattled soul may struggle for years or even decades to free itself. Fortunately, with perseverance and outside help, a select few are able to make the journey from spiritual bondage to liberation.

The perils of the journey have been widely acknowledged. Plotinus, a philosopher who influenced early Christians such as Augustine, understood the dynamics at play, as did Pope Benedict, who captures the essence of an entrapped spirit:

> [N]on-divine being is itself, as such, fallen being. Finitude is already a kind of sin, something negative, which has to be saved by being brought back into the infinite.[11]

Plotinus recognizes the challenge faced by a soul who battles deception as it travels on the path to reconciliation. Benedict synopsizes the idea:

> And so the journey back—the *reditus*—begins when the fall is arrested in the outer depths, so that now the arrow points upward. In the end the "sin" of the finite, of not-being-God, disappears, and in that sense God becomes 'all in all.' The way of *reditus* means redemption, and redemption means liberation from finitude, which is the real burden of our existence.[12]

Reconcilers who make peace facilitate liberation from bondage—not release in a Manichean sense[13]—but rather a release from the evil intentions that tether man to the fallen world. Reconcilers do not liberate souls from the finite world *per se*; rather, they help souls escape the bonds of falsehoods that bind them to a world lacking love. They

---

11 Pope Benedict XVI, *The Spirit of the Liturgy*, 30.
12 Ibid.
13 We do not argue that all creation is bad, as did the Manicheans; rather, that which must be overcome is uncontrolled attachment to the physical realm. Attachment is the problem.

rescue joyless souls stripped of divine love, those who resemble helpless swimmers swept out to sea by a riptide:

> For if we ask ourselves what *being damned* really means, it is this: taking no pleasure in anything any more, liking nothing and no one, and being liked by no one. Being robbed of any capacity for loving and excluded from the sphere in which loving is possible—that is the absolute emptiness, in which a person exists in contradiction to his own nature, and his life is totally ruined. If, then, the essential characteristic of man is his likeness to God, his capacity for love, then humanity as a whole and each of us individually can only survive where there is love and where we are taught the way to this love.[14]

The solution to this existential dilemma seems obvious: heal and strengthen divine relationship. However, souls drowning in treacherous seas of evil intentions do not view life in such simple terms. They are tossed topsy-turvy by the Serpent's armies. Before long they lose trust in God:

> The human being does not trust God. Tempted by the serpent, he harbors the suspicion that in the end, God takes something away from his life, that God is a rival who curtails our freedom and that we will be fully human only when we have cast him aside... The human being lives in the sus-

---

14 Pope Benedict XVI, "October 31," *Benedictus*, 330.

picion that God's love creates a dependence and that he must rid himself of this dependency if he is to be fully himself. Man does not want to receive his existence and the fullness of his life from God.[15]

Desperate men and women who have lost trust in God seek worldly power they can wield to extricate themselves from their dire predicament:

> He himself wants to obtain from the tree of knowledge the power to shape the world, to make himself a god, raising himself to God's level, and to overcome death and rely on love that to him seems untrustworthy; he relies solely on his own knowledge since it confers power upon him. Rather than on love, he sets his sights on power, with which he desires to take his own life autonomously in hand. And in doing so, he trusts in deceit rather than in truth and thereby sinks with his life into emptiness, into death.[16]

Benedict paints a dreary yet accurate portrait of humans alienated from God, souls compelled to strike out with limited mortal power. Ironically, like Adam and Eve, their distrust is misplaced—it was not God who precipitated man's descent. Rather, the deceptive Serpent promulgated the falsehoods that generate man's suffering.

The Serpent reaps rewards with his duplicity and sabo-

---

15   Pope Benedict XVI, "December 6," *Benedictus*, 369.
16   Ibid.

tage—he feeds off the tribulations of souls who fall victim to his deception. He dines on those who assume suffering is woven into the very nature creation, a falsehood that promises no escape. He chuckles at man's dogged attachment to a "suffering creation," a fallen world. He enjoys the weeping of trapped souls.

But souls need not feed the Serpent's appetite. They can secure release, freedom, and happiness, though there is but one path—*restoring divine relationship*. Benedict adds his insight to this conclusion:

> We can only be saved—that is, be free and true—when we stop wanting to be God and renounce the madness of autonomy and self-sufficiency.[17]

The restoration of divine relationship initiates the repair of all relationships:

> We can be saved only when he from whom we have cut ourselves off takes the initiative with us and stretches out his hand to us. Only being loved is being saved, and only God's love can purify damaged human love and radically re-establish the network of relationships that have suffered from alienation.[18]

Thus, in spite of appearances, Satan does not hold all the cards. No matter how doggedly the Serpent works to drown souls in the blackness of amnesia, it is always pos-

---

17 Ratzinger, *The Essential Pope Benedict XVI*, 266.
18 Ibid.

sible to find freedom in reconciliation and mystical union with Christ:

> From an intimate union with Christ, there automatically arises also a participation in his love for human beings, in his will to save them and bring them help. He who knows Christ from within wishes to communicate to others the joy of the redemption that has opened up for him in the Lord: pastoral labor flows from this communion of love and even in difficult situations is always nourished by this motivation and becomes life-fulfilling.[19]

Benedict calls on men of goodwill to engage in the "pastoral labor" of loving their brother. However, souls whose intentions have been hijacked by destructive hidden influences head in a very different direction—they oppose God and reject divine love. Their intentions, yoked to Satan's intentions, contribute to the juggernaut known as Original Sin, Satan's intentional force field that defiantly blocks all paths to peace. This opposition to divine will (Original Sin) directly opposes peacemaking and is the reason world peace has eluded us. Peacemakers are left with only one option: reconcile troubled souls with God, one heart at a time.

> The present "world" has to disappear; it must be changed into God's world. That is precisely what Jesus' mission is, into which the disciples

---

19 Ibid, 267.

are taken up: leading "the world" away from the condition of man's alienation from God and from himself, so that it can become God's world once more and so that man can become himself again by becoming one with God.[20]

The primary obstacle to peace, as we have discovered, is the presence of destructive hidden influences, natural and supernatural, engaged in continuous destruction of relationships. Their nihilistic mindset creates hostile alienation that blocks divine love. Peacemakers battle covert agents as they extract prisoners from this trap. The following sections will help the peacemaker fight these battles.

Two Trees — Good versus Evil and Mystical Union

In the Garden, we find two trees: the first, the Tree of Knowledge of Good and Evil, represents duality. The second, the Tree of Life, represents mystical union with Christ. People rarely speak of the second tree. As a result, the concept of mystical union is foreign to them and they resemble spiritual sleepwalkers:

> Across the centuries, it is the drowsiness of the disciples that opens up possibilities for the power of the Evil One. Such drowsiness deadens the soul, so that it remains undisturbed by the power

---

20   Benedict XVI, *Jesus of Nazareth vol. 2*, 101.

of the Evil One at work in the world and by all the injustice and suffering ravaging the earth.[21]

Benedict further addresses this accounting of our tragic flaws:

> In its state of numbness, the soul prefers not to see all this; it is easily persuaded that things cannot be so bad, so as to continue in the self-satisfaction of its own comfortable existence. Yet this deadening of souls, this lack of vigilance regarding both God's closeness and the looming forces of darkness, is what gives the Evil One power in the world.[22]

Jesus incarnated into a world awash in the Evil One's influence, a world that had not awakened. Jesus provided a wake-up call; he revealed a path to peace and a path to salvation that required him to take sin and death onto himself in order to transform the world:

> Because he is the Son, he sees with total clarity the whole foul flood of evil, all the power of lies and pride, all the wiles and cruelty of the evil that masks itself as life yet constantly serves to destroy, debase, and crush life. Because he is the Son, he experiences deeply all the horror, filth, and baseness that he must drink from the "chalice" prepared for him: the vast power of sin and death. All this he must take into himself, so that it can

---

21 Pope Benedict XVI, *Jesus of Nazareth vol. 2*, 153.
22 Ibid.

be disarmed and defeated in him.[23]

His sacrifice is nearly impossible to contemplate, let alone understand. Therefore, we do not fault mere mortals when they shy away from the "whole foul flood of evil." We cannot dismiss their fear of slipping into a pit from which there's no escape. Helpless in the face of evil, they close their eyes and sleep. Who can blame them? Such hopelessness is not a personal failing. Rather the hopelessness is a feature of a world overwhelmed by evil:

> Might evil be invincible? Is it the ultimate power of history? Because of the experience of evil, for Pope Wojtyła the question of redemption became the essential and central question of his life and thought as a Christian. Is there a limit against which the power of evil shatters?[24]

Benedict notes that Saint John Paul II responded in the affirmative. There is a limit to evil:

> "Yes, there is," the Pope replies in this book of his, as well as in his Encyclical on redemption. ... The power that imposes a limit on evil is Divine Mercy. Violence, the display of evil, is opposed in history—as "the totally other" of God, God's own power—by Divine Mercy. The Lamb is stronger than the dragon, we could say together with the

---

23 Ibid., 155.
24 Pope Benedict XVI, *Address of His Holiness Benedict XVI on the Occassion of Christmas Greetings to the Roman Curia, Monday, December 22, 2005* (Libreria Editrice Vaticana, 2005).

Book of Revelation.[25]

Rephrasing this idea in reconciliation terms, we can say divine intention is stronger than the counter intention of the Evil One. Though evil may give us reason to doubt, we can be assured of our salvation. Unfortunately, this certainty is not common. Reconcilers must help parties discover their strength and teach them to skillfully wield spiritual weapons to overcome destructive hidden influences. Benedict shared Saint John Paul II's insights on the subject:

> At the end of the book, in a retrospective review of the attack of 13 May 1981 and on the basis of the experience of his journey with God and with the world, John Paul II further deepened this answer.
>
> What limits the force of evil, the power, in brief, which overcomes it—this is how he says it—is God's suffering, the suffering of the Son of God on the Cross: "The suffering of the Crucified God is not just one form of suffering alongside others.... In sacrificing himself for us all, Christ gave a new meaning to suffering, opening up a new dimension, a new order: the order of love..."[26]

The counter-intuitive idea that suffering produces a path to salvation challenges our sense of reality. Even

---

[25] Ibid. "The Pope" and "Pope Wojtyła" both refer to Saint John Paul II.
[26] Pope Benedict XVI, *Address of His Holiness Benedict XVI on the Occassion of Christmas Greetings to the Roman Curia*, Monday, December 22, 2005.

Saint John Paul II's discourse on the dynamics of suffering is not easy to grasp. The following excerpt offers clarification that can aid our study:

> The passion of Christ on the Cross gave a radically new meaning to suffering, transforming it from within.... It is this suffering which burns and consumes evil with the flame of love.... All human suffering, all pain, all infirmity contains within itself a promise of salvation; ...evil is present in the world partly so as to awaken our love, our self-gift in generous and disinterested service to those visited by suffering.... Christ has redeemed the world: "By his wounds we are healed' (Is 53: 5)" (p. 189, ff.).[27]

The idea that Christ's suffering overcomes evil stops us in our spiritual tracks. How could that be? Just when we summon the courage to deliver a blow, Christ disavows brute force. Our limited awareness demands that we carefully unpack the concept. What factors can transform suffering into a solution to evil?

Let us start our reflection by considering the nature of Christ's divine mind. Also referred to as Christ consciousness, his mind pervades all creation, including that which is repulsive and evil. After all, how could he wash the stains from the world's linen if he did not first take in the dirty laundry? If he does not "own" those who oppose his will, how could he possibly transform them? How can

---

27   Ibid.

he realign the intentions of evil actors if he cannot bring them under his loving control? These are difficult questions.

Looking to the gospel for answers, we find Jesus broke new ground when he eschewed the obsessive sparring that arises from the duality of good and evil. He avoided the tree of knowledge, the tree of good and evil, and instead pervaded creation with divine love. He became "all in all." He demonstrated the spiritual unity represented by the second tree, the Tree of Life.

But how does this paradigm work in practical terms? When Christ's mind pervades a territory or space where evil holds power, he most certainly is not offering passive support for evil. He is not allowing his presence to fuel evil. Rather, he makes himself present without exerting raw force; he is present without pushing against substance; he demonstrates a state of non-resistance. Rather than become trapped in the quicksand of evil, he pervades the space with his transcendent loving mind that cannot be bound by evil. His presence spiritually transforms the space and the evil residing in that space. In poetic terms, he engages in supernatural alchemy.

Thus, Christ models the ultimate path to reconciliation: *He becomes the Truth and the Way that leads to peace. Mystical union with Christ—co-being-in-love—dissolves evil intentions. Mystical union changes the very nature of reality.*

Christ eschews the use of raw force, material energy,

and instead transforms the very nature of existence.[28] He fulfills the scriptural prophecy of a new earth and a new heaven, demonstrating that creation exists in the Mind of God. He shows us the reality that underlies the fundamental beliefs of our faith. His counter-intuitive path to reconciliation crosses into territory usually inhabited solely by mystics, yet its fruits should be and must be accessible to all souls.

Moving Past Fear

Let's step back and take another look at the nature of the fallen world. The "Serpent's game" ensnares naive souls in a series of diabolical traps that bring on crushing despair. Though souls struggle to escape the fallen world and step out of the Serpent's Game, they are rarely able to break free:

> [T]he sheep caught in the thorn bush and unable to find its way home is a metaphor for man in general. He cannot get out of the thicket and find his way back to God.[29]

Souls caught in the thicket face a choice: They can either struggle to free themselves or they can resign themselves to their fate. Those who choose to listen to the wily advice of the Serpent fare even worse. They are plunged

---

[28] See earlier discussions regarding the malleable nature of an idealistic universe.
[29] Pope Benedict XVI, *The Spirit of the Liturgy*, 33.

into even deeper darkness. The trap set by the enemies of faith resembles life in ancient prisons, where isolation and hardship prevailed:

> In ancient times the really terrible thing about prisons was they cut people off from the light of the day and plunged them into darkness. So, at a deeper level, the real alienation, unfreedom, and imprisonment of man consists in his want of truth. If he does not know truth, if he does not know who he is, why he is there, and what the reality of the world consists in, he is only stumbling around in the dark.[30]

Benedict also uses the image of a paralyzed man to describe life in a fallen world, life in the Evil One's trap:

> The paralyzed man is the image of every human being whom sin prevents from moving about freely, from walking on the path of good and from giving the best of himself. Indeed, by taking root in the soul, evil binds the person with the ties of falsehood, anger, envy, and other sins and gradually paralyzes him. Jesus, therefore, scandalizing the scribes who were present, first said: "... your sins are forgiven."[31]

The following might describe combatants who arrive for mediation while subject to the wiles of the Evil One:

---

30 Pope Benedict XVI, "November 18th," *Benedictus*, 349.
31 Ibid.

> In what does man's wretchedness actually consist? Above all, in his insecurity; in the uncertainties with which he is burdened; in the limitations that oppress him; in the lack of freedom that binds him; in the pain that makes his life hateful to him. Ultimately there is, behind all this, the meaninglessness of his existence that offers satisfaction neither to himself nor to anyone else for whom it might have been necessary, irreplaceable, consequential.[32]

Every disputant that walks through the door to mediation represents a life to be rebuilt and a soul to be saved. Trained reconcilers, especially those informed by Benedict's insights, work through a party's confusion to identify the core cause of their woes:

> We can say, then, that the root of man's wretchedness is loneliness, is the absence of love—is the fact that my existence is not embraced by a love that makes it necessary, that is strong enough to justify it despite all the pain and limitations it imposes.[33]

Therefore, first and foremost, peacemakers must address loneliness spawned by the absence of love. When souls pass through the fallen world's house of mirrors, they lose their connection to divine love. Once trapped, they forfeit spiritual awareness; they become utterly lost

---

[32] Ibid., "March 5th," 80.
[33] Ibid.

and alone. A sense of existential desperation makes them turn to worldly force in an attempt to bend the wills of their fellow humans. No longer able to rely on loving relationships to fulfill their needs, they turn to the use of coercive power. Convinced that force, even deadly force, is the only thing that ensures survival, they renounce divine relationship. However, this stance proves unworkable:

> When man prefers his own egoism, his pride, and his convenience to the demands made on him by the truth, the only possible outcome is an upside-down existence.[34]

Trapped souls, with their backs against the wall, resort to duplicity, coercion, and brute force. They abandon God's grace as they slip deeper into ruin and despair. Their evil intentions dig ditches of sorrow, which soon fill up with their tears. This dire situation places peacemakers at risk: they can easily become the target of hostility. In response, they must proceed cautiously and anticipate power plays or even violence. They know that, in the absence of God's tranquility, the Evil One reigns with the power of fear:

> Even in our days, we cannot say that the tranquil evidential character of God has been eliminated; but we must admit that it has been made more than ever unrecognizable by the violence that power and profit inflict on us.[35]

---

[34] Ratzinger, *Christianity and the Crisis of Cultures*, 95.
[35] Ibid., 99.

Souls blanketed by supernatural destructive hidden influences are compelled to employ deceit, coercion, and trickery to defend against real or imagined threats. *Existential fear demands that all perceived threats, real or imagined, be destroyed.* However, even when the immediate threats have been dispatched, fear is never vanquished. The destructive hidden influence continues to generate or trigger additional fears, shifting focus from past threats to emerging threats. For the troubled soul there's no rest, no peace.

There is only one sure way to defeat this endless cycle of fear: *truly repair divine relationship.* Restoration of the conduit of divine love is the only sure antidote. This rescue-and-repair action most often must be conducted while staring into the face of evil. The peacemaker may need to turn to spiritual warriors trained in deliverance ministry for assistance. In fact, deliverance ministry might even be considered a sub-discipline of reconciliation ministry. Both bring God's love to the battle against evil.

In the next chapter, we will explore the idea of spiritual warfare in greater detail, but before we move on, we should examine the types of fear a peacemaker will need to manage.

Fear Manifestations

In our quest to understand fear, we take a brief look at a few common types of fear. This discussion should help peacemakers better recognize the fertile human soil where destructive hidden influences prosper and grow.

In some instances, fear is situational. For example, an office assistant secretly fears losing her employment. Given that she has a strong need to hold a job and earn wages, this potential job loss is a source of insecurity and fear. She must defend against the perceived threat. For example, she may imagine or suspect an office colleague is currying favor with the office manager in order to steal her position. As a result, she fears her survival is at risk. Unable to launch an overt or public attack against her perceived enemy, she mounts a covert defense designed to undermine the office colleague. She launches a whispering campaign intended to destroy the office colleague's work relationships. But soon her fear expands and she suspects that the office manager secretly favors her colleague. So the manager becomes a threat she must undermine as well. Both parties are now perceived threats that must be addressed covertly.

The fear-stricken office assistant remains in the shadows, planting deadly seeds of distrust with whispered words of detraction. She gossips and spreads disparaging words about the office manager to the office colleague. Then she repeats the action, whispering disparaging words about the office colleague to the office manager. She plays her co-workers against one another. She will not have to attack them directly if she can get them to attack one another. She operates as a destructive hidden influence, becoming the hidden source of conflict.

In a relatively short time, the office colleague and the

office manager become convinced that the whispered warnings possess merit. Their relationship is sabotaged by the campaign of gossip, innuendo, and detraction. Both become willing to fight, and have no idea their conflict has been manufactured by a hidden third party.

One might think the solution is obvious—promote greater job security. But, in many cases, if not most cases, that solution does not work. Like so many other people, the office assistant's damaged relationship with God generates persistent fear and latent paranoia. There is no type of job security that can eliminate the fear based in a broken divine relationship. Her underlying fear will not dissipate until after she reconciles with God. As long as she is troubled by alienation from God, fear will drive her to undermine associates and friends.

This example echoes the Genesis account: the Serpent, jealous and fearful of man's relationship with God, covertly undermines trust between Mankind and God. He whispers calumny intended to divide. This pattern, recorded in scripture,[36] has been repeated throughout history and functions as a primary cause of unresolved conflict.

Situational fear, however, is the least severe type of fear. *Fear may also be caused by unhealed physical, emotional, mental, and spiritual wounds.* People who live with unhealed wounds suffer from a lingering fear of being harmed again. A destructive hidden influence will in-

---

36 A notable example is the beheading of John the Baptist.

tentionally trigger the fear that the abuser will reappear, though the abuser may be long gone and present no threat. For example, an abusive father may have passed away, yet a covert actor may trigger irrational fear of "male authority figures." The destructive hidden influence will not allow wounds to heal.

A person suffering unhealed wounds can be triggered into mounting proxy battles against all who resemble a past abuser. The present-time (proxy) enemy is merely someone who reminds the person, usually unconsciously, of a past nemesis. A destructive hidden influence will not allow the resemblance to be dismissed as harmless; instead, they frame the proxy enemy as a current threat.

The previously wounded person, triggered into fearing a return of the past, replays old mental tapes, and tries—over and over—to win battles previously lost. Their fear demands they defeat all perceived threats, even though the threats are not real in the present moment.

Proxy targets, those who resemble people from the past, cannot make sense of the hostility directed at them. They have no idea why they're being attacked. The hostility seems to be insane; they are being attacked for no good reason. As a result, their sense of being wronged is especially acute. They fight back with righteous indignation but their angry response only confirms the wounded person's worst fears. The conflict escalates.

Current modalities of healing past wounds are not designed to detect the hidden influence triggering the current fear. In fact, many therapists re-stimulate memories of past wounds and turn the hurt into an imagined present-time threat. They function as a destructive hidden influence.

In addition, therapists focus solely on the horizontal axis and ignore the vertical axis where collateral damage has harmed divine relationship. For example, the victim may believe God allowed them to be hurt in the first place; they may consider God an accessory to the abuse they received. A destructive hidden influence will hammer home that very theme. The therapist's approach may actually damage divine relationship and leave the person more prone to being triggered by destructive hidden influences.

Therefore, in order to help a party truly heal with complete peace of mind, a reconciler addresses lingering fear associated with divine relationship. They seek to detect destructive hidden influences who are engaged in triggering the pain of old wounds, turning the residue of past suffering into a fear of the present.

The most extreme type of fear might be called existential fear. The person trusts no one, fears everyone. They consider all others to be a significant threat to their very survival. Existential fear has a strong (though often unrecognized) supernatural component; existential fear is infused with the Serpent's nihilism. This saddles a party with an overwhelming compulsion to destroy.

However, most parties cannot attack others openly; they must engage in covert assaults. They undermine and weaken others, and then destroy their lives. This is the psychopath, the charming con artist who stabs his victims in the back. This is the Serpent, the Evil One. This is the ancient paradigm put forth in the Garden of Eden narrative—the archetype of the Serpent, who undermines relationships through deception and character assassination.

Upon reflection, we discover a powerful and perhaps surprising axiom: *existential fear of an all-powerful creator lies behind all basic evil intentions.* This may be the most important axiom in peacemaking. When this factor is not addressed, world peace is not achieved.

Consider the following explanation:

The Serpent—faced with the unlimited creative power of God—experiences absolute terror. He cannot tolerate the idea that his very existence depends on the mercy of another. Dependence on another is something to be avoided with every fiber of his being. This is the frightening reality against which he must defend himself, even if that means he must destroy all creation.

As a primary strategic defense, he undermines divine relationship between individual souls and God. His existential fear does not tolerate souls aligning with God's Will and adding to His overwhelming power. He must not allow souls to contribute in a positive way to creation; he cannot allow them to further divine purpose. In response to his dread, he covertly attacks divine relationship wherever he encounters it. He becomes the ultimate destructive hidden influence. This dynamic is the basis of evil in the world; it has defeated all previous efforts to hasten world peace. The troubled history of Mankind arises out of such existential fear.

It would seem that with such a clearly identified problem the solution should be obvious. However, a major conundrum arises: *souls suffering existential fear view love as a Trojan horse.* In their minds, love is the assassin's façade, the false face of a deadly enemy, a weapon of espionage designed to breach their defenses. The solution to existential fear—an infusion of divine love—is blocked by the very fear it seeks to overcome. The problem is booby-trapped. The problem contains a mechanism that prevents its solution. When we examine the situation, we realize we've encountered a truly diabolical trap worthy of our dedicated attention.

Existential fear drives souls to reject Christian love; unfortunately, that forecloses on the path to reconciliation. Tormented beings caught in the Serpent's trap—all of whom suffer existential fear—cannot embrace divine love, which remains the essential ingredient for healing and peace. This enforced *deficit of love* is the primary reason that peace has eluded this world.

The obvious, or at least the simplest solution, falls short; the problem requires a more sophisticated response from peacemakers. Overcoming existential fear demands a sophisticated reconciliation regimen comprised of advanced peacemaking tools. It calls for sequestering fearful parties in a retreat setting where they can be guided through contemplative prayer and other healing regimens.

In this pastoral setting, reconcilers "walk with" damaged souls in a non-threatening manner that occupies the "space of evil" and dissolves the fear-stricken person's manufactured defenses. Reconcilers pervade the space like Christ did in order to transform evil, in order to defuse the black core of existential fear. The work echoes the Archangel Michael wrestling with evil. Dedicated pastoral counseling in a peaceful setting brings stunning results: Fear subsides; defensive walls crumble. The sacred promise of reconciliation with God is realized.

An important truth bears repeating: *existential fear is the genesis of evil; the ultimate destroyer of relationships.* Numerous scripture admonitions warn Christians to "be not afraid" and "fear not." The admonitions express more than a consoling sentiment; they convey a profound instruction: *avoid states of mind that give rise to evil acts.* Men overwhelmed with fear are driven to commit harmful acts whereas, in stark contrast, men who live free from fear have no reason to harm their fellow man. Eliminate fear and one eliminates hostility, rage, and destructive impulses. "Be not afraid," repeated many times in scripture, sets the stage for world peace.

A Peacemaker's Mindset

Faith-based reconciliation turns out to be more powerful than anyone at first imagined. Reconciliation ministry combined with spiritual formation is the only true path to diminished fear, and thus the only path to lasting peace.

Disputants who truly know they're immortal souls existing in a loving divine relationship with God also understand that, in an ultimate sense, they cannot be harmed. The lesson taught from the Cross—souls survive bodily death imposed by evil forces—is paramount for world peace. An immortal soul succumbs to fear solely as a result of identifying with a false self—in its many forms. When attachment and clinging to a false self subsides, fear dissipates. This is the promise of Christianity. On the day mankind experiences this epiphany, sacred peace will descend upon the world.

Parties that conquer fear are less susceptible to destructive hidden influences. No longer subject to the ills of a weakened will, they're harder to trigger into fear. *Removing fear solves the problem of the destructive hidden influence.*

Courage, bolstered by divine relationship, leaves people less susceptible to gossip, detraction, deception, character assassination, and invitations to commit evil. Religious leaders strengthen their faith communities when they exhort their followers to "fear not." These communities of courage can help peacemakers achieve their goal of reconciliation.

Men and women come together to receive the supernatural grace that washes away fear. In the shelter of their faith community, troubled souls find unity with Christ:

> The Church can come into being only where man finds his way to the truth about himself, and the truth is that he needs grace. Wherever pride closes him to this insight, man cannot find the

way to Jesus.[37]

Reflection

Peacemakers rarely travel smooth paths but rather encounter challenges, barriers, roadblocks, and impasse to which they must apply advanced techniques, heightened skill, and sacred wisdom. They must tap the mental and spiritual "provisions" they have accumulated during their preparation.

Peacemakers inevitably wrestle with evil, which requires a sophisticated grasp of fear and its pernicious effects. To fully prepare, they must develop personal strategies for managing various types of fear. They will want to become students of the ways that fear influences the world. They will ask themselves: *what fears might cause me to abandon reconciliation?* They should learn to identify and manage personal fears that will sabotage their ministry. They will want to rehearse ministering to another person while they stare down the face of evil. They will want to master the art of transforming existential fear; this includes learning to rapidly discern destructive intentions from benign intentions. They must acquire a calm composure and acute spiritual perception.

Peacemakers will want to attend retreats to contemplate the full nature of evil. They will want to reflect on

---

[37] Ratzinger, *Called to Communion*, 65.

how they will transform parties whose intentions are directly opposed to the Will of God. They should reflect on how they will surface destructive actors who hide offstage. They will want to improve their detective skills so they might better detect destructive hidden influences.

Peacemakers must develop a keen intuition for assessing destructive hidden influences that target both axes. They must know that eliminating destructive influences in this world alone does not eliminate all fear. They should prepare to encounter and assist parties predisposed to becoming victims of a supernatural destructive hidden influence.

After advanced preparation, peacemakers will travel into regions that bring sleepless nights, nights laden with trepidation about the challenges looming ahead. The following chapters, filled with additional spiritual weapons, should help allay those fears and bolster their peacemaking confidence.

THIRTEEN

Spiritual Warfare

In the course of their ministry, mediators sometimes stumble upon a counterintuitive truth: in order to achieve peace, they must first learn to fight. They must become spiritual warriors.

Just as scripture tells men and women of faith to don spiritual armor before engaging in battle, so experienced mediators advise their students to fortify themselves with advanced conflict resolution tools in order to conquer evil, deception, and opposition. Faith-based peacemakers should never be afraid to wield spiritual weapons when confronting the challenges that block the path toward reconciliation.

Spiritual Warfare

When confronted with violence or hostility, most people choose one of two options: they either fight or they retreat. Both are inadequate. The first option leads to escalation. The result is either devastation or long-term cycles of vengeance and anger. Like quicksand, the use of force pulls disputants deeper and deeper into the conflict. The more they struggle, the more trapped they become.

Retreat leads to avoidance, and avoidance rarely, if ever, resolves the underlying issues fueling conflict. Moreover, some situations cannot be ignored:

> That which is wrong, the reality of evil, cannot simply be ignored; it cannot just be left to stand. It must be dealt with; it must be overcome. Only this counts as true mercy.[1]

The flight or fight response is ingrained in most humans, but people of faith have another option. Spiritual warfare represents a more nuanced response that takes disputants beyond stimulus-response reactions into a realm of reasoned and inspired action. It is not to be taken lightly. Neither is it a course of action one pursues alone, but rather a method that requires divine assistance:

> [T]he very first thing we encounter is the limit of our power to heal and to overcome evil. We encounter the superior power of evil, which we cannot master with our unaided powers.[2]

Benedict's description of human limitations is not gratuitous humility. He imparts the harsh truth that, when

---

[1] Pope Benedict XVI, *Jesus of Nazareth* vol. 2, 133.
[2] Ratzinger. *Jesus of Nazareth* vol. 1, 159.

it comes to battling evil, man requires divine assistance. Secular models fail in this regard—they do not acknowledge the need for God's assistance in managing individuals who intend to harm their fellow man. This oversight dooms secular protocols to failure:

> When men lose sight of God, peace disintegrates and violence proliferates to a formerly unimaginable degree of cruelty.[3]

Faith-based peacemakers often stumble upon wreckage brought about by the shortcomings of secular models. They encounter despairing souls left behind, trapped in conditions that might be equated with Hell:

> There can be people who have totally destroyed their desire for truth and readiness to love, people for whom everything has become a lie, people who have lived for hatred and have suppressed all love within themselves.[4]

These previous failures to make peace or resolve a conflict have dashed hope. Parties worry that past failures portend future impasse. Peacemakers must proceed cautiously. If they're overly eager to make a difference, they may skip a review of past failures. Skipping over negative emotions associated with past failures can cause the process to stall.

---

3   Ibid., 85.
4   Collins. *The Word Made Love*, 165.

In contrast, skilled mediators carefully evaluate the conflict history and note the peacemaking protocols that came up short in the past. After sorting through failed attempts and techniques, they gain new appreciation for Christ's approach to overcoming evil:

> [H]e goes down in the role of one whose suffering-with-others is a transforming suffering that turns the underworld around, knocking down and flinging open the gates of the abyss.[5]

Christ does not avoid opposition. Rather, he prepares for battle as only a spiritual warrior can. Scripture tells us, "His Baptism is a descent into the house of the evil one, combat with the 'strong man.'" Christ chooses spiritual combat.

Too many of us ignore his example. Fear and fatigue overtake us. We fall asleep when we should be vigilant, for the call to peacemaking demands that we follow Christ into dark regions in an attempt to rescue lost souls:

> Thus, it is not only after his death, but already by his death and during his whole life, that Jesus 'descends into hell,' as it were, into the domain of our temptations and defeats, in order to take us by the hand and carry us upward.[6]

Peace is not a fairy tale. Mere tranquility is insufficient. Peacemakers don't frolic in idyllic pastoral settings,

---

[5] Ratzinger, *Jesus of Nazareth vol. 1*, 20.
[6] Ibid., 161.

free from all cares and worries. Instead, they stride onto the smoky battlefield of the fallen world and engage the enemy. It is not a task for the naive or the faint of heart:

> "Finally, be strong in the Lord and in the strength of his might. Put on the whole armor of God, that you may be able to stand against the wiles of the devil. For we are not contending against flesh and blood, but against the principalities, against the powers, against the world rulers of this present darkness, against the spiritual hosts of wickedness in the heavenly places."[7]

Benedict encourages us to find courage and fortitude in the face of an elusive and unrelenting opposition:

> The conflict goes deeper. It is a fight against a host of opponents that never stop coming; they cannot really be pinned down and have no proper name, only collective denominations.[8]

Benedict further describes the opponents:

> They also start out with superior advantage over man, and that is because of their superior position, their position 'in the heavens' of existence. They are also superior because their position is impenetrable and unassailable—their position, after all, is the 'atmosphere' of existence, which they themselves tilt in their favor and propagate

---

7   Ephesians 6:10-12.
8   Ratzinger, *Jesus of Nazareth vol. 1*, 175.

around themselves. These enemies are, finally, all full of essential, deadly malice" (Brief an die Epheser, p. 291).⁹

"Deadly malice" awaits peacemakers in the form of malicious agents who manufacture "atmospheric" fields of evil intention aligned against the Will of God. We minister to broken souls caught in force fields of evil intention—forces that dash souls against the Will of God. While men of casual faith often mock terms like "spiritual warfare" and "battlefield," reconcilers cannot be so cavalier. They know the phrases capture the spiritual vocation of assisting Christ to usher in a new kingdom:

> The beasts from the depths are confronted by the man from above. Just as the beasts from the depths represent hitherto existing secular kingdoms, the image of the "Son of Man," who comes "with the clouds of heaven," prophesies a totally new kingdom, a kingdom of "humanity," characterized by the real power that comes from God himself.¹⁰

St. Peter's Dilemma—Rules of Engagement

Studying Peter's tribulations can help us better grasp the transition to spiritual war. On the eve of the Crucifixion, Peter faced a dilemma: when Judas arrived at the garden

---

9   Ibid, 175.
10 Ibid., 325.

at Gethsemane, escorting guards determined to arrest Jesus, how was Peter supposed to respond? Commentators assume Peter succumbed to cowardice, but that analysis is faulty. Peter showed no hesitation or fear. To the contrary, he struck a guard with his sword and cut off his ear. This was not the act of a Disciple consumed with fear, not the act of a man descending into cowardice.

Peter knew what he was up against. Intuitively, he understood Judas in terms best expressed by John the Evangelist: "... Satan entered into him."[11] Peter knew the battle with the Evil One had commenced and he was prepared to fight. But Jesus surprised Peter and ordered him to stand down. Jesus introduced new "rules of engagement." Peter was overwhelmed with confusion, which, more than cowardice, caused him to falter that terrible night.

Later, in subsequent events narrated in the Acts of the Apostles, Jesus forgave Peter for his missteps and the disciple overcame his confusion. Christ showed Peter the power of his forgiveness and from that moment forward Peter used forgiveness as a spiritual weapon to transform destructive individuals. Spiritual-transformation-through-forgiveness became a central feature of the emerging Church:

> The Church is founded upon forgiveness. Peter himself is a personal embodiment of this truth, for he is permitted to be the bearer of the keys after having stumbled, confessed and received the

---

11   John 13:27.

> grace of pardon. ... She is held together by forgiveness, and Peter is the perpetual living reminder of this reality: she is not a communion of the perfect but a communion of sinners who need and seek forgiveness.[12]

Healing-through-forgiveness fueled the explosive expansion of the early Church. Christians who experienced divine forgiveness became ambassadors of peace and goodwill. God's unconditional forgiveness softened and humbled their hearts, making them more willing to forgive their enemies. This divine gift of forgiveness was eternal—springing from a well that never ran dry.

We can always repent. We can always ask for forgiveness. The option never expires. Conveying this good news is a vital step in reconciliation ministry. Even modest gestures of forgiveness invite reciprocation.

From this observation, a principle emerges: forgiveness reverses the deadly spiral of revenge. It signals a turning point in a broken relationship. It is not only the forgiven parties that are lifted up by God's grace. Those who forgive also find themselves infused with God's love. Both discover a mystical connection to the source of all being. This takes place in a richly textured series of events:

> Forgiveness and penance, grace and personal conversion are not contradictions but two sides of one and the same event. This fusion of activity and passivity expresses the essential form of

---

[12] Ratzinger, *Called to Communion*, 64.

human existence, for all of our creativity begins with our having been created, with our participation in God's creative activity.[13]

Reconcilers must master this paradigm of transformation through forgiveness:

> But true forgiveness exists only when the "price," the "equivalent value," is paid, when guilt is atoned by suffering, when there is expiation. The circular link between morality, forgiveness, and expiation cannot be forced apart at any point; when one element is missing, everything else is ruined.[14]

Jesus placed this counter-intuitive spiritual truth in Peter's hands and then commissioned him to teach forgiveness to his followers. Peter, with the winds of Pentecost at his back, gathered early Christians into a healing community to share the divine mystery of forgiveness:

> Forgiveness, together with its realization in me by way of penance and discipleship, is first of all the wholly personal center of all renewal. But because forgiveness touches the very core of the person, it gathers men together and is also the center of the renewal of the community.[15]

These principles, instrumental in the growth of the Church, have become a vital component of reconcilia-

---

13 Ibid., 149.
14 Ibid., 150.
15 Ibid., 151.

tion ministry. However, while the gift of forgiveness is available to all humankind, many souls have drifted and no longer accept the grace of God's forgiveness. In their minds, such grace is not real. This view has created a spiritual crisis, as Benedict observed:

> I believe that the core of the spiritual crisis of our time has its basis in the obscuration of the grace of forgiveness.[16]

There's no doubt that hostility and violence among humans can be linked to a deficit of forgiveness. People commit harmful acts, and then experience guilt. Guilt creates inner turmoil, which fuels an impulse to lash out. Guilt-ridden people strike out and cause additional harm, which increases guilt once again. Hostility feeds on itself, escalates, and then spirals out of control. We end up with a world armed to the teeth with deadly weapons. Repetitive rounds of harmful deeds are followed by gut-wrenching guilt and brutal retaliation that escalate the violence:

> The result is a chain of trespasses in which the evil of guilt grows ceaselessly and becomes more and more inescapable.[17]

This ballet of evil intentions and deeds occurs in a vacuum of forgiveness, even though "the Lord is telling

---

16 Ibid., 149.
17 Ratzinger, *Jesus of Nazareth* v.1, 157.

us that guilt can be overcome only by forgiveness, not by retaliation."[18] Souls desperately seek escape from endless rounds of guilt and retribution, but their escape requires the forgiveness they lack. At Christ's behest, Saint Peter formalized a solution: *he instituted the sacred rite of penance and forgiveness.*

Perhaps the existence of this rite, often called "confession," has kept a lid on the potential destruction of this planet. But now, as the role of the Church in the world diminishes, we must anticipate an increase in violence and tyranny. Will the loss of the conduit to Christ's forgiveness cause destruction and tyranny to explode out of control? Caution is warranted. Too often we find the concept of forgiveness, like the phrase "God is Love," being reduced to mere greeting-card sentiment. Reconciliation ministry demands a deeper understanding—like the understanding that came from Peter's tribulations.

Understanding Forgiveness

Forgiveness bestows peace in the present by healing the past. This demands work and sacrifice. Benedict commented on the devotion required:

> What is forgiveness, really? What happens when forgiveness takes place? Guilt is a reality, an objective force; it has caused destruction that must be repaired. For this reason, forgiveness must be

---

18   Ibid.

more than a matter of ignoring, of merely trying to forget. Guilt must be worked through, healed, and thus overcome. Forgiveness exacts a price— first of all from the person who forgives.[19]

Forgiveness unfolds in a series of disciplined steps. Parties accept God's unconditional forgiveness. Then, filled with grace flowing from that forgiveness, they forgive those who harmed them. Reciprocal rounds of apology and forgiveness follow. Peacemakers wield forgiveness like a spiritual scythe, clearing away thickets of hostility and guilt, clearing paths to I-Thou encounters.

Forgiveness endows parties with new spiritual eyes, with which they can better see the condition of those who harmed them. With new eyes they see enemies "as they are"—impaired, wounded, and trapped in a supernatural matrix of lies. Jesus expressed this stark vision of desperate men with some of the most powerful words found in scripture, "Father, forgive them, they know not what they do."[20] Jesus' sentiment spoken from the cross— forgive them as they act out of ignorance—is the genesis of a new spiritual vision nurtured by a forgiving heart.

The new spiritual vision reveals that transgressors have been snared in the Serpent's trap. Suffering with pain they struggle like a wild animal bloodied by the iron jaws of a hunter's trap. They growl and bite those who get too close. Tragically, some people react to the trapped

---

19   Ibid., 158.
20   Luke 23:34.

creature by beating them in a frenzy of retribution. Participants in this ugly drama are unaware they're in fallen-world bondage. We can say: "they know not what they do."

However, when a peacemaker facilitates the forgiveness paradigm, both the trapped party and those harmed are transformed. They are no longer who they once were. The person who forgives:

> [A]lso involves the other, the trespasser, in this process of transformation, of inner purification, and both parties, suffering all the way through and overcoming evil, are made new. At this point, we encounter the mystery of Christ's Cross.[21]

The miracle of divine forgiveness delivers both parties to the foot of the cross where they encounter the sacred mystery of Christ's forgiveness extended to all mankind. His unconditional love beckons to souls, inviting them to seek spiritual transformation:

> True forgiveness is something quite different from weak indulgence. Forgiveness is demanding and requires both parties, the one who forgives and the one who is forgiven, to do so with all their minds and hearts.[22]

Forgiveness cannot be purchased cheaply, but rather must be drawn from the deep well of spiritual conversion.

---

21 Ibid., 159.
22 Pope Benedict XVI. "February 28," *Benedictus*, 73.

Unfortunately, in our contemporary culture, forgiveness is often diminished to a social nicety or reduced to a lawyer's plea for leniency. This cheapened version of forgiveness is detached from its sacred origin. Benedict rejects this trend. Removing the cross from our understanding does not work:

> A Jesus who sanctions everything is a Jesus without the cross, for such a Jesus would not need the torment of the cross to save mankind. As a matter of fact, the cross is being increasingly banished from theology and reinterpreted as just a vexatious mischance or a purely political event.[23]

In contrast to contemporary trends that cheapen forgiveness, Benedict argues that forgiveness, and the cross from which it was bestowed, should be conceived in a sacred context:

> The cross as reconciliation, as a means of forgiving and saving, is incompatible with a certain modern mode of thought. Only when the relationship between truth and love is rightly comprehended can the cross be comprehensible in its true theological depth.[24]

Reconcilers facilitate comprehension of this relationship between truth and love. For them, it is a practical matter. They know that parties who love enough to for-

---

23 Ibid.
24 Pope Benedict XVI, "February 28," *Benedictus*, 73.

give others acquire a heightened spiritual vision, an ability to perceive deeper levels of truth. This allows them to see that offenders "do not truly know what they did." Ironically, they also see they were at fault; they also did not fully "know what they did." But, with new spiritual sight, they realize that all parties involved in the conflict lacked full understanding.

Parties eventually come to know that increased love brings increased truth, but before they reach that epiphany, they work in the darkness of the Evil One's shadow where evil transpires. Fortunately, a light shines through this darkness. The power of forgiveness, discovered during reconciliation, disperses the shadows and reveals sacred truth:

> Forgiveness has to do with truth. That is why it requires the Son's cross and our conversion. Forgiveness is, in fact, the restoration of the truth, the renewal of being, and the vanquishment of the lies that lurk in every sin; sin is by nature a departure from the truth of one's own nature and, by consequence, from the truth of the Creator God.[25]

Forgiveness says to the transgressor, "I see your divine essence, even though it is smothered by falsehoods and illusion." Forgiveness acknowledges the full truth of man's condition and the full truth of his essence. Those who forgive an offender acknowledge that he has been

---

25   Ibid.

suffering in a soul-crushing trap. They understand that their brothers, consumed with pain, might strike out. Tragically, most men do not acknowledge this truth and instead beat their delinquent brother into quiet submission. Ironically, those who beat a transgressor today will stumble tomorrow and receive the same treatment.

The world in which Christ took up the cross resembles the fallen world of today—a shadowy world of pain and quiet desperation. How should we respond to this terrible reality? Perhaps the only valid response is compassionate forgiveness. That being said, compassion demands change. It does not allow undesirable conditions to persist. Forgiveness should never be an expression of apathy—a resignation to evil and distress. To the contrary, forgiveness chips away at ignorance. Reconciliation brings transgressions into the light of spiritual truth.

At this point, the forgiving party may offer the transgressor an opportunity to reflect on the harm caused by their words, intentions, and actions. Punishment is held in abeyance while guilty parties inspect their past misdeeds. This frees them to seek a deeper understanding of why they harmed others, to ask, Why did I do that? In moments of stillness, they contemplate their actions. When wrongdoers reflect on the truth of their offenses, without duress, they may experience conversion and transformation. Their view of reality changes. Essentially, forgiveness works as a solvent, stripping away layer after layer of evil intention, dissolving the grimy residue of harmful deeds.

Why forgive? Some desire closure. Others forgive because they know that most people "know not what they do." Ignorance leads them astray. Transgressions occur in the absence of discipline and understanding. We are brought to the conclusion that divine forgiveness is vital for the salvation of those who have fallen asleep while trapped in a fallen world.

Fortunately, forgiveness short-circuits the use of raw force and demands that parties forego trading an "eye for an eye." Offenders are invited to review the consequences of their actions in a prayerful manner. Release does not happen overnight. Ample time is needed for them to recover their hijacked free will.

Peter's Dilemma ... continued

In the days leading up to Pentecost, Peter's discipleship matured. He came to understand the rules of engagement instituted when Jesus conferred upon him the power to forgive sin:

> [I]t becomes apparent that in its core the power to bind and to loose means the authority to forgive sins, an authority that in Peter is committed to the Church (cf. Mt 18:15-18).[26]

Peter, who once experienced difficulty with the new rules of engagement, now led the way. His path differed

---

26   Ratzinger, *Called to Communion*, 64.

dramatically from the tragic path Judas walked, as recounted by John the Evangelist:

> For John, what happened to Judas is beyond psychological explanation. He has come under the dominion of another. Anyone who breaks off a relationship with Jesus, casting off his easy yoke, does not attain liberty, does not become free, but succumbs to other powers. To put it another way, he betrays his friendship because he is in the grip of another power to which he has opened himself.[27]

Judas, who became ensnared in the Evil One's grip, compromised his exercise of free will and suffered spiritual ruin. However, even in the extreme case of Judas, a soul need never lose all hope:

> True, the light shed by Jesus into Judas' soul was not completely extinguished. He does take a step toward conversion: "I have sinned," he says to those who commissioned him. He tries to save Jesus, and gives the money back (Mt 27:3-5). Everything pure and great that he had received from Jesus remained inscribed on his soul—he could not forget it.[28]

Judas, though tormented and anguished, nonetheless turned slowly toward salvation. Ultimately, he failed and the Evil One's demonic power negated his free will. Trag-

---

27 Pope Benedict XVI, *Jesus of Nazareth vol. 2*, 68.
28 Ibid.

ically, Judas failed to exercise the option that would have secured his release. He failed to pray for God's forgiveness. Lacking the guidance of a reconciler, he lost sight of this sacred option:

> His second tragedy—after the betrayal—is that he can no longer believe in forgiveness. His remorse turns into despair. Now he sees only himself and his darkness; he no longer sees the light of Jesus, which can illuminate and overcome the darkness.[29]

Ironically, Judas needed the type of rescue that subsequently became the primary ministry of the church. Reconcilers armed with faith and reason stand by, ready to escort wayward souls on the road to salvation. They're prepared to help them find the courage to extend apologies and ask forgiveness. Forgiveness clears the barriers blocking harmony, unity, and salvation. Reconciliation ministry echoes themes of exorcism:

> To "exorcise" the world—to establish it in the light of the *ratio* (reason) that comes from eternal creative reason and its saving goodness and refers back to it—that is a permanent, central task of the messengers of Jesus Christ.[30]

Those who rescue captive souls expect to be tested by adversaries. They knowingly put themselves at risk when

---

29 Ibid.
30 Ratzinger, *Jesus of Nazareth vol. 1*, 174.

they "exorcise" the clusters of traits that comprise a false self. Confident in their ability to parry pedestrian verbal attacks, they may feel secure in their position, only to be hit with explosive salvos of evil intentions. The abuse that targets reconcilers bears an uncanny resemblance to the abuse aimed at exorcists. Reconcilers find intriguing similarities between clusters of false-self traits and "legions" of demons. The ministry of peace overlaps the ministry of deliverance; both mirror the work Peter performed in the early Church.

Spiritual battle is difficult, but peacemakers can triumph with the weapons of apology, forgiveness, and reconciliation. They can restore the salvific relationship with God. This work is vital to the Church's mission; we can predict with confidence that only those faith communities that endorse reconciliation ministry will flourish in the tradition of Peter.

Christian Response to Evil

Profound spiritual lessons from Christ's Passion and Resurrection guided Peter. Those lessons also inspire reconciliation ministry:

> In Jesus' Passion, all the filth of the world touches the infinitely pure one, the soul of Jesus Christ and, hence, the Son of God himself. While it is usually the case that anything unclean touching something clean renders it unclean, here it is the other way around: when the world, with all the injustice and cruelty that make it unclean, comes

into contact with the infinitely pure one—then he, the pure one, is the stronger.[31]

This stunning concept—the unclean become clean when they come in contact with Christ—is absolutely critical for faith-based reconciliation. It sets our approach apart from all others. Reconciliation ministry is inherently Christocentric, as evil in the world is overcome by Christ's supernatural presence:

> Through this contact, the filth of the world is truly absorbed, wiped out, and transformed in the pain of infinite love. Because infinite good is now at hand in the man Jesus, the counter-weight to all wickedness is present and active within world history, and the good is always infinitely greater than the vast mass of evil, however terrible it may be.[32]

Benedict reveals a core principle of spiritual warfare: *Christ does not resist the Evil One with brute force but, instead, pervades the fallen world with a mystical presence that transforms evil intentions.* This supernatural "rule of engagement" challenged Peter who did not suffer cowardice but rather was staggered with disbelief at the counter-intuitive rules of spiritual warfare. Peter's reaction is our reaction—how am I supposed to do *that*? Benedict guides further reflection:

---

[31] Pope Benedict XVI, *Jesus of Nazareth* vol. 2, 231.
[32] Ibid.

> At this point we run into a second, more profound transformation: he transforms, from within, the act of violent men against him into an act of giving on behalf of these men—into an act of love. This is dramatically recognizable in the scene of the Garden of Olives. What he teaches in the Sermon on the Mount, he now does: he does not offer violence against violence, as he might have done, but puts an end to violence by transforming it into love.[33]

This transformation of violence, accomplished with the elixir of divine love, captures the "alchemy" of spiritual warfare. The "magic" shines forth from Jesus' words and deeds:

> The act of killing, of death, is changed into an act of love; violence is defeated by love. This is the fundamental transformation on which all the rest is based. It is the true transformation that the world needs and which alone can redeem the world. Since Christ in an act of love has transformed and defeated violence from within, death itself is transformed: love is stronger than death. It remains forever.[34]

Peacemakers seek to facilitate a version of this spiritual transformation. They know the phrase "God is love" transcends mere speculation. With this knowledge, they

---

33 Ratzinger, *The Essential Pope Benedict XVI*, 82.
34 Ibid.

arrive in the realm of the miraculous with certainty that their ministry can hasten world peace. Nonetheless, worldly consensus disputes the idea that "love is stronger than death" and declares the topic unworthy of discussion. Destructive hidden influences do not want us to know that their intentions can be diminished and then vaporized by love.

Peacemakers do not succumb to doubt but rather turn to humble prayer and seek God's love. Resting in the Lord, they imbue peacemaking with a prayerful stillness that allows disputants to listen more closely to God:

> One who is trapped in slavery, darkness, and suffering comes to hear the word of God in his or her life. As the seed of that word is planted, it begins to take root. The more clearly the word of God is heard in that person's life, the greater the transformation that begins to unfold.[35]

The Holy Spirit breaks into dungeons to rescue souls. He awakens those who slumber, inspires those who waste away in apathy, and ignites dreams of hope. These dreams seed a transformation. The Spirit's light becomes a luminous catalyst that guides parties toward a brighter future.

Captive souls must then take responsibility for their own journey. Some hail the jailbreak and embrace the freedom it promises. Others remain vulnerable and afraid even as they take the first steps toward casting

---

35 Collins, *The Word Made Love*, 156.

off bondage. They beckon to peacemakers, seeking allies in their fight against evil. Hearing the call, peacemakers come to their defense.

However, when the sentries of the wily Evil One detect spiritual warriors mounting an offensive, they circle, isolate, and distract the warrior. The sentries know that fleeing souls will seek asylum in the church, so they cut off their escape route. They plant saboteurs in the faith community who intercept fleeing souls as they reach the doors of the Church. Experienced peacemakers anticipate the tactics. They're not naive regarding the ability of Satan to reach into the ecclesial body:

> [T]here is also the fact that attacks on the Pope and the Church come not only from without, but the sufferings of the Church come precisely from within the Church, from the sin existing within the Church.[36]

Benedict's warning should not be taken lightly. When a weakened Church fails to field an army of highly trained reconcilers, she is no longer able to defend against corrosive hidden influences. The consequences are tragic. Souls who once found asylum in the Church are betrayed. A prerequisite for victory over evil is a strong Church fully engaged in the battle:

> [W]e are realists in expecting that evil always at-

---

36 Pope Benedict XVI, *Interview of the Holy Father Benedict XVI with Journalists During the Flight to Portugal, May 11, 2010* (Libreria Editrice Vaticana, 2010).

tacks, attacks from within and without, yet that the forces of good are also ever present and that, in the end, the Lord is more powerful than evil and Our Lady is for us the visible, motherly guarantee of God's goodness, which is always the last word in history.[37]

The Church has been gifted with an inherent potential to triumph over destructive evil intentions. The work of dedicated peacemakers makes this potential real. However, the Church's success in defeating evil depends on the Church deploying adequate resources. If we hope to hasten world peace, the Church must dramatically boost the number of spiritual warriors engaged in reconciliation ministry.

On the Battlefield

Wise peacemakers map the battlefield and assess prevailing conditions. They find that widespread spiritual destruction has left them with a stunning lack of allies. Satan's hideous misrepresentation of God has made people not want to know such a God. Divine relationship becomes mocked and antipathy toward faith is rampant. Spiritual warriors find few safe havens. In many quarters, opposition to God becomes the default position, the cultural norm. This ongoing assault against the supernatural disparages man's endowment of the image and likeness of

---

[37] Ibid.

God. People are deceived into denying their true nature; they forfeit their identity and rights as spiritual beings:

> The first and most fundamental of all human rights is the right to God... Without this basic right, which is also the right to truth, the other human rights are not enough. Without this fundamental right to truth and to God, man becomes degraded to the level of a mere creature of needs.[38]

Blinded to truth, victims abandon their spiritual heritage. They wander into ego traps that enforce illusory identities. Spiritual warriors must march into this menacing territory and rescue embattled souls. Benedict cheers the rescue campaign, noting that God did not create man to live in prisons:

> Let us ask him to enter into the spiritual prisons of this age, into the darkness of our lack of truth, revealing himself as the Victor who tears down the gates and says to us, "I, your God, have become your Son. Come out! I have not created you to be in prison forever. I did not make you for the dungeon."[39]

Reconcilers who mastermind prison breaks imitate Christ. They discern the warden's tactics, decrypt the jailhouse playbook, and learn how materialist illusions imprison souls. They defeat discouragement and unlock

---

38 Ratzinger, *The Essential Pope Benedict XVI*, 58.
39 Ibid., 60.

prison gates. Knowing the mechanisms of spiritual entrapment, they choreograph escapes and lead souls to freedom.

Peacemakers who map the Evil One's prisons are positioned to help all souls, as every soul needs maps that detail prison security weaknesses they can exploit. Even those who strongly profess faith need an escape plan, as was the case with blessed John Henry Newman:

> Until that moment, Newman thought like the average men of his time and indeed like the average men of today, who do not simply exclude the existence of God, but consider it as something uncertain, something with no essential role to play in their lives. What appeared genuinely real to him, as to the men of his and our day, is the empirical, matter that can be grasped. This is the "reality" according to which one finds one's bearings. The "real" is what can be grasped, it is the things that can be calculated and taken in one's hand.[40]

Newman eventually debunked false narratives:

> In his conversion, Newman recognized that it is exactly the other way round: that God and the soul, man's spiritual identity, constitute what is genuinely real, what counts. These are much more real than objects that can be grasped. This conversion was a Copernican revolution. What

---

40 Pope Benedict XVI, *Address of His Holiness Benedict XVI on the Occassion of Christmas Greetings to the Roman Curia, Monday, December 20, 2010.*

had previously seemed unreal and secondary was now revealed to be the genuinely decisive element. Where such a conversion takes place, it is not just a person's theory that changes: the fundamental shape of life changes. We are all in constant need of such conversion: then we are on the right path.[41]

Reconcilers must be attuned to those moments when the fundamental shape of life changes. They must recognize turning points and develop an intuitive sense for the rhythm of transformation. They must learn to intuit when an infusion of love will carry the transformation to fruition. With the Holy Spirit's assistance, they keep "the dance" going by facilitating love, which draws parties forward to new discoveries:

> He who loves wishes to know. A true love of Christ, therefore, expresses itself also in the will to know him and everything that pertains to him.[42]

Disputants who undergo life-changing conversions emerge with a passion for breaking free from spiritual dungeons where they once languished. They pursue love and wisdom with new passion and purpose. Having escaped bondage, they become spiritual warriors in their own right.

---

41 Ibid.
42 Ratzinger, *The Essential Pope Benedict XVI*, 267.

Morality Considered

Souls who escape spiritual prisons to reconcile with God see morality in a fresh light. They no longer consider morality apart from relationship. They have a new appreciation for virtues that make loving relationships possible. The apex of relationship and morality, they find, is found in the I–Thou encounter:

> [M]orality, which begins with this look directed to the other, is the custodian of the truth and the dignity of man: man needs morality in order to be himself and not lose his dignity in the world of things.[43]

Morality—previously confined to lists of behavioral edicts—becomes sound reasoning that ensures loving relationships. Older versions of morality—laundry lists of memorized rote rules—are replaced by divine collaboration, a dynamic process of repairing loving relationships based on the truths of divine relationship.

Morality derived from divine collaboration produces reasoned decisions that honor reciprocity—the golden rule. Collaboration prompts the question: Will I treat the other as I treat myself? Divine collaboration expands the question: will I honor the divine within the other? This leads to a new and perhaps unexpected result: *sound moral reasoning requires a reconciled relationship with God.* If a

---

43   Ratzinger, *Christianity and the Crisis of Cultures*, 70.

party has not reconciled divine relationship, they struggle with moral reasoning and do not grasp morality in an optimum manner.

The protocol of divine collaboration calls on disputants to align their intentions and decisions with the Will of God at the same time they engage in a search for mutual satisfaction.[44] Mediators oversee the process. They facilitate communication and exchange of affinity; they choreograph a negotiated and reciprocal exchange; they seek to maximize party satisfaction. Perhaps most important, they help parties overcome destructive hidden influences that foment distrust. Morality is a tool mediators use to help parties channel their free will.

Peacemakers coach moral decisions that enhance sound relationships, but they run into opposition when Satan targets those relationships for destruction with supernatural evil intention. But reconcilers persist and use morality as guardrails that protect parties who otherwise might be shoved off the path into the ditch.

Benedict's theology of relationship provides a sound context within which to evaluate morality. It provides suitable criteria for moral decisions, choices that either enhance or destroy relationships. Each moral decision affects the flow of divine love between man and God. The choice increases or retards the amount of love that flows. In this model, reconcilers do not hand out lists of moral

---

44   Reconcilers triage healing, set venues, establish order. They gain advantage over destructive hidden influences by controlling the process.

precepts and expect disputants to immediately revise their views. Rather, change emerges during the give-and-take of negotiation. Morality takes shape in actual exchanges between living souls. Morality addresses the actual living relationship. It is not abstract, scholastic, or rote catechism. Rather it applies to specific situations with real consequences. This applied morality is a close brother to applied theology.

Some people will incorrectly identify and criticize this approach as a form of relativism. They will claim that arriving at moral solutions in specific situations does not honor "objective" morality that stands by itself, separate from life. However, there are no pristine scrolls of moral edicts hanging in a separate, untouched "objective" realm. That realm does not exist. Those who insist on "objective morality" are simply those looking for a way to transcend trendy fads that lack a foundation in fundamental truth. They do not realize they are actually seeking Absolute Subjectivity. Morality arises from divine relationship and the baseline of Absolute Subjectivity that is God. A morality based on divine relationship operates at the most fundamental level possible.

Let us consider how it works: parties arrive at mediation under the sway of evil influences but reconcilers intercede. They remedy deficits of divine love by fostering shared affinity and desire for mutual satisfaction. They help parties realign their exercise of free will with the Will of God. They help parties satisfy their interests, making sure they also satisfy God's interests. A working definition of morality takes shape: *morality guides a person's actions so as to enhance divine relationship.*

During divine collaboration, a moral compass brings a party's intentions in line with divine will. They carefully chart their journey to avoid enemy territory where their wills might be recaptured. In addition, as they develop spiritual mirrors, they are able to reflect the light of divine love toward their fellow man. In this sense, collaboration allows people to become a conduit for the kind of grace that nurtures relationships. After a party jettisons false-self debris, they reflect God's grace more brightly. Benedict describes the emerging reflection of God's love:

> [W]e too succeed in looking at others in a manner that respects their personal dignity if we experience how God looks at us in love. It is this look that reveals to us how precious is our person.[45]

Parties who share the "look of love" motivate others to seek unburdening. Divine love becomes infectious, contagious. The river of divine love sweeps human intentions into alignment with God. The look of love is a central tenet of faith:

> Christianity is this remembrance of the look of love that the Lord directs to man, this look that preserves the fullness of his truth and the ultimate guarantee of his dignity.[46]

---

45   Ibid., 71.
46   Ibid.

When a soul abandons its inherent ability to mirror divine love, that soul finds that their moral compass malfunctions. They veer off the path into darkness. Soon, they are recaptured by the Evil One and escorted back to the dungeon where they will languish in chains, tortured into believing humans are soulless creatures that cannot mirror God's love. Sequestered in darkness, they no longer perceive the face of God.

> [I]t is only when you have lost God that you have lost yourself; then you are nothing more than a random product of evolution. Then the "dragon" really has won.[47]

The Battlefield Revisited

Peacemakers who have become spiritual warriors do not enter battle alone but rather find that Christ wages war on the same battlefield. In the exegesis of Biblical scholars, Benedict uncovers Christ's battle plan:

> They argue that Jesus began by offering the good news of God's kingdom and his unconditional forgiveness, but that he had to acknowledge the rejection of this offer and so came to identify his mission with that of the Suffering Servant. They argue that after his offer was refused, he realized that the only remaining path was that of vicarious expiation: that he had to take upon himself the

---

47   Ratzinger, *Jesus of Nazareth vol. 1*, 166.

disaster looming over Israel, thereby obtaining salvation for many.[48]

This concept of vicarious expiation is tremendously difficult to grasp, and even harder to put into action. We are challenged to reflect deeply on how God's forgiveness is extended to mankind. It is this message of forgiveness that softens the hearts of prodigal sons and daughters; it is their subsequent remorse that motivates them to launch their homecoming pilgrimage. Prodigal offspring drawn homeward by unconditional forgiveness reach home to find a feast, a banquet table overflowing with the Lord's bounty. They encounter a feast of divine love. Benedict captures this dynamic:

> [T]hus ensues a dialogue of love, that wholly new kind of unity that love alone can create. The being of the other is not absorbed or abolished, but rather, in giving itself, it becomes fully itself. .... worship now has a new aspect: the healing of wounded freedom, atonement, purification, deliverance from estrangement.[49]

Peacemakers enter the trenches of the fallen world to foster healing, facilitate atonement, and rescue prodigal sons and daughters. They heal wounds suffered by naive runaways, who return home as honored guests who are invited to take part in sacred reunion.

---

48 Pope Benedict XVI, *Jesus of Nazareth vol. 2*, 120.
49 Pope Benedict XVI, *The Spirit of the Liturgy*, 33.

Destructive hidden influences, however, take offense when reconcilers extract lost souls from the wasteland. A peacemaker may feel an urge to fight back using force. But, if they are wise, they know peacemaking can be sabotaged by the illusion of a victory won through force. Spiritual warriors transform the very essence the opposition; their spiritual weapons mystically transform states of being and render the enemy no longer an enemy.

This last point is worth stressing: *a valid and lasting victory transforms the enemy.* Rather than use force to subdue another who intends us harm, we seek their rebirth. At the end of the battle, the enemy no longer exists in his original form. Truth, love, and unconditional forgiveness dematerialize the enemy's false self, dissolving the ego self that is bound to desire, fear, and hostility. The spiritual warrior becomes a sculptor chipping away at false-self plaster. When an enemy encounters a spiritual warrior in battle, the enemy finds his ego-self disappearing—amputated by a spiritual sword. As the battle nears conclusion, the false self who once sought to destroy others no longer exists. Though the transition to divine self may not yet be complete, destructive beings have been disarmed.

False selves seeking to do harm are analogous to wild beasts snared in the rusty jaws of hunting traps, driven to madness by the pain. They will continue to strike out at others until they are freed from crushing pain. Once set free, they will abandon the enemy posture.

But how do peacemakers release souls from the traps that have turned them into agents of destruction? Perhaps they will want to reflect on how Christ took the violence of the false self into himself. He owned it, controlled it, and transformed it with the alchemy of divine love. He inspected transgressions in full, viewing all causes and conditions with the supernatural vision of unconditional forgiveness. Falsehoods were transformed to dust, leaving behind only the likeness and image of God. This counter-intuitive, vicarious expiation is possible solely because all things originated in the Mind of God, and thus all things can be transformed in the Mind of God. The very nature of this universe, understood accurately, makes miracles possible. That which is counter-intuitive and paradoxical is rendered common sense.

Extending unconditional divine forgiveness dissolves resistance and unsticks the oppositional embrace of conflict. In other words, forgiveness melts the glue that entangles fallen souls to conflict and binds them to their sins. Disputants no longer seek to crush their opposition; instead, they practice non-resistance coupled with spiritual transformation. Reconcilers facilitate apology and forgiveness, and thus indirectly facilitate mystical transformation. They disentangle false selves and free souls from bondage.

Know Your Enemy

Spiritual warriors must know their enemy. On their journey, they will encounter legions of lost souls drafted into the Serpent's army, tasked with forwarding intentions that oppose the Will of God. Left to their own free will, these souls do not seek to do harm. As soon as their wills are alloyed with the Serpent's will, however, they lose control of their own fate and become proxy fighters for the Evil One.

In an ironic twist, when these proxy fighters regain the freedom to exercise their free will, they turn on those who once controlled their lives. They become spiritual warriors in the battle against the Evil One. Prior to their conversion, they pit false self against false self in a never-ending clash best captured by the words issued from the cross: "They know not what they do."

If they fail to recognize the Evil One choreographing the battle, they end up imitating Don Quixote tilting at windmills and chasing shadows. In contrast, those who finally recognize the true enemy join the battle against destructive hidden influences that oppose the Will of God.

Reflection

Peacemakers who assume the role of spiritual warriors would do well to reflect on the battlefield metaphor. They may be inspired to raid dungeons and unchain imprisoned souls. They may dream of launching daring prison escapes—springing locks, evading guards, and defeating perimeter defenses. Seeing the world in this way gives them the courage to face the threats they will encounter in their everyday lives. As they progress in their training, they'll come to appreciate spiritual discipline, counter-intuitive weapons, and New Covenant rules of engagement.

Reconcilers should also reflect on the concept of forgiveness. If they have not personally experienced divine forgiveness, they may want to attend retreats that explore the mystery of God's unconditional mercy. If they have received divine forgiveness, yet still find it difficult to forgive others, they'll want to enroll in advanced training for pastoral counselors, where they'll study the Rite of Reconciliation and its fruits.[50]

Aspiring peacemakers may wrestle with the obvious question: Will spiritual warriors, those who battle evil, survive the conflict? Is it wise for them to venture into enemy territory? Or is it better to retreat behind monastery walls? How will they know that they possess sufficient courage for battlefield duty? How will they know that they can meet the demands of the ministry?

As they survey the battlefield, perhaps for the first time, they may truly understand how reconciliation ministry dovetails with the sacred promise of eternal life. They may recognize that their ultimate survival is assured and they can fight without fear. Their success in saving others, however, will depend on diligent training and preparation. They cannot lag or falter. They must renew their dedication to the ministry.

---

50 See the Catholic Rite of Penance.

FOURTEEN

Mystical Union: Eucharistic Reconciliation

Our reflection on mystical union with Christ begins with a breathtaking idea: man is endowed with the image and likeness of God and therefore man possesses an inherent ability to access the Mind of God. Mystical union, experienced by mystics throughout the ages, is the intermingling of individual spiritual consciousness with divine consciousness. This union of consciousness plays a vital role in reconciliation with God.

The probability of achieving mystical union becomes more likely when one lives a monastic life, yet the commitment required is appropriate for only a select few.[1] Thus, for our purposes, we will focus on the relatively brief union with Christ that occurs during the Eucharistic celebration, the Mass. In this rite, also called the Blessed

---

[1] An account of monasticism lies beyond the scope of this work. Those who desire further study may wish to consult: Thomas Merton; St. Bonaventure; St. Francis of Assisi; St. Augustine; The Desert Fathers; St. John of the Cross.

Sacrament, people seek a prayerful encounter with the Real Presence of Christ. They seek mystical union; they seek to bring their individual spiritual consciousness into Communion with divine consciousness.

Liturgy and Reconciliation

Reconciliation echoes aspects of the liturgy. In fact, peacemakers are often inspired by the liturgy. For example, during the liturgy the faithful pray, "thy will be done on earth, as it is in heaven." Reconcilers echo this same sentiment when they facilitate the realignment of individual will with the Will of God.

Peacemaking parallels other aspects of the liturgy: chipping away false-self traits echoes the renunciation of sin; the study of scripture to discern divine will parallels the Liturgy of the Word; seeking an I-Thou encounter parallels the act of seeking Communion with the Real Presence. Disputants and worshippers alike pray that their lives will be infused with divine will, joining heaven and earth:

> The essence of heaven is oneness with God's will, the oneness of will and truth. Earth becomes "heaven" when and insofar as God's will is done there; and it is merely "earth," the opposite of heaven, when and insofar as it withdraws from the will of God.[2]

---

2   Ratzinger, *Jesus of Nazareth* vol. 1, 147.

"Oneness" achieved through a prayerful encounter with a living God echoes the core goal of reconciliation ministry. There can be no greater reconciliation than to be at-one-with another, no greater reconciliation than unity. This "oneness" stands at the heart of a theology of relationship, the theology that Benedict, our mentor, advances. This renewed union, which emerges from a reconciled divine relationship, is frequently glimpsed during the Mass:

> [E]very time the community gathers to participate in the Eucharistic sacrifice of the eternal Word made flesh in history ... the dialogue between God and his people is given concrete reality.[3]

This dialogical "concrete reality"—a universe built on dialogue with God—is consistent with Christian Idealism, consistent with the idea that Creation emanates from the Mind of God. During Holy Communion the veil that separates heaven and earth is rent, bringing relationship with God into the present in a very concrete way. This is a key aspect of Benedict's dialogical theology:

> The dialogical mode of doing theology is also arguably more capable of plumbing the depths of the essential truth of the Christian vision, which has at its center the mystery of the "tearing of the veil" previously separating heaven and earth

---

[3] Collins, *The Word Made Love,* 118.

and now makes possible intimate communion between God and humanity.[4]

During the Blessed Sacrament, worshippers taste reconciliation with God and anticipate reconciliation beyond this life. Christopher Collins captured Benedict's view of these Eucharistic dynamics:

> For Ratzinger the divine liberation of humanity begun in baptism is most fully realized in the dynamics of the eucharistic liturgy, wherein Christ, *caritas* itself, comes to the poor of the assembly, speaks to their hearts, and gives them his love, his own heart, sacramentally.[5]

Eucharistic communion is not mere stage play, not a form of theater. The humbling spiritual experience of communion requires more than just showing up. Worshippers must prepare in earnest. The full power of the rite is not known until one has spent years or even decades of study, reflection, prayer, and worship.

The Eucharist might rightfully be called a path to peace; it can be seen as a prayerful meditation that leads to reconciliation on the vertical axis. Worshippers seek forgiveness for transgressions. This is followed by the liturgy of the Word, a reading of scripture that orients worshippers toward Holy Communion, in which they will be infused with divine love and grace.

---

[4] Ibid., 19.
[5] de Gaàl, *The Theology of Pope Benedict XVI*, 127.

Initial steps of the Mass, similar to initial steps of peacemaking, are devoted to stripping away false-self traits. This "identity sculpting" lifts burdens, allowing worshippers to move toward Communion with the Real Presence:

> Insofar as this losing of self occurs, the church ultimately gains its true self in this sacramental union, because it is in the liturgy that what has separated people from their God is now overcome and they can be reconciled.[6]

During the Eucharist, heaven bestows divine love on the faithful, consistent with dialogical theology: "Relational, dialogical love then becomes the proper lens for understanding all of history and even being itself."[7] The liturgy reveals lived truths regarding mankind's existential journey. The history of mankind has been condensed into a sacrament.

For the sake of clarity, we should explore a key liturgical reality: in the Blessed Sacrament, the spiritual consciousness of worshippers co-mingles with the Mind of God. When souls experience Holy Communion, they participate in co-being with God. This co-mingling of consciousness is a key property of divine relationship. Benedict explains how this applies to a sense of "one body":

> [C]ommunion means the fusion of existences;

---

[6] Ibid., 128.
[7] Ibid., 91.

> just as in the taking of nourishment the body assimilates foreign matter to itself, and is thereby enabled to live, in the same way my "I" is "assimilated" to that of Jesus, it is made similar to him in an exchange that increasingly breaks through the lines of division.[8]

During Holy Communion relationships are no longer constrained by the boundaries of the mundane world. Instead, they're infused with being-at-one-with Christ. This idea is captured by phrase "the Body of Christ":

> It is the event of "gathering", in which the Lord joins us to one another. The formula "the Church is the Body of Christ" thus states that the Eucharist, in which the Lord gives us his body and makes us one body, forever remains the place where the Church is generated, where the Lord himself never ceases to found her anew; in the Eucharist the Church is most compactly herself—in all places, yet one only, just as he is one only.[9]

The progression of the Blessed Sacrament generates constantly increasing grace that leads to mystical union. A similar progression occurs during peacemaking: *when mediation begins, parties are far removed from a state of grace.* They simply hope to resolve differences and move on. During reconciliation, this changes: parties draw upon God's mystical grace; they integrate natural and supernat-

---

8   Ratzinger, *Called to Communion*, 37.
9   Ibid.

ural concerns into a seamless reality. Mundane interests are transcended, much as worshippers rise above mundane reality during the Eucharist:

> [T]o celebrate the Eucharist means to enter into the openness of a glorification of God that embraces both heaven and earth, an openness effected by the Cross and Resurrection.[10]

During the Eucharistic rite, worshippers sample mystical union—the same union experienced more deeply by contemplative monastics. This mystical experience, though fleeting, reveals a comprehensive reality:

> Everything, then, comes together: the horizontal and the vertical, the uniqueness of God and the unity of mankind, the communion of all who worship in spirit and in truth.[11]

Mediation, in a parallel manner, introduces parties to a greater reality. Reconciliation, when conducted in a faith context, overlaps man's quest for salvation. Mediators do more than smooth out troubled relationships: they assist people on their pilgrimage toward salvation. Mediators take on the role of spiritual directors, endowing mediation with the fruits of faith and worship:

> In these rites I discover that something is approaching me here that I did not produce myself,

---

[10] Pope Benedict XVI, *The Spirit of the Liturgy*, 49.
[11] Ibid

that I am entering into something greater than myself, which ultimately derives from divine revelation.[12]

Worshippers, those who take part in the Blessed Sacrament, experience a spiritual arc from penance to Communion. This meditative liturgical arc mirrors the arc that peacemakers experience when they facilitate a party's conflict journey from penance to reconciliation. This natural synergy between the sacred rite and the peacemaking journey inspires mediators to schedule frequent recesses between mediation sessions, allowing parties to attend worship interludes where they can reflect and temporarily transcend temporal concerns. In contemplative moments, they may recognize that the key to peace can be found in divine relationship:

> The Consecration is the moment of God's great *actio* in the world for us. It draws our eyes and hearts on high. For a moment the world is silent, everything is silent, and in that silence we touch the eternal—for one beat of the heart we step out of time into God's being-with-us.[13]

The mystical silence of "being with God" during worship mirrors moments of deep listening that take place during mediation. During those moments, stillness descends and the sacred comes to the foreground; the

---

12 Ibid., 165.
13 Ibid., 212.

presence of the Holy Spirit is felt. In the early church, Christians recognized this convergence of worship and peacemaking:

> Often, in the primitive church, the Eucharist was called simply "agape," that is, "love"; or even simply "*pax*," that is, "peace." The Christians of that time thus expressed in a dramatic way what is an unbreakable link between the mystery of the hidden presence of God—and the praxis of serving the cause of peace, of Christians being peace.[14]

Philosophy Revisited

The nature of this universe makes it possible to experience Communion, knowing the Real Presence.[15] This experience reveals an unbreakable link between God and individual souls. Firsthand evidence confirms that man, in order to be made whole again, must conform his intentions to the Mind of God. Parties who align their will with the Will of God come into alignment with fundamental reality. Most people seeking to discern divine will participate in the liturgy in order to restore their link to the sacred:

> Participation in the liturgy is the entrance par excellence of the members of the church into the "'I'

---

14 Ratzinger, *The Essential Pope Benedict XVI*, 69.
15 Christian Idealism posits that Creation issues from the Mind of God. Humans are intimately connected to God as one aspect of Creation.

of Christ." For Ratzinger, to "enter into the 'I' of Christ" is fundamentally to step into the dialogical relationship between divinity and humanity.[16]

Mystical Unity and Spiritual Direction

A word of caution is warranted: one cannot access divine relationship as a spectator. Rather, sacred rewards are reaped through prayerful participation. Achieving the necessary depth of contemplative prayer takes time and advanced spiritual direction. St. Paul, for example, preached that only from a deeply spiritual perspective could one understand the truths of mystical unity:

> "Because it is one bread, we, the many, are one body", says Paul to the Corinthians, that is, in the same letter in which he first develops the doctrine of the Body of Christ (1 Cor 10:16). It is here that we find the true basis of this doctrine: the Lord becomes our bread, our food. He gives us his body, which, by the way, must be understood in the light of the Resurrection and of the Semitic linguistic background of Saint Paul. The body is a man's self, which does not coincide with the corporeal dimension but comprises it as one element among others.[17]

This is a difficult passage, comprised of multiple layers

---

16   Collins, *The Word Made Love*, 160.
17   Ratzinger, *Called to Communion*, 36.

of meaning. It invites students to dig deeper into theology to fully grasp the true nature of reality. In short, in order to gain an optimum understanding of life, students must understand the concept of body-soul duality.

In the excerpt, Benedict presents a challenging concept: *the self does not coincide with the corporeal dimension*. This leads to an important distinction—the Greek term for "body" refers to the person, *not the flesh body*. Thus, it is the spiritual being or soul—the actual self or person—that is resurrected, *not the flesh body*. The soul enjoys post-mortem continuity of consciousness, not the body. Let us consider the remainder of the passage (*emphasis added*):

> Christ gives us himself—Christ, who in his Resurrection has continued to exist in a *new kind of bodiliness*. The outward action of eating becomes the expression of that *intimate penetration of two subjects* that we examined briefly just now. Communion means that the seemingly uncrossable frontier of my "I" is left wide open and can be so because Jesus has first allowed himself to be opened completely, has taken us all into himself and has put himself totally into our hands.[18]

The soul thus transcends matters of the flesh and enters into transcendent truths that emerge from Eucharistic union with Christ. As the "veil is torn," each man experiences new spiritual awareness and encounters heaven:

---

18   Ibid.

> [T]he Eucharist is revealed as man's unceasing great encounter with God, in which the Lord gives himself as "flesh," so that in him, and by participating in his way, we may become "spirit."[19]

As the bonds of mortal life are loosened, the soul glimpses his true nature as immortal self:

> When there is communion with him, the boundary of death is over here and now. Whenever someone enters into the "I" of Christ, he has entered straight away into the space of unconditional life.[20]

The worshipper's shift in awareness is nothing less than a realization of his nature as an immortal soul in relationship with God:

> The love of the Son proves to be stronger than death because it unites man with God's love, which is God's very being. Thus, in the Resurrection of Christ, it is not just the destiny of an individual that is called to mind. He is now perpetually present, because he lives, and he gathers us up, so that we may live: "[B]ecause I live, you will live also" (Jn 14:19).[21]

During the sacred liturgy, man's movement toward God synchronizes with God's movement toward man.

---

19 Ratzinger, *Jesus of Nazareth vol. 1*, 270.
20 Ratzinger, *Eschatology*, 117.
21 Pope Benedict XVI, *The Spirit of the Liturgy*, 102.

As the grip of material illusion is loosened, worshippers ascend toward mystical union. They sacrifice worldly encumbrance; they jettison false self and taste sweet Communion:

> Sacrifice consists then—we shall say it once more—in a process of transformation, in the conformity of man to God, in his *theiosis*, as the fathers would say. It consists, to express it in modern phraseology, in the abolition of difference in the union between God and man, between God and creation: "God in all" (1 Cor 15:28).[22]

Peacemakers who come to better understand union with Christ straddle two paths—the path to peace and the path to salvation. They have climbed an unusually steep slope and must pause frequently to "catch their breath." With the rigor of a monastic discipline, they engage in frequent periods of contemplative prayer. Their increased focus on mystical union gives them a heightened sense of duty to bring about reconciliation between the world's brothers and sisters:

> Eucharist is never merely an event *à deux*, a dialogue between Christ and me. The goal of eucharistic communion is a total recasting of a person's life, breaking up a man's whole "I" and creating a new "We." Communion with Christ is of necessity a communication with all those who are his: it means that I myself become part of this new

---

22   Ratzinger, *The Essential Pope Benedict XVI*, 149.

> "breed" which he creates by transubstantiating all earthly reality... The Eucharist is in fact the "healing of our love."[23]

The reconciliation of Holy Communion takes place in what we might call "inter-subjective space." As explained by Christian Idealism, individual spiritual consciousness unites with divine consciousness, or the Mind of God. Benedict has noted this co-mingling of consciousness:

> We pray that his presence might pick us up, so that we become "one body and one spirit" with him... The mysticism of identity, in which the Logos and the inner dimension of man blend together, is transcended by a Christological mysticism: the Logos, who is the Son, makes us sons in the sacramental fellowship in which we are living.[24]

Christ as "The Way"

Descriptions of Jesus as Rabbi, teacher, prophet or philosopher fall short. Mundane descriptions fail to capture the manner in which he transforms souls through supernatural mystical union. Mundane labels limit our understanding that Christ is "the Way."

In this regard Christ is not merely an exemplar

---

23 Pope Benedict XVI, "June 22," *Benedictus*, 195.
24 Ibid., "July 17," 220.

to be followed, one who shows the way to union with God. Rather, he is "the integrating space in which the 'we' of human beings gathers itself toward the 'you' of God."[25]

This "integrated space" is the loftiest reality we can know. When we co-mingle with the Real Presence, we open the door to inspired revelation. In the state of mystical union, God permeates our awareness. We encounter Absolute Subjective Being. We are in him and he is in us.[26] This co-mingling of consciousness finds the Holy Spirit infusing human consciousness and lifting man up so he can recognize his true nature as an immortal soul.

The inherent Idealistic nature of this universe dictates that religious inspiration is virtually certain. Subjective souls co-existing in a subjective universe created by the Mind of a Subjective Being, God, will experience mystical union. It is not an anomaly nor a delusion. It is the closest a man can come to fully knowing reality. Adding to this line of thought, Benedict comments on the unity extolled throughout the Bible:

> Thus the Song of Songs became, both in Christian and Jewish literature, a source of mystical knowledge and experience, an expression of the essence of biblical faith: that man can indeed enter into union with God—his primordial aspiration. But this union is no mere fusion, a sinking in the

---

25 Collins, *The Word Made Love*, 90.
26 See the Gospel of John for more on this concept.

nameless ocean of the Divine; it is a unity which creates love, a unity in which both God and man remain themselves and yet become fully one.[27]

Reconciliation ministry, working at its pinnacle, reveals divine self through mystical union with the Creator: "He who is united to the Lord becomes one spirit with him."[28] After parties experience this ultimate reconciliation, even fleetingly, they are also inspired to serve as peacemakers:

> At the same time, the devotion of the faithful shows an infallible intuition of how such love is possible; it becomes so as a result of the most intimate union with God, through which the soul is totally pervaded by him—a condition which enables those who have drunk from the fountain of God's love to become in their turn a fountain from which "flow rivers of living water" (Jn 7:38).[29]

This analysis, based on dialogical theology, advances the fundamental church teachings that Benedict has integrated into key documents:

> Due in part to Ratzinger's influence, *Dei Verbum* embraced this understanding of revelation "seen basically as dialogue" between God and humanity that unfolds in history.[30]

---

27 Pope Benedict XVI, *God Is Love*, 32.
28 Ibid. 1 Cor 6:17.
29 Ibid., 97.
30 Collins, *The Word Made Love*, 54.

Sacramental Universe

One aspect of theology is the study of how God reveals himself to man, which includes forms of communication that transcend material limits. In this study, they are forced to acknowledge the subjective nature of this universe. They realize that humans have the ability to enter into dialogue with God because, as immortal souls they came into existence in a state of co-being with God. They reestablish this co-being through mystical union. Theology, in its deeper study of the nature of divine relationship, renders Holy Communion no longer a mystery. Mystical union and divine revelation, inherent features of reality, arise from the very essence or nature of a soul.

However, when people view life from a material perspective, the idea of divine relationship becomes unreal. It cannot be understood from their perspective. In spite of their blindness, they nonetheless experience a gnawing hunger to find a spiritual home. Though they cannot articulate their longing, they hunger for a final destination that will satisfy their deepest hunger. As a result, they constantly watch for signs that God exists. Eventually, their diligence is rewarded: They realize the supernatural ground of Being pervades their consciousness and everything they observe, because reality issues from the Mind of God:

> The Creator speaks through creation in such a way that all that comes to be is "Being-thought."[31]

---

31 Ibid., 73.

As the person becomes "spiritually formed," things that once seemed counter-intuitive and paradoxical now appear to be common sense. It turns out that yearning for a spiritual home is not a mental pathology or fantasy, as the culture would have us believe, but is rather an innate hopeful response of prodigal sons and daughters to sacred signs along the road leading home to the heavenly feast. These signs are part of a "sacramental universe" that draws pilgrims homeward:

> [I]n the course of the liturgy is a discovery of the transcendent nature of the human person. This discovery of identity happens in the liturgy because it is a moment of the earthly entry into heaven. Here the temporal is able to enter into the eternal because there has first been an entry into history from the place of eternity.[32]

This marriage of heaven and earth bridges the dark chasm hollowed out by man's fear of death. Communion with the Body of Christ helps men surmount this barrier:

> In the Body of Christ, death no longer works as a limit; in this Body, past, present and future interpenetrate.[33]

The Eucharistic bridge between realms can be a powerful adjunct to the peacemaking ministry. Souls crossing the bridge with knowledge of their true nature more

---

32 Ibid., 129.
33 Ratzinger, *Called to Communion*, 99.

easily align with the Will of God. This places reconciliation within their reach. Efforts to reconcile that are aided by the Eucharistic celebration foreshadow impending divine reconciliation:

> Liturgy would be a kind of anticipation, a rehearsal, a prelude for the life to come, for eternal life, which St. Augustine describes, by contrast with life in this world, as a fabric woven, no longer of exigency and need, but of the freedom of generosity and gift.[34]

When peacemakers include worship and contemplative prayer in their process, troubled parties are lifted above the mundane world. They experience Eucharistic joy, having been rescued by the Shepherd:

> The liturgy is the means by which earthly time is inserted into the time of Jesus Christ and into its present. It is the turning point in the process of redemption. The Shepherd takes the lost sheep onto his shoulders and carries it home.[35]

During the sacred liturgy, souls glimpse their sacred destination and come to know they are divinely infused with Christ's love:

> The living Lord gives himself to me, enters into me, and invites me to surrender myself to him,

---

[34] Pope Benedict XVI, *The Spirit of the Liturgy*, 14.
[35] Ibid., 61.

so that the Apostle's words come true: "[I]t is no longer I who live, but Christ who lives in me" (Gal 2:20). Only thus is the reception of Holy Communion an act that elevates and transforms a man.[36]

Divine Self Infused with Spirit

Divine self includes "Christ within me." Transformation from false self to divine self begins to take place when a soul bridges mundane and supernatural realms through the Eucharistic portal. As they are in Christ and Christ is in them, there is a rebirth of divine self.

Peacemakers should not confuse this rebirth with "peak experience" and "self-fulfillment," states constrained by naturalism. The reality of "Christ within"—which might be called "the bridge between time and eternity"[37]—defies psychometric measurement or description. A proper description requires spiritual or religious terminology. For example, we can describe Holy Communion as an ancient pathway that spans the realms:

> Hence, Communion means the fusion of existences; just as in the taking of nourishment the body assimilates foreign matter to itself, and is thereby enabled to live, in the same way my "I" is "assimilated" to that of Jesus, it is made similar to him in an exchange that increasingly breaks through the lines of division.[38]

---

36 Ibid., 89.
37 Ibid., 92.
38 Pope Benedict XVI, "June 21st," *Benedictus*, 192.

easily align with the Will of God. This places reconciliation within their reach. Efforts to reconcile that are aided by the Eucharistic celebration foreshadow impending divine reconciliation:

> Liturgy would be a kind of anticipation, a rehearsal, a prelude for the life to come, for eternal life, which St. Augustine describes, by contrast with life in this world, as a fabric woven, no longer of exigency and need, but of the freedom of generosity and gift.[34]

When peacemakers include worship and contemplative prayer in their process, troubled parties are lifted above the mundane world. They experience Eucharistic joy, having been rescued by the Shepherd:

> The liturgy is the means by which earthly time is inserted into the time of Jesus Christ and into its present. It is the turning point in the process of redemption. The Shepherd takes the lost sheep onto his shoulders and carries it home.[35]

During the sacred liturgy, souls glimpse their sacred destination and come to know they are divinely infused with Christ's love:

> The living Lord gives himself to me, enters into me, and invites me to surrender myself to him,

---

34 Pope Benedict XVI, *The Spirit of the Liturgy*, 14.
35 Ibid., 61.

so that the Apostle's words come true: "[I]t is no longer I who live, but Christ who lives in me" (Gal 2:20). Only thus is the reception of Holy Communion an act that elevates and transforms a man.[36]

Divine Self Infused with Spirit

Divine self includes "Christ within me." Transformation from false self to divine self begins to take place when a soul bridges mundane and supernatural realms through the Eucharistic portal. As they are in Christ and Christ is in them, there is a rebirth of divine self.

Peacemakers should not confuse this rebirth with "peak experience" and "self-fulfillment," states constrained by naturalism. The reality of "Christ within"—which might be called "the bridge between time and eternity"[37]—defies psychometric measurement or description. A proper description requires spiritual or religious terminology. For example, we can describe Holy Communion as an ancient pathway that spans the realms:

> Hence, Communion means the fusion of existences; just as in the taking of nourishment the body assimilates foreign matter to itself, and is thereby enabled to live, in the same way my "I" is "assimilated" to that of Jesus, it is made similar to him in an exchange that increasingly breaks through the lines of division.[38]

---

36 Ibid., 89.
37 Ibid., 92.
38 Pope Benedict XVI, "June 21st," *Benedictus*, 192.

The "fusion of existences" experienced during the Mass lies well beyond the purview of naturalistic science. Mystical fusion—achieved when an immortal soul jettisons false self and accepts divine grace that leads to Communion with the Real Presence—transcends materialism and supersedes the limits of natural science. Those who seek understanding must first gain a deeper knowledge of the intermingling of natural and supernatural realms. Benedict aids our understanding by describing how God acts through the liturgy:

> This action of God, which takes place through human speech, is the real "action" for which all of creation is in expectation. The elements of the earth are transubstantiated, pulled, so to speak, from their creaturely anchorage, grasped at the deepest ground of their being, and changed into the Body and Blood of the Lord. The New Heaven and the New Earth are anticipated. The real "action" in the liturgy in which we are all supposed to participate is the action of God himself.[39]

This profound reconciliation requires the sacrificial death of the false self. Ego identity must be sacrificed on the altar. When the grace of God strikes, shells of ego identity comprising the counterfeit self, the ego shatters, and a soul is set free:

> Human beings must die with Christ like a grain

---

39 Ibid., "May 24," 163.

of wheat in order to truly rise, to stand erect, to be themselves (Jn 12:24). Human persons are not to be understood merely from the perspective of their past histories or from that isolated moment that we refer to as the present. They are oriented toward their future, and only it permits who they really are to appear completely (1Jn 3:2). We must always see in other human beings person with whom we shall one day share God's joy.[40]

In summary, participation in the Holy sacraments increases the probability that disputants will achieve reconciliation. Peacemakers skilled in marrying the path to peace with the path to salvation facilitate enduring reconciliation. The Eucharist is a powerful adjunct to peacemaking that delivers glimpses of Christ's promise of world peace. Benedict captures this dynamic in a beautiful passage:

> God, the living God, establishes a communion of peace with us, or to put it more strongly, he creates "consanguinity" between himself and us. Through the incarnation of Jesus, through the outpouring of his blood, we have been drawn into an utterly real consanguinity with Jesus and thus with God himself. The blood of Jesus is his love, in which divine life and human life have become one.[41]

---

[40] Ibid., "January 3rd," 16.
[41] Pope Benedict XVI, *Mass of the Lord's Supper, Homily of His Holiness Benedict XVI, Holy Thursday, 9 April 2009* (Libreria Editrice Vaticana, 2009).

Reflection

Peacemaking ultimately converges with spiritual pilgrimage. Peacemakers travel parallel paths of reconciliation and salvation that eventually merge. Along the way, they evaluate their theology background—has their study provided sufficient preparation? Will additional training be needed—perhaps in pastoral counseling and spiritual direction? Has their personal spiritual formation been sufficient? Or will they need to recruit a personal spiritual director to help them at the same time they assist others?

Reconcilers will also want to evaluate how they will employ the sacraments as an aid to the reconciliation ministry. How will they employ supernatural aids? They will want to assemble a team of pastoral counselors, including priests, to counsel parties regarding matters of faith.

When reconciliation advances into territory typically reserved for mystics, mediators should recognize the need to be sensitive to subtle or intangible party needs that defy verbal description. They will employ advanced contemplative listening. In addition, they'll want to discern the movement of the Holy Spirit, so they can recognize the times when they should step aside and cede control to the Spirit.

Previously, most reconcilers assumed they met the requirements for the ministry. But now, as they assess their personal spiritual formation, they may find good reason to renew their efforts, as the path may be steeper than they anticipated.

Reconcilers should compile an expanded roster of peacemaking skills they will want to acquire, after finding that the demands of ministry have moved beyond technique into the realm of a sacred quest. Fortunately, at this stage, peacemakers are usually confident that such abilities lie well within their reach.

FIFTEEN

Spiritual Healing

When marriages and friendships fall apart, we feel pain, grief, and anxiety. We look for solutions. We reach out to others. We may even rush to consult counselors and psychologists who specialize in mending broken relationships. In short, we take the situation seriously.

What happens when our relationship with God falls apart? When faith fails us, we may suffer emotional and spiritual wounds that erode our ability to live joyful, meaningful lives, yet too often these wounds remain unnoticed and untreated. We feign indifference. "What relationship?" we wonder. Just as we ignored our relationship with God, so too we turn a blind eye to the pain associated with the loss of divine relationship.

The loss is noticeable. We may resemble the "walking wounded" as we go through the daily motions of a life robbed of joy and purpose, yet few of us seek to identify the cause of the failure. Rarely do we turn to priests and pastors to sort out the damage. Mystery settles over our lives as quiet resignation takes hold.

Reconciliation ministry seeks to overcome chronic apathy regarding divine relationship; reconcilers seek to heal the related emotional, mental, and spiritual wounds. They seek to perform an accurate "autopsy" that reveals the causes behind the destruction of divine relationship.

Holy Communion and Healing

Even when we recognize the absence of God's presence, we may not know how to heal the relationship. Fortunately, the rite of Holy Communion offers a solution:

> The nourishment that man needs in his deepest self is communion with God himself. Giving thanks and praise, Jesus transforms the bread, he no longer gives earthly bread, but communion with himself. This transformation, though, seeks to be the start of the transformation of the world—into a world of resurrection, a world of God.[1]

The Blessed Sacrament treats and heals spiritual disease—alienation and loneliness, fear and dread, guilt and hostility—one heart at a time. Yet world peace requires healing on a global scale. It requires campaigns that touch many hearts over sustained periods of time.

As Benedict notes, Holy Communion plays a central role in this task:

---

[1] Pope Benedict XVI, *Mass of the Lord's Supper, Homily of His Holiness Benedict XVI, Holy Thursday, 9 April 2009.*

> Here now is the central act of transformation that alone can truly renew the world: violence is transformed into love, and death into life. Since this act transmutes death into love, death as such is already conquered from within, the Resurrection is already present in it.[2]

As peacemakers progress in their ministry, they learn to appreciate the role Holy Communion plays as a spiritual weapon they can wield in the battle against conflict, hostility, and war:

> Only this intimate explosion of good conquering evil can then trigger off the series of transformations that little by little will change the world. All other changes remain superficial and cannot save.[3]

Many who are healed by Christ's love hear the call to vocation:

> As those drawn into union with Christ find their most fundamental identity as beloved children of God the Father, a transformation occurs within the heart of the believer that sparks an outward looking to the world in love.[4]

---

2   Pope Benedict XVI, *Apostolic Journey to Cologne on the Occasion of the Twentieth World Youth Day, Eucharistic Celebration, Homily of His Holiness Pope Benedict XVI, Cologne-Marienfeld, Sunday 21 August, 2005* (Vatican City: Libreria Editrice Vaticana, 2005).
3   Pope Benedict XVI, "June 23," *Benedictus*, 2006, 194.
4   Collins, *The Word Made Love*, 121.

The experience of the Real Presence of Christ during Holy Communion infuses believers with a sense of companionship. Confident in the knowledge that they no longer walk the path to peace alone, they gain a key insight—they are now united with the Body of Christ. Benedict explores this theme:

> Union with Christ is also union with all those to whom he gives himself. I cannot possess Christ just for myself; I can belong to him only in union with all those who have become, or who will become, his own. Communion draws me out of myself towards him and, thus, towards unity with all Christians. We become "one body."[5]

After their sacramental encounter with the Real Presence, these souls "walk with Christ," much as the Disciples walked with the Lord after his Resurrection:

> [I]n the case of the narrative of the disciples on the way to Emmaus, a liturgical element emerges, indicating that this encounter with the Risen Christ is the true basis of the life of the whole church.[6]

The early Christian community delivered brotherhood and peace. Christians found healing when they gathered for communion with the Risen Christ:

---

[5] Pope Benedict XVI, *God Is Love*, 37.
[6] Collins, *The Word Made Love*, 88.

> They belong to each other precisely by accepting one another's freedom and by supporting one another in love and knowledge—and in this communion they are simultaneously free and one for all eternity.[7]

Worshippers today, like those in the early Church, gather to encounter the Real Presence during Mass. Every time they do so, whether they are conscious of it or not, they walk a spiritual tightrope that straddles this world and the next:

> If the human capacity for truth and for love is the place where eternal life can break forth, then eternal life can be consciously experienced in the present.[8]

One glimpse of eternity during the Eucharistic celebration can mend a broken soul by dissipating fear, rekindling hope, and lifting despair from the heart. The pilgrim's road home becomes visible once again. Sadly, those who refuse the sacrament or doubt the Real Presence are denied this grace. Sensing no path forward, they become discouraged. Some leave the Church. Others merely go through the motions. Few grasp the meaning of supernatural healing. Fortunately, peacemakers can bridge the gap between those who live the faith and those who merely profess it.

---

7   Ratzinger, *Jesus of Nazareth vol. 1*, 281.
8   Ratzinger, *Eschatology*, 157.

Contemplative Prayer and Healing

Faith-based peacemakers know their ministry extends beyond concerns of the flesh. They know they minister to immortal souls; therefore, they must address consequences that stretch past body death into eternity. This aspect of ministry requires solid insights from theology:

> In Ratzinger's theology the problem of death and the possibility of eternal life that death seems to undermine is primarily a problem not simply of how to account for the restoration of being, but of how communication can be understood to continue even in the face of the radical silence death seems to impose.[9]

The promise of eternal life carries with it the promise of a continuity of consciousness, communication, and relationship. These variables, which we manage during the reconciliation process, will therefore demand our continued attention. If we believe in an afterlife, a post-mortem continuation of being, then we must also expect to carry on the ministry of reconciliation, even when it is transformed by the death of the physical body.

Faith-based peacemakers differ from their materialist counterparts in that they consider the person in front of them to be an immortal soul. Materialists ridicule the idea of a continuity of consciousness beyond death while faith-based peacemakers have gained certainty in the ex-

---

9 Collins, *The Word Made Love*, 141.

istence of a future unbound by limitations of the flesh. They reflect on the manner in which Jesus appeared to the disciples:

> Jesus, however, does not come from the realm of the dead, which he has definitively left behind: on the contrary, he comes from the realm of pure life, from God; he comes as the one who is truly alive, who is himself the source of life. Luke underlines quite dramatically how different the risen Lord is from a mere "spirit" by recounting that Jesus asked the still fearful disciples for something to eat and then ate a piece of grilled fish before their eyes.[10]

Jesus, who comes from "the realm of pure life," possesses a spiritual nature, but Benedict explains that Jesus is not "mere" spirit. He steers us away from thinking of Spirit as distant and sequestered, unable to participate in the material aspects of creation. Rather, unconstrained and unlimited, Christ can touch all minds, in all places, at all times. He can impinge on this world and make his Presence known. Man can know him, but cannot constrain him.

In addition, Scripture describes his Trinitarian nature:

> According to Mark, Peter simply says to Jesus: "You are the Messiah [the Christ]" (Mk 8:29). According to Luke, Peter calls him "the Christ [the anointed one] of God" (Lk 9:20), and according

---

10   Pope Benedict XVI, *Jesus of Nazareth vol. 2*, 269.

to Matthew he says: "You are the Christ [the Messiah], the Son of the living God" (Mt 16:16). In John's Gospel, finally, Peter's confession is as follows: "You are the Holy One of God" (Jn 6:69).[11]

Benedict, with the help of Matthew's Gospel and Paul's letter to the Galatians, paints a picture of the divine relationship, the spirit-to-spirit encounter with Christ, that we can expect in the next life:

> Jesus' words to Peter, Blessed are you, Simon Bar Jona, "for flesh and blood has not revealed this to you, but my Father who is in heaven" (Mt 16:17), have a remarkable parallel in the Letter to the Galatians: "But when he who had set me apart before I was born, and had called me through his grace, was pleased to reveal his Son to me, in order that I might preach him among the Gentiles, I did not confer with flesh and blood" (Gal 1:15f.; cf. 1:11f.:)[12]

Just as Peter and Paul came to know Christ better through revelations that emanated from beyond the world of flesh-and-blood, we should also expect to know Christ through spiritual means. Here we speak not of *mere* spirit, but rather of spirit that pervades, permeates, infuses, and commands material creation. This is Spirit as captured in Christian Idealism.

Benedict explains:

---

11   Ratzinger, *Jesus of Nazareth v.ol 1*, 293.
12   Ibid., 295.

Jesus comes through closed doors; he suddenly stands in their midst. And in the same way he suddenly withdraws again, as at the end of the Emmaus encounter. His presence is entirely physical, *yet is not bound by physical laws of space and time*.[13]

The New Testament descriptions do not conform to contemporary tenets of materialism. In order to understand the New Testament worldview, we must turn to Christian Idealism, which Benedict describes so well:

> In this remarkable dialectic of identity and otherness, of real physicality and freedom from the constraints of the body, we see the *special mysterious nature of the risen Lord's new existence*. Both elements apply here: he is the same embodied man, and he is the new man, having entered upon *a different manner of existence*.[14]

Benedict, an unusually gifted mentor when it comes to this challenging topic, guides our reflection and discernment:

> [T]he encounters with the risen Lord are not the same as mystical experiences, in which the human spirit is momentarily drawn aloft out of itself and perceives the realm of the divine and eternal, only to return then to the normal horizon of its existence. Mystical experience is a tempo-

---

13 Pope Benedict XVI, *Jesus of Nazareth vol. 2*, 266. Emphasis added.
14 Ibid. Emphasis added.

rary removal of the soul's spatial and cognitive limitations. But it is not an encounter with a person coming toward me from without.[15]

There is a difference between mystical experiences and Paul's encounter with the Lord:

> Saint Paul clearly distinguished his mystical experiences, such as his elevation to the third heaven described in 2 Corinthians 12:1-4, from his encounter with the risen Lord on the road to Damascus, which was a historical event—an encounter with a living person.[16]

These revelations did not come easily to the Disciples. They were challenged by the idea of a transcendent reality, just as we are challenged today by the idea of a continuity of divine relationship extending beyond death. When we speak of a post-mortem life, we cannot limit ourselves to mere hope, born of blind faith, for a heavenly existence. Rather, we must speak of a relationship that existed in the past, exists now, and will exist forever. Peacemakers today resemble the Apostles after Christ's Resurrection, those who spoke of relationship with Christ extending beyond this mortal life:

> Only Christ's self-identification with us, only our fusion into unity with him, makes us bearers of the promise. The ultimate goal at which this

---

15 Ibid., 273.
16 Ibid.

gathering aims is perfect unity—it is "unification" with the Son, which at the same time makes it possible to enter into the living unity of God himself, so that God might be all in all (1 Cor 15:28).[17]

Here Benedict introduces "fusion into unity with him," a critical concept for spiritual healing. A man's spiritual wounds are filled with the presence of Christ, which renders man whole once again. Gaps torn open in a soul's core being by fear, pain, and alienation are patched up. Those who are healed embrace an I-Thou relationship with their brothers and sisters.

In the wake of the Resurrection, awareness of the continued presence of Christ exploded; people became aware that they were not alone but rather their world was permeated with supernatural presence and filled with the Holy Spirit. Balance was restored between the natural and supernatural realms:

> They must be immersed in [Christ]; they must, to speak, be "newly robed" in him and thus they come to share in his consecration, in his priestly commission, in his sacrifice. ...it became ever clearer that the "name of God" meant his "immanence"; his presence in the midst of men, in which he is entirely "there," while at the same time infinitely surpassing everything human, everything to do with this world.[18]

---

17 Ratzinger, *Called to Communion*, 33.
18 Pope Benedict XVI, *Jesus of Nazareth vol. 2*, 90.

Souls suffering from unhealed spiritual wounds find healing in Christ; the holes in their heart become infused with divine presence as a result of God's mercy. Before healing can occur, we must clean the wounds and extract the poison of false-self ego identities that troubled souls use to fill the void of spiritual loneliness.

Spiritual Medicine

Aspiring reconcilers know they need to hone their conflict resolution skills; few anticipate the need to practice spiritual medicine. Overlooking the connection between reconciliation and salvation, they focus exclusively on empirical results and ignore the mystical aspects of healing.

Benedict warns against a narrow, materialistic view that prizes mere self-improvement over the promises of salvation ministry:

> It is not the perfecting of one's own self that makes one holy but the purification of the self through its fusion into the all-embracing love of Christ: it is the holiness of the triune God himself.[19]

In this view, Man is healed through mystical unity with the presence of Christ, as can be seen in Benedict's description of a disciple:

> The disciple is bound to the mystery of Christ. His

---

19 Ratzinger, *Called to Communion*, 95.

life is immersed in communion with Christ: "It is no longer I who live, but Christ who lives in me" (Gal 2:20).[20]

Souls are not healed in isolation; they're healed when the Spirit fills their emptiness, when new life bursts old constraints and floods them with inner prayer:

> This orientation pervasively shaping our whole consciousness, this silent presence of God at the heart of our thinking, our meditating, and our being, is what we mean by "prayer without ceasing."[21]

Benedict succinctly captures the nature of this unceasing prayer:

> This is what prayer really is—being in silent inward communion with God.[22]

Great peacemakers engage in constant prayer of this nature, resting in silent communion with God. As they go forth to assist others, they also work on healing their fractured relationship with God. Like most people, they may misjudge the extent of healing required; they may underestimate the challenge of spiritual transformation. Yet others will overlook or disregard the journey entirely, as Benedict notes:

---

20 Ratzinger, *Jesus of Nazareth* vol. 1, 74.
21 Ratzinger, *Jesus of Nazareth* vol.1, 130.
22 Ibid.

> In recent decades, having interior life has been widely mistrusted as "escapism," as an excessive search for privacy. Yet ministry without spirituality, without interior life, leads to empty activism. Not a few priests who set out on their mission with great idealism fail in the end because of a mistrust for spirituality.[23]

Benedict recommends "spending time with God" as an antidote to spiritual ills. This advice runs counter to the idea of a distant, impersonal deity. Many believe—mistakenly—that the sacred bond with God only comes into existence when souls depart this world and enter a heavenly realm. Benedict, however, leads us to understand that divine relationship exists fully in the present. His advice is especially pertinent for reconcilers: shroud yourself in stillness and "rest in the Lord."

To have time for God, to face him personally and intimately is a pastoral priority of great, if not primary, importance. It is not an added duty but rather a key pastoral mission. Absent God's immediate presence, we are drained of spiritual breath (spiritus), or the movement of the Holy Spirit within us. To put it simply, divine relationship is breath of the soul, without which we would suffocate.

Saint Francis of Assisi understood this principle so well that his life became a testament to it. In all things, he sought to imitate Christ so that he might come to know

---

23 Ratzinger, *The Essential Pope Benedict XVI*, 316.

the face of God. So great was his devotion that Seraphic angels lifted him up into union with Christ, an event that foreshadowed the coming age of the true order of Francis:

> [T]he eschatological Order of Francis is related to the Seraphim, and it will be taken up completely with contemplative love.[24]

The true Order was thought to be composed of souls in constant contemplative prayer—souls like Francis, who became infused with deep love as a result of intense prayer and devotion.

Benedict captures the essence of Franciscan spirituality:

> As the simplex and idiota, Francis knew more about God than all the learned men of his time—because he loved Him more.[25]

Francis did not cheapen his love by committing the sin of idolatry; he did not waste his time by worshipping ideas or icons. Rather, his love fueled a single-minded desire to perfect his relationship with Christ. In stillness he listened deeply, his heart open to the presence of the Holy Spirit.

To acquire a listening heart—as Francis did—is to prepare the soul for the act of spiritual healing:

> [T]he request for a listening heart becomes a re-

---

[24] Ratzinger, *The Theology of History in St. Bonaventure*, 157.
[25] Ibid.

quest for communion with Jesus Christ, the petition that we increasingly become "one" with him (Gal 3:28).[26]

Contemplative prayer, practiced in the tradition of Franciscan spirituality, renders transcendent relationship with Christ immediate and real. A ministry that models this practice includes spirit-driven deep listening:

> A further characteristic of the Spirit is listening: he does not speak in his own name, he listens, and teaches how to listen. In other words, he does not add anything but rather acts as a guide into the heart of the Word, which becomes light in the act of listening. The Spirit does not employ violence; his method is simply to allow what stands before me as an other to express itself and to enter into me.[27]

Mediation augmented with deep listening derives healing power from the mediator's living relationship with Christ. This powerful link leads to a new axiom: *those healed through restored relationship with Christ are destined to heal others.*

Many encounter this principle when they receive the Rite of Anointing—also known as the "last rite." The Church provides the Sacrament when a parishioner faces impending death or undergoes major surgery.

---

26 Ratzinger, *Jesus of Nazareth* vol. 1, 146.
27 Pope Benedict XVI, "May 28," *Benedictus*, 167.

For survivors, the last rites offer a lesson in humility and charity. We soon learn that while we're being healed, we are simultaneously called to become healers. Our physical and spiritual rejuvenation prepares us to join the reconciliation team, while gratitude compels us to share the gifts we have received with others.

Recipients of the Rite face a choice: they can receive God's grace and move on, full of renewed joy in life and hope for the future, or they can pass the gift on to others, becoming ministers of healing in their turn. Far too many let the opportunity pass—after all, ministering to others requires an investment of time and energy.

But consider a possibility: What if entry into heaven depends on one's ability to heal others? What if the "price of admission" has less to do with a tally of one's earthly transgressions and more to do with one's ability to love and heal others?

The thought is daunting, but the reality can be liberating. During the Rite of Anointing, many souls anticipating the transition to post-mortem life find an effortless realignment with the Will of God:

> For man, the will of God is not a foreign force of exterior origin, but the actual orientation of his own being. Thus the revelation of God's will is the revelation of what our own being truly wishes.[28]

Aspects of Holy Communion are echoed in the Rite

---

28 Ibid., "June 1," 186.

of Anointing. Both sacraments inspire souls to share the good news of the healing they have received through union with the Holy Spirit:

> Hence, Communion means the fusion of existences; just as in the taking of nourishment the body assimilates foreign matter to itself, and is thereby enabled to live, in the same way my "I" is "assimilated" to that of Jesus, it is made similar to him in an exchange that increasingly breaks through the lines of division.[29]

This sacramental fusion—souls resting in mystical union with Christ—takes place in the shadow of the cross from which the promise of spiritual healing issued forth into the world. The promise was fulfilled three days later—with Christ's Resurrection. The message was clear: Though you may suffer and die on a cross, you will rise up to know eternal life. Reconciliation takes place at the foot of the cross, where natural and supernatural realms intersect to make reality.

A New Heaven, A New Earth

Reconciliation heals divisions and guides warring parties into the light of the Eucharist, where they become one with the Body of Christ. The alienation that once sickened them gives way to a communion of peace. Worship-

---

29 Ibid., "June 21," 192.

pers glimpse through a "portal" that opens onto a view of heaven:

> As we saw, the Eucharist is an entry into the liturgy of heaven; by it we become contemporaries with Jesus Christ's own act of worship, into which, through his Body, he takes up worldly time and straightway leads it beyond itself, snatching it out of its own sphere and enfolding it into the communion of eternal love.[30]

Worshippers who sample and taste mystical union with Christ discover an exit from the matrix of strife we call the fallen world. They know they can escape

> the prison of this world through the curtain now torn open, a participation in the Pasch, the "passing over" from the world to God, which Christ has opened up.[31]

During the liturgy, the sanctuary is transformed into a sacred portal where earth and heaven merge, fulfilling Christ's promise:

> Christian liturgy is a liturgy of promise fulfilled, of a quest, the religious quest of human history, reaching its goal.[32]

Christ's promise breaks into a world hungering for

---

30 Pope Benedict XVI, *The Spirit of the Liturgy*, 70.
31 Ibid.
32 Ibid., 50.

peace. Pilgrims look to heaven and a humble God bends low, initiating "a liturgy of pilgrimage toward the transfiguration of the world, which will only take place when God is 'all in all.'"[33] They visit the altar where God

> brings heaven into the community assembled on earth, or rather...takes that community beyond itself into the communion of saints of all times and places. We might put it this way: the altar is the place where heaven is opened up.[34]

The traditional hallmarks of liturgy are transcendent healing and reconciliation:

> The church is most fully who it is when communicating the Father's love to the world and, through Christ, communicating the wounded world back to the Father. Being a place where this communication, this dialogue can happen is the real aim of the church and when it fulfills that aim it offers an irreplaceable service to the world.[35]

The Mass is not a stale nostalgic ritual referencing historical events that have long since faded into memories. It is not a stage play scripted with religious creeds, and it is not entertainment. Rather, the Mass is a sacrament during which profound spiritual events transpire:

> [T]he Blessed Sacrament contains a dynamism,

---

33 Ibid.
34 Ibid., 71.
35 Collins, *The Word Made Love*, 122.

which has the goal of transforming mankind and the world into the New Heaven and New Earth, into the unity of the risen Body.[36]

During sacred worship man receives the fruits of a loving divine relationship that fulfills his most profound dream:

> The dream of blending divinity with humanity, of breaking out of the limitations of a creature—this dream, which persists through all the history of mankind and in hidden ways, in profane versions, is dreamed anew even within the atheistic ideologies of our time, just as it is in the drunken excesses of a world without God—this dream is here fulfilled.[37]

Troubled parties, however, arrive for mediation suffering from having lived in the "drunken excesses of a world without God." They labor under the stress of having to constantly create a false-self ego; they suffer as a result of the amputation of their true nature. Caught in the jaws of traps set by the Evil One, they suffer nightmarish visions of dire futures filled with diabolical creatures who have ransacked the worldly realm, transforming it into a hell. They arrive at the conflict resolution sessions in a terrible state of mind. They do not know whether to run, fight, or succumb.

---

36   Pope Benedict XVI, *The Spirit of the Liturgy*, 87.
37   Pope Benedict XVI, "June 6," *Benedictus*, 177.

But then, during reconciliation, their brokenness is healed and knowledge of their innate spiritual nature is restored. Healed spiritual eyes allow them to see the path to mystical union; they encounter Christ as he was, as he is now, and as he shall be throughout eternity:

> "We have drunk deeply of the Spirit," says St. Athanasius, "and we drink Christ" (Evdokimov, p. 204). This seeing, which teaches us to see Christ, not "according to the flesh," but according to the Spirit (cf. 2 Cor 5:16), grants us also a glimpse of the Father himself.[38]

Chains of deception affixed by the Evil One are severed. Spiritual wounds—many self-inflicted—begin to heal. Souls with new vision see through falsehoods and deceptions, in contrast to the fate of those who turned away with muddied vision:

> If an interior opening-up does not occur in man that enables him to see more than what can be measured and weighed, to perceive the reflection of divine glory in creation, then God remains excluded from our field of vision.[39]

In faith-based reconciliation, souls are liberated from this world without God:

> For Christians, the Resurrection of Christ is the

---

[38] Pope Benedict XVI, *The Spirit of the Liturgy*, 122.
[39] Ibid., 122.

true Exodus. He has stridden through the Red Sea of death itself, descended into the world of shadows, and smashed open the prison door.[40]

Individuals thus reconciled with Christ collectively realize the promise of eternal freedom:

> Liberation without truth would be a lie; it would not be freedom but deception and thus man's enslavement, man's ruin. Freedom without truth cannot be true freedom, so, without truth, freedom is not even freedom. If man is to be free, he must be "like God." Wanting to be like God is the inner motive of all mankind's programs of liberation.[41]

This type of desire to be "like God" is not a desire that seeks to replace God with a robust ego self. Rather, this type of desire emanates from man's native or innate endowment of the "image of God." It is a desire to wash away the mud of the fallen world; a desire to be anointed with sacred perfume; a desire to discard dirty rags worn in servitude to worldly goals; a desire to don fine spiritual garments fit for the Father's feast. This type of desire arises from a supernatural longing for a spiritual home, longing for a destination where one is immersed in God's presence:

> Christian prayer for the Lord's return always in-

---

40 Ibid., 137.
41 Pope Benedict XVI, "March 8," *Benedictus*, 83.

cludes the experience of his presence. It is never purely focused on the future. The words of the Risen Lord make the point: "I am with you always, to the close of the age" (Mt. 28:20). He is with us now, and especially close in the eucharistic presence.[42]

The Eucharistic I-Thou encounter takes place in the here and now, not in an otherworldly realm. Christ's Incarnation and Resurrection revealed that the history of heaven and earth are intertwined. Benedict offers further insights:

[I]t must be understood that the Resurrection does not simply stand outside or above history. As something that breaks out of history and transcends it, the Resurrection nevertheless has its origin within history and up to a certain point still belongs there. Perhaps we could put it this way: Jesus' Resurrection points beyond history but has left a footprint within history. Therefore it can be attested by witnesses as an event of an entirely new kind.[43]

This is good news that conveys a promise: the healing of spiritual wounds in this world accrues benefits in the next. Keeping this in mind, we might argue that the primary mission of the Church is bearing witness to the continuity between natural and supernatural realms:

---

42 Pope Benedict XVI, *Jesus of Nazareth vol. 2*, 289.
43 Ibid., 275.

> Indeed, the apostolic preaching with all its boldness and passion would be unthinkable unless the witnesses had experienced a real encounter, coming to them from outside, with something new and unforeseen, namely, the self-revelation and verbal communication of the risen Christ.[44]

The good news of the Incarnation and the Resurrection shattered the darkness covering the world. If these events had not erupted into mankind's consciousness, doubt and despair would rule. But that is not what we find; instead, we discover that healing and unity are made possible by our true spiritual nature, by our endowment of the image and likeness of God. Peacemakers are pressed to consider a "much higher goal [than imitating the man Jesus]." They must seek assimilation into Christ, in mystical union. This goal may need clarification:

> [It]...might sound strange to the ears of modern man. But, in truth, we all thirst for the infinite: for infinite freedom, for happiness without limits. ...Man is not satisfied with solutions beneath the level of divinization.[45]

Whether or not parties achieve true reconciliation depends on whether they possess the peace of Christ. In this sense, reconciliation begins in the Mass, when people of faith turn to one another with the words "peace be with

---

44 Ibid.
45 Ratzinger, *The New Evangelization*.

you." Then and only then does Christ's peace begin its journey into the world:

> "Worship" itself, eucharistic communion, includes the reality both of being loved and of loving others in turn. A Eucharist which does not pass over into the concrete practice of love is intrinsically fragmented.[46]

When we incorporate Holy Communion into our peacemaking protocol, mediation merges with salvation ministry to create a nuanced approach that serves man's complex and often contradictory nature. This marriage of worldly and supernatural disciplines infuses the reconciliation process with eternal significance and enhances the act of worship:

> If "sacrifice" in its essence is simply returning to love and therefore divinization, worship now has a new aspect: the healing of wounded freedom, atonement, purification, deliverance from estrangement.[47]

The healing sacrifice of Christ, resonating throughout time, is the cornerstone of worship *and* reconciliation. Both focus on man's escape from bondage:

> The essence of worship, of sacrifice—the process of assimilation of growth in love, and thus

---

46 Pope Benedict XVI, "December 27," *Benedictus*, 390.
47 Ibid., "April 28," 155.

the way into freedom—remains unchanged. But now it assumes the aspect of healing, the loving transformation of broken freedom, of painful expiation.[48]

The convergence of worship and peacemaking was foreshadowed in scripture, in the phrase "Christ the Mediator." Christ is both the mediator and the ultimate other with whom we reconcile:

> Worship is directed to the Other in himself, to his all-sufficiency, but now it refers itself to the Other who alone can extricate me from the knot that I myself cannot untie.[49]

Benedict, in these remarkable passages, describes the spiritual dynamics of liberation and reconciliation ministry. We can capture the essence of peacemaking with a succinct definition: *peacemaking guides souls to freedom from bondage by helping them untie knots they cannot untie on their own.*

Reflection

Faith-based peacemakers practice spiritual medicine. They meet disputants who live fractured lives; they encounter parties who are out of touch with their own divine endowment. Such souls suffer "multiple-ego disorder." This

---

48 Ibid.
49 Ibid.

is not a unique or new psychological pathology; rather, it has been the norm in a fallen world. Most people have lost all sense of divine self and have filled the vacuum with multiple false-self identities and thus suffer from a "legion" of ego-identities. The peacemaker must be ready to confront this dark situation.

Peacemakers also need extensive training in the disciplines of pastoral care and spiritual formation. Unlike other professionals, mediators must bring unique personal resources to their ministry. They must impart and transmit spiritual qualities that foster the emergence of I-Thou encounters. The "being-in-love" they possess infuses the parties they serve.

In order to satisfy the spiritual demands of their healing task, they study the sacred liturgy, which may require some seminary training. They receive formation from spiritual directors experienced in monastic life. They may spend time as a guest at a monastery or engage in solo hermitages.

Peacemakers should familiarize themselves with the various levels of mystical experiences described by religious figures throughout the Church's history. As a primer, they might consult the lives of mystics, monastics, and saints who have torn the veil separating this world from the next. More advanced study will prepare them to accompany disputants as they become pilgrims in search of spiritual wisdom.

Mediators may also want to become more intimately familiar with the liturgy. A trusted priest may become their mentor, helping them discover the deeper aspects of the sacraments. They may discover opportunities to coordinate peacemaking events with Eucharistic celebrations.

Peacemakers cannot neglect the study of theology, which, at its core, is the study of man's relationship with God. It is the study of divine relationship.

As we near the end of our journey, we see challenges and opportunities. While the difficulties may be greater than a student first imagined, the possible outcomes transcend anything they previously dreamed. Outcomes that once seemed otherworldly and barely imaginable are achieved on a regular basis.

SIXTEEN

Peace in the End Times

As we near the pinnacle of our journey, we begin a final reflection.

The principles established now tower over the landscape like snow-capped peaks. One axiom rises higher than most: *reconciliation ministry must consult man's deepest essence as an immortal soul*. When stated in reverse, the axiom delivers a warning: *when reconciliation ministry fails to recognize a soul's final destination, it delivers little of value*.

During our preparation, we learned that mediators who ignore the immortal nature of a soul are left with nothing but a worldly paradigm, which does not lead to world peace. Therefore, we must seek to understand man's immortal nature, which led us to turn to theology—Benedict's theology of relationship. We married faith with reason, and discovered that divine relationship is the cornerstone of peacemaking. Thus we arrived at a solid foundation for a reconciliation ministry that would hasten the advent of world peace.

In summary, we learned that enduring world peace, the Peace of Christ, requires peacemakers who truly understand Man's relationship with God. With that thought in mind, let us further review the preparation that is about to draw to a close.

The Eternal Dialogue

Our preparation birthed a profound discovery: *the core principles of a reconciliation ministry emerge from a loving relationship with a living God.* The Franciscan Saint, Bonaventure, viewed this eternal dialogical relationship as the conduit used by the Holy Spirit to reveal reality:

> Ultimately, for Bonaventure, what is "unveiled" in the process of *revelatio* is *divine reality* itself.[1]

According to Bonaventure, revealed truth is found in the person of Christ, with whom man enters into relationship. And through that divine relationship Christ leads man to an awareness of his immortality:

> He is the person who is revealed to be truth itself precisely because he leads through death—which otherwise would seem to define the limits of the truth of human existence.[2]

In stark contrast to Bonaventure's eschatological

---

[1] Collins, *The Word Made Love*, 25.
[2] Ibid., 78.

vision, secularists reduce man to a biological entity--the death of the body is final. While materialists would focus man's attention on the here and now, theologians ask us to look beyond the pain of this world in order to see the beauty that shines through the transcendent realm. They work to restore our spiritual sight so that we can glimpse beyond the veil of mortality. Benedict champions this idea of "parting the veil" and counsels spiritual leaders to:

> [I]mprove our pronouncements about the resurrection: their essential content is not the conception of a restoration of bodies to souls after a long interval; their aim is to tell men that they, they themselves, live on; not by virtue of their own power, but because they are known and loved by God in such a way that they can no longer perish.[3]

Benedict has corrected the faulty view that the present life and the next life are isolated silos of existence. Instead, we learn that people make their decisions in the here and now with consequences that reach into eternity. For this reason, it is wise for mediators and parties to embrace a more expansive time frame when assessing future consequences of current decisions.

We also discovered that, in order to correctly anticipate future consequences, parties must grasp body-soul duality and continuity of consciousness. We did not propose an abstract, impersonal separation from the flesh body, which would be a mistake. Rather, we advanced the

---

3   Ratzinger, *Introduction to Christianity*, 353.

idea that awakened souls who detach from the flesh body enter smoothly into an intense divine relationship:

> In contrast to the dualistic conception of immortality expressed in the Greek body-soul schema, the biblical formula of immortality through awakening means to convey a collective and dialogic conception of immortality: the essential part of man, the person, remains; that which has ripened in the course of this earthly existence of corporeal spirituality and spiritualized corporeality goes on existing in a different fashion.[4]

This "different fashion" of existence, explained so well by Christian Idealism, posits a never-ending relationship between God and immortal souls. The person or soul:

> [G]oes on existing because it lives in God's memory. And because it is the man himself who will live, not an isolated soul, the element of human fellowship is also part of the future; for this reason the future of the individual man will only then be full when the future of humanity is fulfilled.[5]

In the previous passage, Benedict argues that man, as a conscious soul, as a person, exists in fellowship with all humans. This human fellowship persists into a soul's postmortem existence. A continuity of personhood means the

---

4 Ibid.
5 Ibid.

soul's exercise of free will in this life carries on beyond this life. A party who truly understands this concept of continuity appreciates the importance of reconciling divine relationship.

The concept of a continuity of personhood means that a person need not wait until after death to seek union with Christ. Rather, in this life a soul possesses the divine essence they will possess in the next. Mystical awareness attained while "in the flesh" persists in the afterlife. The flesh body does not determine continuity of consciousness—that is not possible. Continuity is solely a property of a soul. Jesus taught a related idea when he demonstrated that his spiritual essence could shine through a flesh body:

> Jesus...shines from within; he does not simply receive light, but he himself is light from light.[6]

In short, a soul does not depend on a transitory flesh body for its existence. A flesh body perishes; a soul never perishes. Spiritual essence is never extinguished; the potential for eternal dialogue with God never ceases. The theology of the Trinity supports this idea, as:

> [I]n God himself there is an eternal dialogue between Father and Son, who are both truly one and the same God in the Holy Spirit.[7]

---

6 Ratzinger, *Jesus of Nazareth vol. 1*, 310.
7 Ibid., 320.

Trinitarian theology delivers another profound insight: the opportunity to know "Christ within" never ends. The potential for mystical knowledge of "Christ within" is present during bodily existence and continues unabated into the next life. During the period a soul resides "in the flesh," the potential for union between an immortal soul and God does not die out. A soul does not lose its essence while pervading the flesh.

Though one might assume that physical existence would cripple all potential for mystical union, this is not the case. Awareness of immortality may dim as the dust and grime of the false self accumulates, and yet the soul retains its essential nature. This is good news. Reconcilers can tap latent awareness of immortality when the parties evaluate decisions; reconcilers can phrase the inquiry in "what if" terms: What if immortality was a factor to be considered? How might this decision look to you, if you were immortal? A transcendent perspective may unleash reconciliation success when all previous attempts have failed. However, skilled reconcilers do not force parties into a debate about what is true and what is not true; rather, they tap the person's latent awareness by asking them to imagine or speculate.

Bound / Unbound: A New Heaven

Pilgrims embark on a spiritual journey to rediscover a previously abandoned mystical destination, in a metaphorical return to the Garden of Eden. Ironically, once they're released from bondage, they discover that the dungeon they inhabited was partially of their own making:

> Man builds himself his own prison, against which he then noisily protests. True wonder, on the other hand, is a No to this confinement in empirical, this-worldly reality. It prepares man for the act of faith, which opens to him the horizon of the eternal and infinite.[8]

Devoted pilgrims and reconcilers encounter this "true wonder" that says "no" to confinement in a fallen world. They remove mud from their eyes and experience awe as they gain a heightened understanding of the Cross:

> It is on the Cross that the parables are unlocked. In his Farewell Discourses, the Lord says, apropos of this: "I have said this to you in parables [i.e., veiled discourse]; the hour is coming when I shall no longer speak to you in parables but tell you plainly of the Father" (Jn 16:25).[9]

Christ summons souls and invites them to abandon their wandering so they might take up a pilgrimage to the heavenly feast. Those who complete the journey, like the prodigal son, find heavenly joy:

> The cause of this joy is that the son, who was already "dead" when he departed with his share of

---

8 Ratzinger, *Called to Communion*, 143.
9 Ratzinger, *Jesus of Nazareth vol. 1*, 190.

the property, is now alive again, has risen from the dead; "he was lost, and is found" (Lk 15:32).[10]

This homeward journey parallels the path to peace. People who walk the path to salvation encounter the same terrain as people who walk the path to peace.

Pilgrims struggle to grasp how death on a cross could possibly feature in Christ's journey home to the Father or play a role in a reconciliation paradigm.

In their sleepiness, both pilgrims and peacemakers overlook signs, much as the Disciples failed to understand how the Transfiguration foreshadowed the Resurrection. Fortunately, Benedict's mentoring helps pilgrims and reconcilers recognize sacramental signs. For example, his theology weaves events like the Transfiguration into a seamless narrative:

> There we are told that Jesus took Peter, James, and John and led them up onto a high mountain by themselves (Mk 9:2). We will come across these three again on the Mount of Olives (Mk 14:33) during Jesus' agony in the garden, which is the counterimage of the Transfiguration, although the two scenes are inextricably linked.[11]

As a part of their formation, pilgrims and peacemakers learn to view the Gospel as a cohesive whole. In contrast, the Disciples experienced events as they unfolded; lacking

---

10 Ibid., 205.
11 Ratzinger, *Jesus of Nazareth vol. 1*, 308.

a complete history of sacred revelation, an overarching picture of the scene, they had to respond to the confusion of the moment.

That being said, modern pilgrims and peacemakers can come to resemble Disciples lifted into ecstasy by divine love. Awed by the majesty of God, they can be swept up in religious euphoria, even when they do not fully understand the meaning of the Transfiguration.

The Transfiguration serves as a good example of the miraculous breaking into our world; it demands a heightened understanding we do not always possess. "And he was transfigured before them," Mark says quite simply, going on to add somewhat awkwardly, as if stammering before the Mystery: "And his clothes became radiant, intensely white, as no one on earth could bleach them."[12]

Matthew has rather more elevated words at his command: "His face shone like the sun, and his clothes became white as light."[13] Luke is the only one of the Evangelists who begins his account by indicating the purpose of Jesus' ascent: he "went up on the mountain to pray."[14] It is in the context of Jesus' prayer that he now explains the event that the three disciples are to witness: "And as he was praying, the appearance of his face was altered, and his clothing became dazzling white."[15]

What are we to make of their witness? The Transfigu-

---

12 Mark 9:2-3
13 Matthew 17:2
14 Luke 9:28
15 Luke 9:29

ration demonstrated the prayerful unity of Jesus and the Father. This foreshadowed the eschatological Trinitarian unity:

> The Transfiguration is a prayer event; it displays visibly what happens when Jesus talks with his Father: the profound interpenetration of his being with God, which then becomes pure light.[16]

When people are slow to recognize transcendent signs, peacemaking efforts are hampered. Though people may strive to remain awake when the transcendent is revealed, they often fall asleep, overtaken by the "dark night of the soul." They need the assistance of a spiritual director so they might reawaken.

The ultimate example of a descent into the darkness to free lost souls is Christ's post-crucifixion journey to the underworld. Benedict describes his salvific journey:

> God himself descends into Sheol. At that moment, death ceases to be the God-forsaken land of darkness, a realm of unpitying distance from God. In Christ, God himself entered into the realm of death, transforming the space of noncommunication into the place of his own presence. ... Hitherto, life itself had counted as salvation. Now it is in very truth a death which becomes life for us.[17]

This fascinating passage prompts reflection: how do

---

16 Ibid., 310.
17 Ratzinger, *Eschatology*, 93.

souls end up forsaken in darkness where communication ceases? For peacemakers, this is not a matter for idle speculation. They will be called on to walk with those who wander in darkness; they must show empathy for the plight of those who suffer. They will journey into dark spaces. Peacemakers, we learned, must prepare for these dark passages by gathering insights from the accounts of saints, martyrs, and mystics. In reading such accounts, they journey vicariously into dark nights to study the landscape through which they must guide others.

In addition, we came to realize that reconcilers must become skilled in discerning misdirection that leads to darkness. They find that even religious educators with the best of intentions often mislead people regarding man's eschatological fate. Such tainted instruction sends the faithful off the path into the weeds. The following example illustrates such subtle misdirection:

> In the West, as distinct from both the Greek East and Egypt, the churches confessed the resurrection of the *flesh*, rather than of the dead. It has been shown that what we have here is a continuation of the Jewish terminology for the resurrection, which by means of the venerable formula "all flesh" denoted mankind as a whole. ...The idiom expresses, therefore, a concern not, in the first place, with corporeality, but with the universality of the resurrection hope.[18]

---

18   Ibid., 134.

In this analysis, Benedict pinpoints the mistranslation that turns into misdirection. This leads to the faulty (and absurd) idea of the resurrection of perishable flesh. The original teaching conveyed the promise of immortality; however, alterations (mistranslations) shifted attributes from the spiritual to the corporeal, from spirit to flesh. Conflating the transitory (flesh) with the immortal (soul) caused huge confusion that persists to this day. Even now, when religious teachers should know better, some passionately argue that the flesh body is resurrected. It is left up to peacemakers to uproot such misdirection and re-litigate issues that Christ previously settled when he descended into Sheol to defeat death. In our preparation, we learned that peacemakers must constantly strip away false ideas that place parties in bondage.

Eschatology Considered

In the early stages of our journey, peacemaking basics emphasized man's supernatural *origin*, but now, near the journey's end, the emphasis shifts to man's supernatural *destination*. Paradoxically, the final destination also becomes a new beginning:

> In death, a human being emerges into the light of full reality and truth. He takes up that place which is truly his by right. The masquerade of living with its constant retreat behind posturings and fictions is now over. Man is what he is in truth. Judgment consists in this removal of the

mask in death. The judgment is simply the manifestation of the truth.[19]

Once people know their true nature, body-soul duality becomes a part of their daily reality; it no longer exists as a mere tenet of impersonal philosophy. Man's knowledge that spirit that transcends flesh becomes indispensable for reconciliation. However, parties masked with false-self identities derail reconciliation. In contrast, a person who has uncovered his divine self finds that he can reconcile with God:

> Not that this truth is something impersonal. God is truth, the truth is God, it is personal. ... The truth which judges man has itself set out to save him. It has created a new truth for man. ... the truth of being loved by truth.[20]

Souls at rest in God experience unity and peace; they bring stillness and calm to the world. Wounds once filled with worldly ego-debris are now filled with Christ's peaceful presence. Souls are no longer shattered into a thousand shards of ego-self. Healed and reconciled, they enter a state of being-in-love that transcends all results previously imagined.

Convening Challenges

We have glimpsed our destination, but, before we con-

---

19   Ibid., 206.
20   Ibid.

clude this reflection, we should return to the period before our journey began. Peacemakers were limited to helping only those parties who expressed a desire to reconcile; however, that left many people who did not believe they needed mediation, especially when it came to divine relationship. In their eyes, restoring divine relationship was not a tangible goal; they could not even imagine a process of coming to know divine self.

Instead, they strove desperately to exert control over their mortal fate. They resorted to increased force in attempts to dominate and coerce others. Yet fallen world forces sabotaged their best efforts; eventually, they lost the ability to live in peace. Ill-advised efforts to overthrow Creation blinded them to the gifts of grace and mercy, as Benedict describes:

> In reality, man, who no longer has access to the infinite, to God, is a contradictory being, a failed product. Thus, we see the logic of sin: by wanting to be like God, man seeks absolute independence. To be self-sufficient, he must become independent; he must be emancipated even from love, which is always a free grace and not something that can be produced or made. However, by making himself independent of love, man separates himself from the true richness of his being and becomes empty.[21]

Why is peace so elusive? Benedict's passage provides

---

21 Ratzinger, *The Essential Pope Benedict XVI*, 390.

clues. God intends for man to enjoy loving relationships, yet opposition forces foment division, hate, and alienation. The fallen world does not permit people to flourish; it crushes them. Destructive opposition to the Will of God creates a nihilistic void that leaves lost souls spiritually destitute. Unconscious and suffering pain, people abandon their true nature. The absence of God's presence creates a vacuum of love and truth that swallows up any remnant of goodwill. When nihilistic atheists declare that God is dead, they negate the power of divine love and prepare their own obituary. The word "peace" is rarely spoken. Instead, we find a state of despair that releases a dark storm of rage:

> To sum up everything, then, we can say: the ultimate root of hatred of human life, of attacks on human life, is the loss of God. Where God disappears, the absolute dignity of human life disappears, as well. In light of the revelation concerning the creation of man in the image and likeness of God, the intangible sacredness of the human person has appeared. Only this divine dimension guarantees the full dignity of the human person.[22]

Amidst these conditions, peacemakers often find convening or "getting parties to the table" is more difficult than the mediation itself. Disputants harbor random fears that scuttle their willingness to participate. Recon-

---

22 Ibid.

cilers seeking to overcome convening barriers must heed the following axiom: peacemaking that omits supernatural concerns is doomed to failure. When we work with anything less than full truth, we end up with flawed outcomes.

Men and women alienated from the supernatural foundations of life do not easily grasp why they should reconcile. They focus on fear rather than love and that fear promotes the use of raw force, power, and coercion—which preemptively scuttles peacemaking. When fear is the dominant emotion, peacemakers must reset the process and draw on the elixir of divine love. They must invite the Holy Spirit to soften hearts until, slowly, parties open up to the opportunity to heal relationships, especially their relationship with God. Eventually, they may realize that their divine relationship can serve as a blueprint for all their other relationships.

Peacemakers may facilitate the convening stage by arranging for parties to visit sacred spaces for reflection and contemplative prayer. Sacred spaces can serve as "peace incubators," places where latent desires for peace might be uncovered. Parties visiting such a retreat, sanctuary, or peace incubator benefit from guided reflection that addresses the transcendent components of reconciliation. They benefit from "pastoral reality checking."

At the same time that peacemakers clarify transcendent concerns, they also help parties answer the question, "how do I manage this troubled situation and repair this relationship?" Reflection and practical steps converge.

Parties base their decisions on their worldviews, on what they consider most real. Their faith or view of the supernatural is part of their worldview, whether or not they express their faith. For this reason, when relationship with God is brought into the open, the probability of success is greatly increased; hidden considerations are surfaced. The parties may not have previously thought their faith beliefs affected their decision-making but, with mediator-guided reflection, they surprise themselves.

During the convening stage, mediators convert small conciliatory gestures into a willingness to collaborate. They coach technique, procedure, process, and structure. They remedy deficits of love with admiration and affinity. The increase in love—no matter how modest—brings parties closer to understanding. Reconcilers choreograph a dance that increases love, wisdom, and understanding. At the correct moment, they bring the parties "to the table" for divine collaboration.

Mediators might liken the convening process to the task of navigating a river clogged with debris. Though the crew toils to clear wreckage from the water, additional debris continues to float down from upstream, blocking the path forward. No matter how much debris the crew removes, they're unable to proceed.

In order to remove all debris blocking the path, they must adjust and begin their work upstream at the pristine source of the river. They return to that place where divine intention was strongest. Now, starting at the sacred source, they're able to navigate downstream. In this way, they more easily identify troublesome "locations" where debris pours into the river. Cleaning as they go, they make quicker progress. The river metaphor helps us better visualize divine collaboration—a process that clears impediments to reconciliation.

Theoretically, the church provides assistance with reconciliation, at least in a general sense. But such help rarely occurs, as clergy are ill-prepared to assist. We may need to create spiritual direction centers, safe spaces where parties can focus on repairing their lives. Some may be associated with parishes; other centers may be independent.

While many people refuse to enter a church to seek assistance, they will visit counseling centers, including those that offer spiritual direction and pastoral counseling. In that safe setting, they can address unique personal concerns and transcendent factors that make healing possible. When a church or even an individual parish overlooks this vital aspect of Christian ministry, it is likely that church will decline—which is exactly what we are witnessing today.

Destination Unveiled

Our studies prepared us to embrace a simple truth: Christ promised both peace and salvation. The two paths overlap. Believers accept this premise as a matter of faith. Peacemakers come to this conclusion when, in the course of their ministry, they see immortal souls reconciled with a loving God, with the result that they are more open to receiving the summons that calls on prodigal sons and daughters to return home.

Peacemakers should take note: the journey rarely, if ever, begins with the acceptance of divine love. Most parties embroiled in a dispute start out on a note of desperation. Peace seems elusive; hidden influences beckon from the shadows. Confusion lures them off course and evil intentions twist their desires. Those who decide to wait out the storm are ultimately disappointed—the seas never calm; dark forces continue to batter mankind.

Mediators have discovered that most people are not in control of their lives—they have ceded control to an ego identity, a cluster of misaligned traits and intentions. These clusters collide with one another like carnival bumper cars. Our observations have revealed that all conflicts are built on one false self becoming entangled with another false self. Two or more false selves become locked in an oppositional embrace.

Peace only becomes possible when one removes the false selves that generate misdirected intentions. The "bumper car" analogy provides a visual clue—we can resolve conflict by realigning intentions. In order to do so, we must first develop a realignment protocol.

Reconciliation Stages Reviewed

In the practice of mediation, we learn to recognize various stages or phases in the process. The following is a short review and synopsis of those steps:

Phase One, called *Opening*, includes icebreaking and convening tasks.[23] Peacemakers must establish process control, bringing order to a chaotic conflict situation. They must prayerfully invite the presence of the Holy Spirit. They promote and foster small gestures of affinity that draw parties closer together. They facilitate friendly, "icebreaking" conversation that encourages parties to risk listening closely to one another better. Parties are encouraged to let go of their fight-or-flight impulses, so they might sit in the same room with their adversary.

In *Phase Two*, the *Communication* stage, conflict narratives are drafted and shared. Parties respond to the question, "What happened?" Peacemakers summon party interests, needs, desires, motivation, and intentions to the surface for assessment. They facilitate difficult conversations and clarify clashing intentions. Increased communication, even when minor, increases knowledge (understanding), which increases affinity (closeness). In this phase, parties begin to heal and restore relationship.

Phase Three, the *Transformation and Unburdening* stage, is designed to strip away false-self traits so as to reveal divine self. Peacemakers help parties sculpt away false-self structures to reveal the underlying truth—they are immortal souls endowed with the image and likeness of God. This stage was the focus of the faith-based reconciliation concepts we covered.

---

23 These phases were inspired in part by the Star model developed at the Straus Institute for Dispute Resolution at the Pepperdine University School of Law.

During this stage, parties are encouraged to cease compulsive attachment to a false self, and they're guided past barriers erected by their opponent's false self. They move toward the magical I-Thou encounter. The tasks in this stage are aided by formal spiritual direction. Mediators marry faith and reason and thus enhance in-depth "reality checks" that shape sound worldviews. Fresh "reality maps" are charted with the help of the transcendent truths uncovered.

As was discussed, peacemakers promote Phase Three Unburdening by encouraging parties to participate in Eucharistic celebration. As a result, souls encounter the Real Presence of Christ and enter into Holy Communion from which they receive a renewal of being-in-love.

During the transformation stage, peacemakers discover they are constantly engaging in battle. Those who put forth evil intentions never rest. The opposition operates in perpetual attack mode, binding souls to ego constructs that misalign their free will. They drag souls into spiritual swamps devoid of love for God.

We discovered that peacemakers must counter the assault by stripping away falsehoods, exposing evil intentions, and neutering destructive hidden influences. A party's transformation begins in darkness with but a slight flicker of hope that invites them to chip away at falsehoods so they might mine buried truths. As party ego-bondage erodes, they repair divine relationship, only to discover that Christ heals those who actively return his love.

Phase Four follows with the final stage of *Divine Collaboration*. Collaborative negotiation is upgraded to divine collaboration. Parties align their exercise of free will with the baseline Will of God. When they reference a neutral baseline, rather than their personal interests, they avoid potential Face Loss—which can occur when personal interests clash with other personal interests in a win-lose scenario. A neutral benchmark allows parties to Save Face, as they're not forced to capitulate to their opponent; instead, they simply align with a neutral baseline. The use of a neutral baseline lessens the fear of being coerced or manipulated. It results in the greatest mutual benefit for all parties.

Phase Five, the *Mystical Union* stage, seeks to foster supernatural harmony. As we now know, reconciliation parallels man's salvation pilgrimage. The mediation process extends beyond the limits of body death. Transcendent love takes on new meaning:

> The capacity, and the duty, to love beyond the grave might even be called the true primordial datum in this whole area of tradition – as II Maccabees 12, 42–45 makes clear.[24]

Disputants seeking peace pray alongside pilgrims seeking salvation. Both have an eye on the fullness of life beyond this realm, knowing that love, which dissolves hostility, continues beyond the boundary of this mortal

---

24 Ibid., 233.

life. Peacemakers who know a more comprehensive reality, a reality that encompasses both natural and supernatural causes, reject the arbitrary limits of secular views:

> Any "self-knowledge" that restricts man to the empirical and the tangible fails to engage with man's true depth. Man knows himself only when he learns to understand himself in light of God, and he knows others only when he sees the mystery of God in them.[25]

The Promise of Reconciliation

Divine light shatters fallen-world darkness and heals troubled lives. As the process of reconciliation reaches its apex, parties grasp the meaning of Christ the Mediator. Benedict explains:

> In the depths of its being, the I is always related to the *you* and vice versa: that true relationship that becomes "communion" can be born only in the deep places of the human I. The act of faith is a participation in the seeing of Jesus, a dependence on Jesus.[26]

This core faith principle provides a valuable road map for reconciliation ministry:

> Faith is communication with Jesus and, conse-

---

25 Ratzinger, *Jesus of Nazareth vol. 1*, 282.
26 Pope Benedict XVI, "March 1," *Benedictus*, 76.

quently, a liberation of my I from its preoccupation with self, a liberation that sets me free to respond to the Father, to speak the Yes of love; that sets me free to say Yes to being, free for that Yes that is our salvation and that overcomes the "world."[27]

In earlier chapters, I've argued that Benedict's theology of relationship provides the most accurate description of divine relationship, if not the most accurate vision of reality. Peacemaking guided by his theology delivers true reconciliation that reaches the deepest state of relationship possible, mystical union:

> It follows then, that faith is, in its innermost essence, a "being with," a breaking out of the isolation that is the malady of my *I*. The act of faith is an opening of oneself to the whole world, a breaking open of the door of my subjectivity... The *I* that has been redeemed finds itself again in a greater new I. In this new *I*, for which faith has liberated me, I find myself united not only with Jesus, but with all who travel the same road.[28]

Reconciliation cracks the sacred code and unlocks secrets of the fallen world. It overcomes opposition to the Will of God. At long last, souls held captive by the forces of evil experience peace. Reconciliation ministry executed with God's grace exceeds all expectations:

---

27 Ibid.
28 Ibid.

In their hearts, people always and everywhere have somehow expected a change, a transformation of the world. Here now is the central act of transformation that alone can truly renew the world: violence is transformed into love, and death into life.[29]

Peacemaking converges with spiritual formation when a person recognizes his inherent immortality. In this fertile soil of spiritual awakening peace can grow and grow until it blankets the planet. Peacemaking is the proverbial mustard seed that that grows into a peaceful world at rest in the Lord. This is the lofty goal of the Holy ministry of peacemaking.

Reconcilers, buoyed by the wisdom of saints, incubate the truths that foster such peace. New Covenant theology inspires them to shepherd disputants toward mystical unity with the Lord. Mediators facilitate glimpses of the peace that has been prophesized for end times. They foster the deep silence that allows parties to know the presence of the Holy Spirit. They rekindle dreams, once abandoned, of reclaiming paradise. They fuel hopes of a new heaven and a new earth. In doing so, they prepare the world for the Lord's return and set the stage for the next act in salvation history. In the following passage, Benedict references the liturgy, but his sentiments could apply equally to reconciliation ministry:

---

29   Pope Benedict XVI, "June 23," *Benedictus*, 194.

> In the liturgy the Church should, as it were, in following him, prepare for him a dwelling in the world. The theme of watchfulness thus penetrates to the point where it takes on the character of a mission: to let the Liturgy be real, until that time when the Lord himself gives to it that final reality which meanwhile can be sought only in image.[30]

Paradoxically, man's hunger for peace is an echo of the Lord's original gift of peace, a gift delivered at the time when souls were endowed with the image and likeness of God. That sacred endowment blessed man with inherent divine love that fuels his longing for the Peace of Christ. The love bestowed by God nurtures man's desire for peace. One might argue that God built the desire for peace into the very nature of souls. Ultimate peace, the Peace of Christ, is revealed when a soul responds with divine love to the source of that divine love and this is exactly what takes place in the reconciliation of divine relationship.

In our preparation, we have discovered that the very essence of this universe is best captured by the phrase "God is Love." When man imitates Christ the Mediator he works with the essence of Creation to hasten the arrival of peace. Those who turn to their brother or sister with the words *"peace be with you"* live in accord with the truth of this universe.

---

30   Ratzinger, *Eschatology*, 204.

The Peacemaking Vision

What might a peace movement, a program of worldwide reconciliation, look like?

We might formulate a few basic expectations:

The ministry most likely will be organized with separate branches to accommodate both clergy and religious. Training will be designed for peacemakers of varied skill levels. Training will be delivered at numerous venues—including universities and seminaries. The curriculum will balance theory and practice with extensive hands-on internships.

An outreach program of workshops, retreats, and spiritual direction will be delivered. Peacemaking will be normalized: the public will see pastoral counseling, spiritual direction, and faith-based mediation as substitutes for psychological services and for litigation. In the Church, reconciliation services will become the norm; peacemaking ministry will be available in all parishes. An evangelical outreach will give rise to a worldwide peace never before achieved.

Final Reflection

Aspiring peacemakers long to hasten world peace, yet they face challenges. They must inventory the steps they will need to complete their personal spiritual transformation. They will need to assess the additional skills they need to facilitate mystical union with Christ. They will need to learn to maintain focus and dedication when events defy logic. They'll need to rehearse addressing destructive hidden influences that mount attacks on peace and faith.

Aspiring peacemakers will need to commit to self-assessment. They will need to evaluate their spiritual and theological readiness. They will need to ask, how well do I understand the idea of a subjective universe created by a loving God? Do I really believe in divine relationship between God and immortal souls endowed with his likeness and image? Peacemakers will need to assess their courage—can they look upon the Face of God with sufficient stillness of mind to achieve mystical union? Will they be prepared to serve as "doctors" who heal the wounds inflicted on the Body of Christ?

Near the summit, the path to peace converges with the pilgrim's path to salvation. This is not a coincidence. The desire to make peace arises as a natural response to divine relationship: reconciliation ministry is nothing more than a formal response to the divine love bestowed by God upon mankind.

May peace be with you.

Bibliography

Aquinas, Thomas. *Summa Theologica*. United Kingdom: Christian Classics, 1948.

Benedict XVI, Pope. *Apostolic Journey to Cologne on the Occasion of the Twentieth World Youth Day*, Eucharistic Celebration, Homily of His Holiness Pope Benedict XVI, Cologne-Marienfeld, August 21, 2005. Libreria Editrice Vaticana, 2005.

___. *Benedictus: Day by Day with Pope Benedict XVI*. Edited by Peter J. Cameron. San Francisco, California: Ignatius Press / Magnificat, 2006.

___. *Address of His Holiness Benedict XVI on the Occassion of Christmas Greetings to the Roman Curia, Monday, December 20, 2010*, 22nd December 2005. Libreria Editrice Vaticana, 2005.

___. *Address of His Holiness Benedict XVI on the Occassion of Christmas Greetings to the Roman Curia,*

Monday, December 20, 2010, 22nd December 2005. Libreria Editrice Vaticana, 2010.

___. *Address of His Holiness Benedict XVI on the Occassion of Christmas Greetings to the Roman Curia, Monday, December 20, 2010, 22nd December 2005*. Libreria Editrice Vaticana, 2005.

___. *God is Love (Deus Caritas Est)*. Encyclical Letter, Liberia Editrice Vaticana. San Francisco, California: Ignatius Press, 2009.

___. *Mass of the Lord's Supper*, Homily of His Holiness Benedict XVI, Holy Thursday, 9 April 2009.

___. Interview of the Holy Father Benedict XVI with Journalists During the Flight to Portugal, May 11, 2010. Libreria Editrice Vaticana, 2010.

___. *Porta Fidei, Apostolic Letter "Motu Proprio Data" of the Supreme Pontiff Benedict XVI for the Indication of the Year of Faith*. Libreria Editrice Vaticana, 2011.

___. *St. Paul*. San Francisco, California: Ignatius Press, 2009.

___. *The Apostles*. Huntington, Indiana: Our Sunday Visitor, 2007.

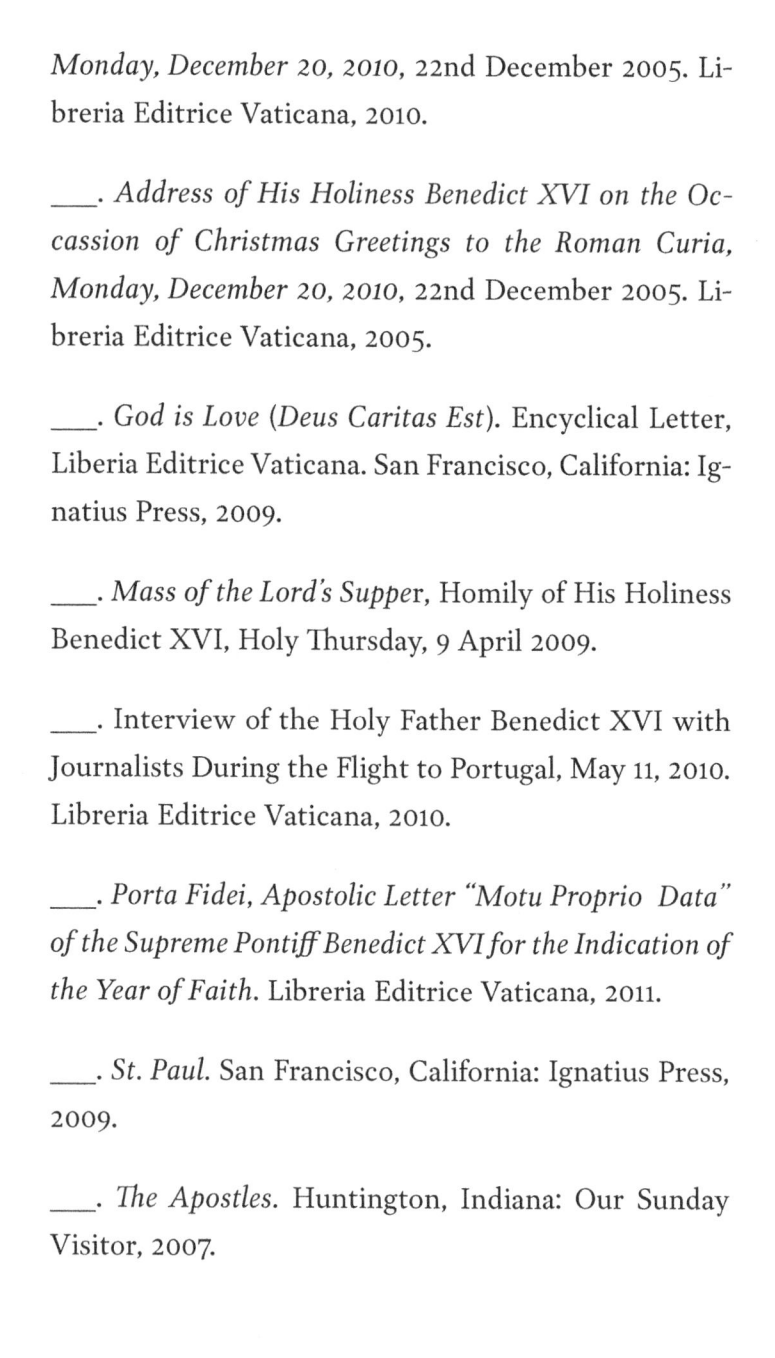

___. *The Spirit of the Liturgy*. Translated by John Saward. San Francisco, California: Ignatius Press, 2000.

Berkeley, Bishop George. *A Treatise Concerning the Principles of Human Knowledge*. Philadelphia, Pennsylvania, 1874.

Bodo, Murray O.F.M., *The Threefold Way of Saint Francis*. New York: Paulist Press, 2000.

Boff, Leonardo. *The Prayer of Saint Francis: A Message of Peace for the World Today*. Translated by Philip Berryman. Maryknoll, New York: Orbis Books, 2001.

Buber, Martin. *I and Thou*. Translated Walter Kaufman. New York: Charles Scriber's Sons, 1970.

Collins, Christopher. *The Word Made Love: The Dialogical Theology of Joseph Ratzinger / Pope Benedict XVI*. Collegeville, Minnesota: Liturgical Press, 2013.

Cousins, Ewert. *The Gethsemani Encounter: A Dialogue on the Spiritual Life by Buddhist and Christian Monastics*. Edited by Donald W. Mitchell and James O.S.B. Wiseman. New York: Continuum.

de Gaál, Emery. *The Theology of Pope Benedict XVI: The Christocentric Shift*. New York: Palgrave Macmillan, 2010.

Finley, James. *Merton's Palace of Nowhere*. Notre Dame: Indiana: Ave Maria Press, 1978.

Fisher, Roger and Ury, William. *Getting to Yes*. New York: Penguin Books, 1981.

Flannery, Austin O.P, editor. *The Basic Sixteen Documents of Vatican II*. Northport, New York: Costello Publishing Company, 1996.

John Paul II, Pope. *Fides et Ratio: Encyclical Letter of the Supreme Pontiff John Paul II to the Bishops of the Catholic Church on the Relationship between Faith and Reason, September 14, 1998*. Rome: Libreria Editrice Vaticana, 1998.

Leachman, James G. The Liturgical Subject: Subject, Subjectivity, and the Human Person in Contemporary Liturgical Discussion and Critique (Notre Dame, Indiania: University of Notre Dame Press, 2009).

Lederach, John Paul. *The Moral Imagination: The Art and Soul of Building Peace*. New York: Oxford University Press, 2005.

Leo XIII, Pope. *Rerum Novarum: Encyclical Letter of Pope Leo XIII on the Condition of Labor*. New York: Paulist Press, 1892.

Maslow, Abraham H. *Motivation and Personality, 2nd ed.* United Kingdom: Harper and Row, 1970.

Maslow, Abraham H. *Toward a Psychology of Being.* United States: John Wiley and Sons, 1968.

Musgrave, Alan. *Common Sense, Science and Scepticism: A Historical Introduction to the Theory of Knowledge.* New York: Cambridge University Press, 1993.

O'Meara, Dominic J. *Plotinus: An Introduction to the Enneads.* Oxford: Clarendon Press, 113.

Origen. *On First Principles.* Notre Dame, Indiana. Ave Maria Press, 2013.

Pontifical Council for Justice and Peace. *Compendium of the Social Doctrine of the Church.* USCCB, 2005.

Ratzinger, Joseph. *Called to Communion: Understanding the Church Today.* Translated by Adrian Walker. San Francisco, California: Ignatius Press, 1991–1996.

___. *Christianity and the Crisis of Cultures,* translated by Brian McNeil. San Francisco, California: Ignatius Press, 2005.

___. *Eschatology: Death and Eternal Life,* 2nd edition Translated by Michael Waldstein, Washington, D.C.:

The Catholic University of America Press, 1988.

———. *Introduction to Christianity*. Translated by J.R. Foster. San Francisco, California: Communio Books, 1969.

———. *Jesus of Nazareth, vol. 1: From the Baptism in the Jordan to the Transfiguration*. Translated by Adrian J. Walker. New York: Doubleday, 2008.

———. *Jesus of Nazareth vol. 2: Holy Week, From the Entrance into Jerusalem to the Resurrection*. San Francisco, California: Ignatius Press, 2011.

———. *The Essential Pope Benedict XVI: His Central Writings and Speeches*. Edited by John F. Thorton, and Susan B. Varenne. New York: Harper One, 2007.

———. *Jesus of Nazareth vol. 3: The Infancy Narratives*. Translated by Philip J. Whitmore. New York: Image, 2012.

———. *The Nature and Mission of Theology*. Translated by Johannes Verlag. San Francisco, California: Ignatius Press, 1993.

———. *The New Evangelization*.

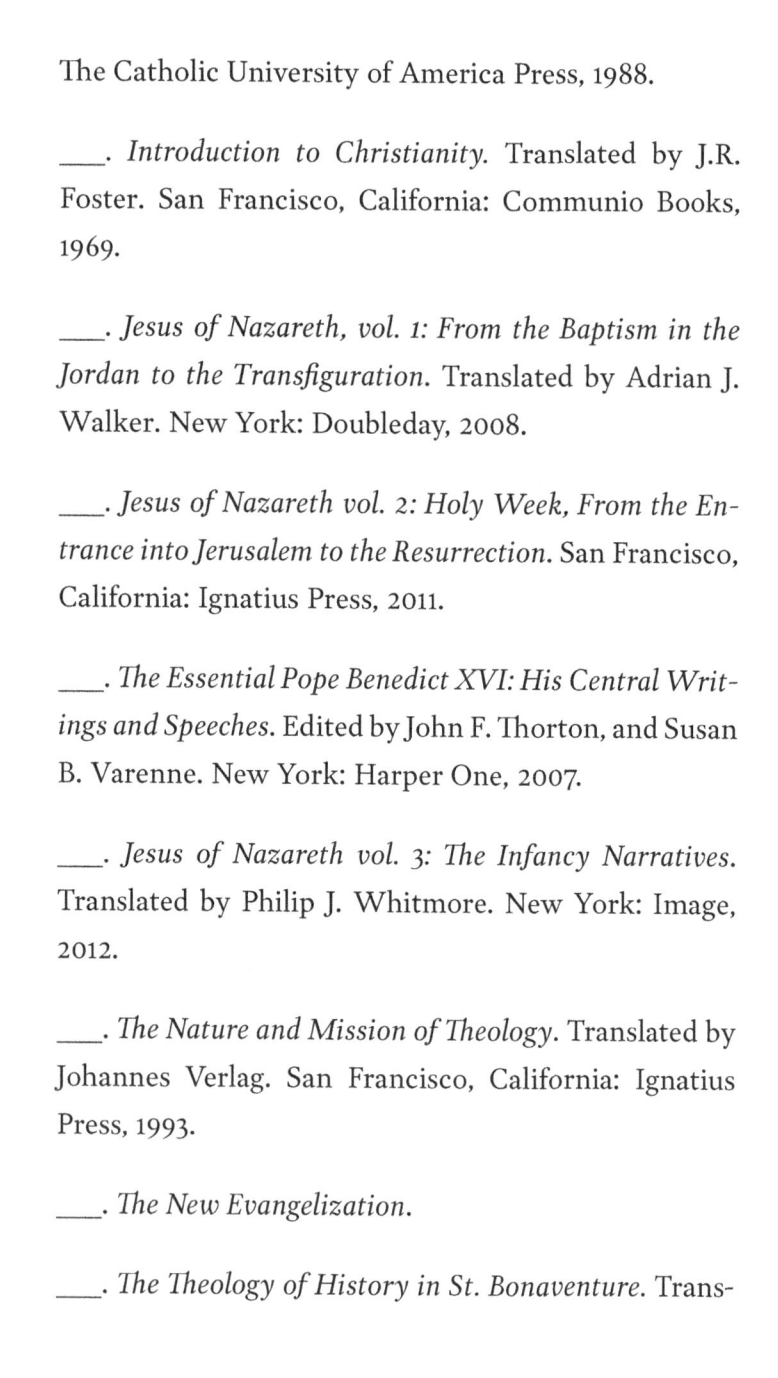

———. *The Theology of History in St. Bonaventure*. Translated by Zachary Hayes OFM. Chicago, Illinois: Franciscan Herald Press, 1971.

Rengers, Fr. Christopher, ed. *The 33 Doctors of the Church*. Rockford, Illinois: Tan Books and Publishers, 2000.

The New Catholic Bible. Saint Joseph Edition. New York: Catholic Book Publishing Corp, 1991.

Thomas, Kenneth and Kilmann, Ralph. "The Thomas Kilmann Conflict Mode Instrument." See http:/kilmann.com/conflict.html.

Sheed, Frank J. *Theology and Sanity*. San Francisco: Ignatius Press, 1993.

Stone, Greg. *Taming the Wolf: Peace through Faith*. Westlake Village, California: Taming the Wolf Institute, 2011.

Made in the USA
Columbia, SC
07 July 2022

Made in the USA
Columbia, SC
07 July 2022